TEACHING IN SPECIAL EDUCATION

Managing the Chaos

Lisa A. Ferrelli

University Press of America,® Inc.
Lanham · Boulder · New York · Toronto · Plymouth, UK

Copyright © 2010 by
University Press of America,® Inc.
4501 Forbes Boulevard
Suite 200
Lanham, Maryland 20706
UPA Acquisitions Department (301) 459-3366

Estover Road
Plymouth PL6 7PY
United Kingdom

Library of Congress Control Number: 2009940625
ISBN: 978-0-7618-5025-0 (paperback : alk. paper)
eISBN: 978-0-7618-5026-7

Dedication

To:
The special education teachers and their students--
who participated so willingly in this study

All special education teachers and their students faced with "Managed Chaos"

And

Carolyn Fluehr-Lobban, Ph.D.
Rhode Island College

CONTENTS

List of Figures

List of Tables

Preface

The study of American education has produced a vast literature. Within that literature are works documenting all aspects of schooling— its components, its history, its reform efforts, its successes and its failures, teacher development, and the practices of teachers in educating students. This literature indicates that schools are complex settings where teachers seek to educate a diverse group of students under a diverse set of circumstances. Within that diverse group of students in schools is a population of students with special needs. As a teacher, myself, these works are of significant attraction. Taken as a whole, these works tell an interesting and intriguing story of how children in our society are educated. What teachers think, know, and do in general education classrooms is well represented and often eloquently stated.

Yet, as I examined the literature, one question stood out among the many that I had—where were the students with special needs and their teachers in this vast literature of educational practice and reform? The unique challenges of teaching in special education make up a much smaller percentage of that literature. I became determined on making a contribution to the literature on teacher knowledge and practice that might be seen as an example that places special education in the spotlight.

The book is organized into two parts. The first part presents a review of the literature that supports and grounds the work as well as a rationale for it. The Introduction presents a brief sketch of the history of special education. Chapter One examines the research literature that informs the topic of teacher practice. This chapter presents relevant research literature addressing teacher practice, integration and inclusion, the effects of standards-based reform on instruction for students with disabilities, and the effects on the participation in standards-based reform for students with significant disabilities. The latter part of the chapter also highlights literature addressing methods of studying the context of teaching and teacher practice. This work provided the background material that I needed to fine-tune the methodology to examine my own practice and then to design the larger study. Chapter One also describes the creation of the "normative model of teaching" used in a pilot study that led to the development of the interview protocol, as well as the general framework for the study. Chapter Two consists of the presentation of a self-study of personal teaching practice. This self-study led to the larger study of special education teachers.

Part II presents the study of six special education teachers. Chapter Three describes in detail the development of the methodology employed in the larger study. Chapters

Four, Five, and Six describe the findings of the study. Chapter Four presents the interview data. The teachers offer descriptions and thoughts on their experiences as special education teachers. The elements of special education teacher practice emerge from the their words. Chapter Five examines what these teachers do as they go abut their teaching. Observation data allows for the creation of teacher vignettes—samples of typically occurring events in their classrooms. Chapter Six presents a discussion of the meaning of the teachers' experiences. Chapter Seven presents an analysis of the data. The data from the interviews and observations are coded for their important themes. Chapter Eight provides a closing discussion of the study's findings. Finally, Chapter Nine presents recommendations concerning the present status of special education practice based upon the experiences of the teachers as documented in this study as well as recommendations for future research. The chapter closes with my final thoughts as a participant member of the group of special education teachers introduced in this study.

Lisa Ferrelli
Woonsocket, RI
September 2009

Acknowledgements

Over the years, I've learned to understand and appreciate the power of writing for bringing clarity to my thoughts and experiences. It was the task of documenting such thoughts and experiences that brought me to the idea of writing a book about those experiences.

The journey to the completion of the research that became the book presented before you began with the question—where do my students with special needs and I fit in the larger world of elementary school and in general education? The road to providing some answer to this question has seen significant high points as well as near psyche rending low points. The high points include thinking that I was actually going to achieve the goal of earning a doctorate, learning to "name" and understand the variables that so powerfully impacted what I did in my classroom and in school, being center stage during an entire class session as special education issues became the main topic of discussion—something that does not often happen in standard education class discussions, and finally, the forming of significant friendships as my cohort mates and I grew close over the time spent together both in and out of class. The low points came in the form of multiple difficulties that nearly brought my working to a permanent halt during the mid-point of my studies. That period was characterized by a sense of abandonment that still bears significant reflection and pain. This being said, there are several people to acknowledge as I bring this activity to its conclusion.

I would like to thank the members of my cohort, Cohort 2000 (DJ, Sylvia, and Nancy), who were always there to provide assistance and support when necessary. They have been with me throughout both the high points and most significantly through those low points as well—reminding me that I was capable of getting through the process.

I would like to thank my doctoral advisor, Carolyn Fluehr-Lobban. Without her guidance and support, there would be no book. She accepted me as her doctoral student despite the baggage that came hand-in-hand with that acceptance. She counseled me to start with a clean slate, move forward, and keep my eye on the prize. She was instrumental in assisting me to select the questions that most needed answering from the massive amount of data that I had collected. Her skills as a writer and an editor were invaluable Her belief in me will always be treasured. In addition, I thank my committee members, Dr. Patricia Cordeiro, Dr. Sandra-Jean Hicks, and Dr. David Byrd. Their guidance has been of great value. I also thank Dr. John Gleason for helping me to develop the plan for the study that this dissertation became.

Many thanks are given to Helen, Angie, Janet, and Kathleen, peers and friends from school. They held me together during the darkest days of this project, on those days when the last place I belonged was in front of students in a classroom.

I would like to thank my family who have put up with me during this entire seven-year process. Their support has been invaluable.

And lastly, I would like to thank the special education teachers who so willingly shared their ideas, practices, and expertise with me. They are at the heart of this work.

Part I
Introduction
Brief History of Special Education

Any answer to the question of where those with special needs might be found must begin with the history of special education. It is this history that provides the broad setting for the work that follows. The first educational and institutional arrangements that became the profession we now call special education were formally established during the Enlightenment, an intellectual movement that swept Europe beginning in the 18th century. It was during this period that people from all levels of society became interested as never before in social questions (Winzer, 1993). Philanthropy became a kind of fashion among the elite of European society. At the beginning of special education, society was interested in how to care for those individuals considered "exceptional." By the close of the 18th century, special education had become an accepted branch of education. However, charity, not education, was the driving force behind efforts to care and educate these individuals. The charitable and philanthropic efforts of this period resulted in wide-ranging pedagogical experiments, educational enterprises, the establishment of charitable foundations, and the emergence of professional teachers (Scheerenberger, 1983; Winzer, 1993).

During the late eighteenth century, medicine began to dominate the goal of understanding humanity. Successes with individuals who were blind and deaf meant that opportunities could be extended to other groups with disabilities, first to those labeled insane and then to those labeled as mentally retarded. However, initial efforts to work with these latter populations were subsumed within the newly emerging medical disciplines of psychology and psychiatry rather than education (Safford & Safford, 1996; Scheerenberger, 1983; Winzer, 1993). Medicine at this time was shaped by a prevailing belief in the taxonomic point of view, in the "conviction that general laws could be derived from the collection and analysis of particular facts and that genera and species had a natural and independent existence apart from the subjective perceptions of a human observer" (Winzer, 1993, p.59). Physicians believed that just as plants and minerals could be classified, so could diseases. Special education as it known today grew from these roots in the field of medicine. The medical roots developed during this period would stay with special education until the present.

Important figures during the beginnings of special education include Philippe Pinel (1745-1826), Jean-Marc Gaspard Itard (1775-1850), and Eduoard Seguin (1812-1880). Pinel's work with individuals in insane asylums led to the understanding that people with mental illness still required humane treatment. With humane treatment, their life conditions improved. Itard worked with the feral child, Victor. He saw an opportunity to use educational intervention to restore a child deprived of a place in civilized society to that society (Winzer, 1993). His work with Victor is documented in *The Wild Boy of Aveyron*. While it was acknowledged that Itard had not fully succeeded with Victor, it was determined that his lack of success was due to Victor and not the methodology that was employed with him. Placing the lack of educational success on Victor ultimately had important implications to the further development and practice of special education. Seguin continued to build on Itard's methods of practice. He believed that children with mental retardation could learn if taught through "specific sensory motor exercises", an approach he developed into a systematic sequence of training (Safford & Safford, 1996; Winzer, 1993). His works became the standard references in the field of special education for many years.

The idea of reforming society remained prominent through the remainder of the 19th century. As it is today, a primary mode for such improvement was the school system. Individuals such as Henry Barnard and Horace Mann offered important and insightful commentary on learning environments. In addition to championing the further development of the common school, individuals such as these involved themselves in campaigning for the development of institutions to serve the special needs of individuals who were deaf, blind, mentally retarded, or delinquent. Others, such as Samuel Gridley Howe and Thomas Gallaudet, established learning institutions for students with disabilities. Along with such schools, came larger facilities—the state institutions. A major characteristic of this period was the fact that these institutional developments were occurring alongside advances in the common school movement (Winzer, 1993). Throughout the 19th century, increasing numbers of students with disabilities received their education and training in the institutions that were developing. Two separate educational systems were clearly developing alongside each other.

The institutions that developed during the 19th and early 20th centuries were notable for the achievements that they made in the education of individuals with disabilities and for the historical records that they generated. The individuals that administered these institutions amply documented their methodologies and communications with peers. Among the issues that their communications addressed were placement, curriculum, vocational training, and early intervention. Debate around these issues continues in schools today. However, the reports generated by the institutions did little to preserve information regarding the daily practice of teachers or the experiences of the children in these facilities (Winzer, 1993).

At the same time that the institutional movement was providing some benefit in the education for individuals with disabilities, there was potentially a darker side to it. As the 19th century became the 20th, increased urbanization, industrialization, and immigration brought with them an apparent increase in deviant behavior. Social Darwinism and the Eugenics movement sought to explain the successes of an establishment and failures of misfits through a theory of inherited intellectual development. The mainstay in these movements was the IQ test. The IQ test introduced both scientific method into a field where previously only subjective judgment was possible, purported to demonstrate the superiority of specific groups, and upheld popular biases about inassimilable and inferior European heritage. Such thinking helped to perpetuate the notion that controlling and managing exceptionality was best achieved through segregation (Osgood, 2005; Safford & Safford, 1996; Scheerenberger, 1987; Winzer, 1993).

Meanwhile, schools were also struggling with the problem of what to do with students with exceptionality. Compulsory school attendance laws meant that schools could no longer ignore students with disabilities; they had to find solutions to the problems of educating such students within the system. Teachers were often unwilling to handle such children in regular classes. Administrators, seeking to establish order, discipline, and high standards in schools were averse to placing such students in regular classes. Thus, schools created the special segregated class (Winzer, 1993). These segregated classes were an obvious way to satisfy the requirements of the law and meet the needs of the schools. Children that posed problems were removed from the mainstream classrooms so that they could not interfere with the learning of normal children or lower the standards of a school.

This model of service delivery through a special class placement has persisted well into the 1970s (Osgood, 2005; Winzer, 1993). The use of the special class is especially used as a placement option for certain, more involved, groups of students with disabilities (Lipsky & Gartner, 1997). Removing children from the mainstream continues to persist in schools, though such removal is frequently more positively interpreted as being in the interest of the student with special needs rather than in the interest of interfering with the learning of other, normal children or lowering school standards.

Special classes developed in response to specific disability categories—there were classes for blind children, deaf children, and children with speech impairments. But it was with the development of classes for children with mental retardation that the use of IQ test scores began to figure most prominently. IQ test scores were used to classify students according to their ability to be educated despite cautions from experts in the field who noted that testing was best used to assist in educational planning rather than in tracking and segregating students (Winzer, 1993). However, some students with special needs were not always welcomed into the world of the public school. According to Winzer (1993), public schools made it clear that they did not want "untrainables" in their classrooms.

By the 1950's many school districts in the country had special education programs. However, concerns related to such programs were abundant. The examination of such programs documented that students there were often without an opportunity to learn academic skills; instead they spent their instructional time learning manual or adaptive living skills. Manual skills might include such tasks as bead stringing, simple assembly, or sorting, while adaptive living skills might include such tasks as tooth-brushing, hair-brushing, or other personal hygiene skills. Research also began to note that students who were not removed from general education classrooms learned more than students who were removed. Finally, parents began actively advocating improving the educational opportunities offered to their children (Friend & Bursuck, 2002). Reactions such as those of experts to the not-so-appropriate uses of IQ tests; of researchers to the not-so-outstanding outcomes of special education programs; and of parents to the questionable educations their children were receiving would set the stage for the developments in special education that were to come as we entered the 1960s and 1970s.

In addition, the expanding civil rights movement of the period began to influence the development of new approaches to special education. While this movement initially addressed the rights of African Americans, it expanded to influence the thinking about individuals with disabilities (Friend & Bursuck, 2002). The pre-eminent case of the civil rights movement was Brown v. Board of Education. This case, a landmark decision of the United States Supreme Court, ruled that arbitrary discrimination against any group of people was unlawful and explicitly outlawed racial segregation in public schools. The case ruled in this way on the grounds that the doctrine of "separate but equal" public education could never truly provide black students with an education similar to that available to white students. Separate education was not equal! When extended to the population of children with disabilities, the discrimination occurred when they were denied access to local public schools because of their disabilities. The decision in Brown v. Board of Education paved the way for the introduction of the concept of integration into public education (Friend & Bursuck, 2002). All students could and should be educated in public schools.

The quality of life and education for children and adults with disabilities, especially those with mental retardation, improved greatly through the 1960s. Parents, often supported by the courts, were increasing demands that their children be provided with educational services in local school districts (Center for the Future of Children, 1996; Friend and Bursuck, 2002). In addition, educators were beginning to critically examine and question the value of special classes. The humanistic trends of the 1960s continued into the 1970s. A key goal of society became the normalization of all individuals with disabilities. Such a goal meant treating individuals with disabilities fairly and humanely. Special classes began to be abandoned in favor of placement in general education classrooms along with appropriate special education support services (Winzer, 1993). Educators came to agree that all children, disabled or not, had the right to a free, appropriate public education. The concept became law with the passage of Public Law 94-142, the Education for All Handicapped Children Act of 1975. The concepts of mainstreaming, integration, and inclusion began to achieve a prominence in thought and to appear regularly in the research literature.

The chief tool of implementation for PL94-142 was the principle of the least restrictive environment (LRE). This principle held that students with disabilities need not be removed from general education classes. In the early years of its implementation, LRE was expressed through the concept of mainstreaming. While not a term that is not actually found in the law, mainstreaming emphasized the place in which special education took place. According to Lipsky and Gartner (1997), mainstreaming assumed the existence of two separate educational systems, one in general education and one in special education. They further noted that mainstreaming was typically applicable to those students considered to be most like "normal". In the 1980s, the term "mainstreaming" gave way to the term "integration." Integration was borrowed from the civil rights perspective on race relations and viewed students with disabilities as targets of discrimination and disenfranchisement. Lipsky and Gartner (1997) also stated that both mainstreaming and integration suffered from fundamental flaws inherent in the LRE principal. These flaws included the following: 1) LRE legitimates a restrictive environment in assuming that there may be certain students who must be removed form the general education environment, 2) LRE confuses segregation and integration with the intensity of services, more intensive services are typically associated with more restrictive environments, 3) LRE is based upon a readiness model—students must prove their readiness for an integrated setting rather than be presumed able to be in a given environment, and 4) LRE directs attention to the physical setting rather than to necessary services and supports (Taylor, 1988).

In response to such critiques of the LRE and to research regarding the efficacy of special education classrooms, the 1980s saw the proposal of the Regular Education Initiative (REI), initiated by Madeleine Will, then the assistant secretary of the Department of Education (Lipsky & Gartner, 1997; Osgood, 2005). REI was essentially a series of proposals defining the parameters of integration for students with special needs. Skrtic (1990) stated that the REI proposals all, to some degree or another, called for eliminating the pull-out approach to mainstreaming. Each proposal also planned for restructuring the two separate educational systems into a new single system in which most or all students who needed help in school were provided with in-class support. The initiatives included within the REI departed from earlier reform efforts of mainstreaming and integration in their appreciation of the need for broader structural reform. They further became the initial steps in a movement that suggested that all students should be included in general education classrooms from the start of their educational careers rather than be separated from those classrooms (Lipsky & Gartner,

1997). REI proposals called for "purposeful integration" of students with special needs; that is, all students with disabilities, regardless of severity, would be educated in general classrooms, with necessary supports (Lipsky & Gartner, 1997, p. 79). Proponents of REI proposals have noted that "the curriculum that special education has enacted over the years, and the whole school context in which special education takes place, have interacted to disenfranchise students from access to a broad, rich, and meaningful education" (Pugach and Warger, 1993, quoted in Lipsky & Gartner, 1997, p. 80). Variations of the thinking first proposed during these initiatives continue to characterize present school practices.

Presently, schools have entered the era of standards-based education and accountability. With the 1997 and 2004 federal reauthorizations of the Individuals with Disabilities Education Act (formerly PL94-142), students with disabilities must demonstrate progress in the general education curriculum and participate in state and district assessments. Issues regarding standards and accountability noted by teachers and administrators were quickly identified. Educators became concerned with how to deliver standards-based instruction to students with special needs. The need to create high standards and demonstrate accountability in schools has only recently been addressed for students with special needs (Kleinert & Kearns, 2001). These requirements clearly have the potential to impact the practice of special education teachers. This brief history provides the broad framework for the work that follows.

Chapter One

Studying Special Education Teachers

Why Study Special Education Teachers?

This chapter examines the literature that surrounds what teachers know and do in their classrooms as well as methodologies that have been used to study those experiences. Research literature addressing the connection between teacher beliefs, knowledge, and practice states that, in general, teachers demonstrate variety in their belief systems and in their practices and expectations for student performance (Barnes, 1992; Collins, 1986; Cuban 1993; Gamoran, Nystrand, Berands, & Lepore, 1996; Lipman, 1997; Peterson, McCarthey, & Elmore, 1996; Richardson, 1990; Rist, 1970; Swanson-Owens, 1986). This literature reveals that individual teacher belief systems and expectations play a determining role in the education students receive. The contents that make up these belief systems include teachers' experiences, knowledge, and new learning. Each of these areas directly impacts the activities that occur in the classroom.

The types of education that many students receive are subject to frequent reform. This is no less true for special education. One current reform initiative is the inclusion of students with significant cognitive disabilities in standards-based reform and statewide assessment. The mandate to participate in general curriculum and assessment may bring about changes in classroom practice while raising several significant questions. These questions include: (1) How do teachers respond to these reforms? (2) How does reform change what teachers do in the classroom? (3) What changes appear in practice? (4) Specifically, does participating in standards-based instruction and an alternate assessment process for students with moderate or significant cognitive disabilities have an effect on the practice of special education teachers?

While there is an existing literature on the practice of general education teachers, there is limited research documenting the practice of special education teachers. The present study documents the influence of special education teachers' knowledge and experience, their belief systems, on their daily practice.

Three major research trends inform teacher practice and potential changes in that practice brought about by the movement to standards-based instruction and assessment for students with significant disabilities. These research trends are: (1) teacher beliefs, knowledge, and practice, (2) the practice of inclusion, and (3) the effect of standards-based reform on instruction for students with disabilities. The literature on the relationship between teacher knowledge, special education, and the teaching practices of inclusion in standards-based reform provide a means for organizing the literature review.

Literature on Teacher Knowledge and Practice

The thinking, planning, and decision-making processes of teachers have come to form their own branch of educational research. Investigations in this area seek to understand and explain why teaching is difficult, how teachers manage the complexity of teaching, and how teachers' personal backgrounds impact their classroom actions. The vast majority of this type of research, research on understanding teacher knowledge and practice, has been done since 1976 (Clark & Peterson, 1986). It is a branch of research that has developed steadily (Malouf & Schiller, 1995; Richardson, 1994). It is a body of research that emphasizes the importance of what teachers know and do in the classroom. This research is a result of what Richardson (1994) identifies as a shift in understanding of what teachers do. She points out that conceptions of teaching have shifted from a view of teachers as the recipients and consumers of research to a view of teachers as producers or mediators of knowledge.

Research on the practice of teaching has shifted from a focus on teacher effectiveness to a focus on understanding how teachers make sense of teaching and learning. This research examines a wide range of variables that contribute to such important aspects of schooling as learning to teach, teachers' classroom action, and changes in practice (Richardson, 1994). These variables include teacher knowledge and learning, teacher attitudes and beliefs, and the teaching context itself (Malouf & Schiller, 1995; Pajares, 1992; Richardson, 1990; Richardson, 1994). Teacher knowledge and learning, teachers' attitudes and beliefs, and the teaching context influence the significance of the impact of research on practice (Malouf & Schiller, 1995; Richardson, 1990). It is logical to suggest that teacher knowledge and learning, teachers' attitudes and beliefs, and the teaching context also impact the effects of change efforts on teacher practice.

Richardson (1990) suggests teachers "filter" research-based practices through their personalities and belief systems. This is to say that teachers absorb and adjust new knowledge to fit their personalities and belief systems. This process of filtering can alter the practice significantly as the assimilation of new knowledge takes place (Richardson, 1990). Malouf & Schiller (1995) suggest that Richardson's (1990) conception of a filter for assimilating new knowledge and changing existing knowledge is accurate. Teacher learning is not simply an additive process but an assimilative one. Examples of the assimilative nature of teacher knowledge and learning occur frequently in the literature (Clandinin & Connelly, 1986; Elbaz, 1981; Peterson et al., 1996; Swanson-Owens, 1986).

Elbaz (1981) suggests the work of teaching should be seen as an exercise of a particular kind of knowledge. She identified four categories of teacher knowledge: (1) subject matter knowledge, (2) personal knowledge, (3) interaction knowledge, and (4) practical knowledge. Of particular importance to this study is practical knowledge. Practical knowledge is defined as knowledge derived from practice. A teacher's practical knowledge includes five orientations: (1) situational, (2) theoretical, (3) personal, (4) social, and (5) experiential. Teachers confront all manner of tasks and situations and draw on a variety of sources of knowledge to help them manage events in the classroom. While the focus of activity in the classroom is teaching, teachers' lives in their totality affect what happens in the classroom in terms of activities and organization (Clandinin & Connelly, 1986).

Other studies of teacher knowledge illustrate Elbaz's point that teachers exercise particular kinds of knowledge when they teach. In a qualitative study of how teachers enacted selected reform efforts with regard to the teaching of writing, Peterson et al. (1996) demonstrate that teachers taught writing in a variety of ways despite having the opportunity to participate in similar ongoing professional development. Teachers implemented what they were taught in a manner consistent with their personal levels of ease in teaching writing. Some were better able to change instruction as a result of the training on writing than others.

Adapting a case study methodology as employed by Elbaz, Swanson-Owens' (1986) study of teaching writing in a high school yields similar results. Swanson-Owens identifies each teacher's "curricular system of meaning". This term, "curricular system of meaning", refers to an analytic set of categories that identify specific areas of teacher thinking. In this study, the analytic categories consisted of teacher knowledge, materials and activities, teacher characteristics, and student characteristics. Swanson-Owens employed data from multiple sources including interviews, observations, and analyses of students' written artifacts. Both teachers in her study taught writing based on their understanding of its purpose in their classrooms. Practices varied because each teacher had a different conception of the purpose for writing.

These studies indicate the importance of teacher perceptions about their knowledge of teaching and the content taught in the classroom. Also important to understanding teacher practice is the role that beliefs and attitudes play in what occurs in the classroom.

There are a number of terms used in the literature to describe teacher beliefs and attitudes. These terms include values, judgments, assumptions, rules of practice, and perspectives (Pajares, 1992). In his review of the literature on teacher beliefs, Pajares (1992) states, "few would argue that the beliefs teachers' hold influence their perceptions and judgments which in turn affect their behavior in their classrooms (p. 307)." Pajares further suggests this is likely because attitudes and beliefs are more affective and evaluative than general knowledge; general knowledge tends to be more objective. Because of the affective orientation of beliefs and attitudes, they function as filters for interpreting reality in a manner similar to what Richardson (1990) describes when she discusses teacher knowledge. Again, the literature contains numerous research examples of teacher attitudes and beliefs shaping practice (Barnes, 1992; Collins, 1986; Gamoran et al., 1995; Lipman, 1997; Rist, 1970).

In his book designed to teach teachers how to set up exploratory talk in the classroom, Barnes (1992) points out that there are specific communication patterns employed in the classroom. These patterns impart the content learned as well as serve to convey the hidden curriculum. This hidden curriculum shapes and is shaped by cultural understandings, beliefs, and values of both students and teachers. Research also shows that cultural understandings, beliefs, and values contribute to teachers' various forms of knowledge (Clandinin & Connelly, 1986; Elbaz, 1981). The perceptions of performance, as well as the expectations for performance or behavior that result from the teacher's knowledge systems as identified in the research may influence the education students receive (Clandinin & Connelly, 1986; Elbaz, 1981). Several additional studies illustrate the role that teacher perceptions of performance and their expectations play in the classroom.

In a case study focusing on differential instruction in reading groups, Collins (1986) found that individual aptitude was not the sole determinant of continued placement in an ability group, particularly placement in low-ability groups. While studying the reading and discourse styles of different ability groups, he found instruction in the higher-ability groups concentrated on comprehension. Instruction in the lower groups tended to focus on linguistic instruction.

In a study of the effects of ability grouping in middle and high school, Gamoran et al. (1995) offer confirmation of Collins' results. They looked at achievement data, distribution of instruction, and the effects of ability grouping in 92 classes. Students at different levels in the Gamoran et al. study received a consistent amount of instruction, although the content of that instruction was very different. Discourse in the higher-ability groups focused on literature while discourse in lower-ability groups focused on skills that did not necessarily emphasize academic work.

In a case study of teacher collaboration and decision making in restructuring a junior high school and the subsequent implications for low-achieving African-American students, Lipman (1997) demonstrates the effect of economic, political, ideological, and cultural influences on teacher participation in school restructuring. She found that efforts toward school change occur in contexts that are neither neutral nor isolated from larger social forces. In this study, teachers failed to examine their beliefs regarding their students, narrowing their vision of ways to alter their existing practices. In these instances, their practice was less likely to change.

If teachers fail to examine their beliefs regarding students as demonstrated by Lipman's (1997) work, they may also demonstrate a low expectation of certain students' success in the school mainstream (Rist, 1970). Rist examines the way in which a classroom teacher formed opinions concerning the capabilities and potential of various children in her classroom. In an ethnographic study of a classroom composed of African-American students in a low socioeconomic setting, Rist found that the teacher's opinions of the children were more often based on social characteristics rather than academic characteristics. Students with less desirable characteristics were less likely to be active in the classroom. Expectations for the less active group of students were also generally low. Low expectations for success led to certain students receiving a less-than-adequate education. According to Rist (1970), such low expectations of success can ultimately lead to students seeing themselves as inadequate and consequently as failures.

Several of the works cited emphasize the influence of situational factors in the development of and change in teacher practice. Situational factors included setting, perceptions and expectations of teachers and students, curriculum, and training opportunities. Other barriers to the development of teacher knowledge and to change in practice include externally imposed curriculum and materials, the relative isolation of the teacher, lack of collegiality, heavy workloads, ambiguity about goals, and insufficient time and resources (Malouf & Schiller, 1995). These factors form a large part of the basis for Cuban's (1993) argument that classrooms have a greater tendency to remain stable rather than change.

Cuban's arguments concerning the influence of situational factors in teachers' acceptance of and ability to reform their practice have recently been newly demonstrated in Kennedy's (2005) study addressing classroom life. In that study, Kennedy worked with teachers she described as "average", that is, her teachers worked in school settings that were "not necessarily noted for their own local reform efforts". She used videotaped lessons and interviews that focused on what she defined as the essential tasks of teaching. Her data were analyzed for themes and patterns that illustrated the teachers' lines of thinking concerning the actions that they took during specific lessons. Her analysis shows how carefully teachers think about their teaching and the various ways in which that teaching can go awry. Kennedy uses the teachers' own practice to illustrate the complex situations into which reform efforts must fit. She demonstrates that reform efforts do not always take into account the difficulties that teachers can encounter on a daily basis. Most importantly, she convincingly demonstrates that teachers are not acting to prevent reform. Kennedy shows that teachers are interested in reform and attend to reforms, although they often make numerous adjustments to those reforms that suit their own beliefs and practices.

On the surface, Cuban's (1993) argument that classrooms tend to remain relatively stable makes sense; however, both Cuban and other research literature indicate teachers and activity in classrooms do change. At issue may be the directionality of the relationship between beliefs and practice. The question becomes, "Do beliefs change first or does practice change first?" In a four-year long case study of one teacher, Hunsaker and Johnston (1992) use reflective and collaborative writing to understand the change process. They demonstrate that in the process of learning new educational practices, the teacher's belief system also changed (Hunsaker & Johnston, 1992). In this instance, the teacher learned new practices first; these changes in practice led to changes in belief systems. Change in practice leading to change in belief is the generally accepted model of staff development as outlined in 1986 by Guskey (Richardson, Anders, Tidwell, & Lloyd, 1991).

However, in a study of teacher beliefs and the teaching of reading comprehension, Richardson et al. (1991) point out that while beliefs of teachers do relate to their classroom practices, this is not always the case. They also note the relationship between beliefs and practice may operate in a manner opposite to that described by Hunsaker and Johnston (1992). Richardson et al. (1991) document instances where teacher beliefs do not relate to teaching practices, proposing that in these instances, the teacher may be in the process of changing beliefs and, consequently, practices. They demonstrated that beliefs changed first, with practice following.

Although the literature on teacher practice is developing, much of the research in this area focuses on general education. The literature on teacher practice is less developed for special education (Malouf & Schiller, 1995). Information on what is occurring in special education is found in the literature on mainstreaming (or integration) and inclusion.

Literature on Integration and Inclusion

The integration of students with disabilities has long been a subject of study (Kavale & Forness, 2000; Scruggs & Mastropieri, 1996). The literature on the subject is vast; among the topics addressed are its outcomes, its methodology, its sustainability, and perceptions of integration and inclusion. Issues related to the integration of students with disabilities can be traced historically to the beginning of special education in the 18th century (Scheerenberger, 1983). "Mainstreaming" refers to the process of integrating students with disabilities into general education classes in order to meet the requirement of placing students in the "least restrictive environment" as mandated by the Education for All Handicapped Children Act of 1975 (PL 94-142, now the Individuals with Disabilities Education Act) (Scruggs & Mastropieri, 1996). Inclusion is a concept employed to describe schools that meet the needs of all students by establishing learning communities for students with and without disabilities by educating them together in age-appropriate general education classrooms in neighborhood schools (Kavale & Forness, 2000).

In their review of the literature on integration, Kavale and Forness (2000) identified several significant research areas, including: (1) perceptions and attitudes of general education teachers toward inclusion, (2) practices and actions in the regular education classes, (3) social outcomes of general education placement, as well as, student perceptions of general education placement, and (4) teacher skill and ability. Of these identified research areas, the perception and attitude of general education teachers receives frequent attention (Janney, Snell, Beers, & Raynes, 1995; Lieber, Capell, Wolfberg, Horn, & Beckman, 1998; Scruggs & Mastropieri, 1996; Soodak, Podell, & Lehman, 1998). Various studies look at the relationship of teacher perception of inclusion efforts to additional factors such as the move toward increased integration (Janney et al., 1995), the nature of the affective relationship of teachers' responses to inclusion (Soodak, Podell, & Lehman, 1998), and the enactment of teacher beliefs within the context of classroom practices related to inclusion (Lieber et al., 1998).

Scruggs and Mastropieri (1996) conducted a quantitative synthesis of the survey research on general education teachers' perceptions of including students with disabilities in their classrooms. They analyze the results of 28 survey studies, conducted over the period from 1958-1995. They found that two-thirds of the general education classroom teachers represented in the cumulative sample supported the concept of mainstreaming/inclusion. They also found that fewer than one-third of these teachers expressed the belief that the general education classroom was the optimal placement or would produce greater benefits than other placements for certain students. While some teachers were willing to include students with disabilities in their own classes, their willingness to include was directly affected by the level of student disability and the amount of additional teacher responsibility required of having the student with disabilities in the classroom. Although many of the teachers felt mainstreaming/inclusion could provide some benefits, only one-third or fewer of the teachers felt they had sufficient time, skills, training, or resources necessary for effectively implementing mainstreaming/inclusion.

Scruggs and Mastropieri's (1996) results are qualitatively supported in a study of the impact of teachers' beliefs and perceptions within the context of integrating students with moderate and severe disabilities (Janney et al., 1995). The researchers interviewed 26 classroom teachers from five school districts that were undertaking a planned change from segregated to integrated models of special education service delivery. School districts were selected from a group of fourteen school districts using stratified purposeful sampling. They were chosen to maximize variation in the amount of integrated programming being provided. Interviewees were general education teachers in the schools in districts that served as local demonstration sites. Additionally, the teachers interviewed were experienced in the process of integration. Data were analyzed inductively, with interviews coded for themes related to beliefs and attitudes toward the integration effort, how teachers' beliefs and attitudes altered during implementation, and any factors that teachers credited as having influenced those alterations. The results of the analysis indicated that the degree of energy required of teachers to move toward integration and the rewards of increased integration were significant factors in the acceptance of integration as a change in practice, supporting Scruggs and Mastropieri's finding that the amount of required teacher responsibility was important to the acceptance of mainstreaming/inclusion. Further, a clear understanding of the purpose of the change and the clarity of its implementation methods were also noted as being important in the acceptance of increased integration, supporting the Scruggs and Mastropieri finding that teachers often felt that increased training was required in order to successfully implement mainstreaming or inclusion.

Soodak, Podell, & Lehman (1998) confirm a relationship among teacher, student, and the school as prominent factors in predicting teachers' responses to inclusion as described by Scruggs and Mastropieri (1996). Soodak, Podell, and Lehman's, participants were surveyed regarding their response to inclusion, self-efficacy, use of differentiated teaching methods, and school climate. The study found there to be two affective dimensions of teachers' responses to including a child with disabilities in their general education classrooms. The first dimension, the hostility/receptivity dimension, reflected teachers' willingness to include students with disabilities in their classes. The second dimension, the anxiety/calmness dimension, reflected teachers' emotional tension when actually serving a student with disabilities. Following multiple tests of reliability for the two identified dimensions, regression analysis was performed using each dimension as the dependent variable. Overall, teacher attitudes and beliefs, students' characteristics, and school climate related to both the hostility/receptivity dimension and the anxiety/receptivity dimension.

The study additionally found that the type of student disability (e.g. physical or cognitive disability) was most strongly related to teachers' responses to inclusion. Receptivity toward inclusion was associated with higher teacher efficacy, use of differentiated teaching practices, teacher collaboration, and physical rather than cognitive disabilities. Teachers were more hostile to including students with mental retardation, learning disabilities, and behavioral disorders as opposed to students with physical handicaps. Additionally, teachers' receptivity toward including students with learning disabilities diminished with experience. This response may be related to not having the desired degree of success with these students. If teachers felt themselves to be unsuccessful with students with learning disabilities then they were less receptive to having these students in their classrooms. Lower anxiety about inclusion was also associated with high incidence handicaps, high teacher efficacy, and small class size.

Lieber et al. (1998) provide an example of the enactment of teacher beliefs about inclusion. This study used interview and classroom observation to determine themes and to identify practices related to inclusion. Data were analyzed using Glaser and Strauss' constant comparative method. The data were sorted and categorized for the purpose of identifying important themes regarding teacher beliefs and inclusion. Several themes regarding inclusion were identified. These themes included such beliefs as all the children are equal parts of the whole, the world is not made up of thirty typically developing children, the students have so much to offer one another, and the students learn a lot by watching other students. The authors indicate that these results were consistent across the teachers in this study and also with teachers' responses in similar studies. While the themes of inclusion were similar, there was considerable variation in the way in which the themes were enacted in the classroom.

New literature addressing teachers' responses to inclusion and the methodology for achieving the practice is published regularly. One such study looks at teachers' response to collaborative professional development (Brownell, Adams, Sindelar, Waldron, and Vanhover, 2006). In this study, case study methodology was employed to study eight general education teachers response to collaborative professional development. The researchers used formal and informal classroom observations, interviews, and fieldnotes to investigate the use of Teacher Learning Cohorts (TLC)—a professional development process driven by collaborative problem solving, focusing on what teachers felt they needed to make changes in their practice geared toward improving the education of students with disabilities and other high risk students. Results indicated various levels of adoption of the TLC model. High adopters of the model had the most (a) knowledge of curriculum and pedagogy, (b) knowledge and student friendly beliefs about managing student behavior, (c) student-focused views of instruction, and (d) ability to carefully reflect on students' learning and then adapt strategies for individual students. The data here demonstrate how teacher knowledge, beliefs, skills, and reflective ability work together to influence teachers' responses to inclusion and their ability to benefit from collaborative professional development efforts.

The studies cited on integration or inclusion stress the importance of the teacher in the acceptance of, or resistance to, change. In illustrating and emphasizing the role of teachers' perceptions and beliefs in practice, these studies also support the idea that what teachers know and do directly influence what goes on in the classroom. Lieber et al.'s (1998) findings regarding teacher beliefs and inclusion confirm other researchers' work regarding teacher practice; teachers confront all manner of tasks and situations and draw on a variety of sources of knowledge to help them manage the events in their classroom (Clandinin & Connelly, 1986; Elbaz, 1981). This study further supports the notion that practices differ because individual teachers have different conceptions of the subject matter they teach and different orientations to student learning (see Peterson et al., 1995; Swanson-Owens, 1986). Brownell et al. (2006) demonstrate that successful implementation of inclusive efforts remains a work in progress dependent on teachers' ability and beliefs.

Most recently, Williamson, Mcleskey, Hoppey, & Rentz (2006) support this assumption that inclusion remains a work in progress by noting that while progress has been made in placing students with disabilities in general education classrooms, the trend in such placement may have reached plateau. Inclusion with general education peers can be a function of the degree of cognitive disability that a student displays. Placement further tends to be influenced by the changing context of policy and practice. Finally, some states are more successful at creating inclusive practices than others.

The primary focus in these studies tends to be the response of general education teachers in mainstreamed or inclusive situations. Limited mention is made of special education teachers. This limited mention of special education teachers continues as the literature that addresses school reform expands.

Reform movements in special education have occurred in response to the issue of gaining greater access to general education environments. Mainstreaming is a process (Scruggs & Mastropierri, 1996) and inclusion a movement (Kavale & Forness, 2000). In practice, both mainstreaming and inclusion tend to address the location of instruction more than the content of instruction. The necessary supports for integration are often lacking. The movement to standards-based instruction addresses the content of the instruction offered in the general education setting but not the location of the instruction. In practice, the content of instruction often becomes associated with traditional conceptions of curriculum and student ability. Such traditional conceptions of curriculum often reveal that there is a great deal of material that must be covered and that there is often not enough time to adequately achieve that end. Since teachers' knowledge influences the practice of integration and mainstreaming or inclusion, their response to the newest educational reform mandate of providing access to standards-based instruction is significant for the education of students with disabilities.

Literature on the Inclusion of Students with Disabilities in Standards-Based Reform

While the literature cited above indicates a heavy emphasis on general educators' practice, this does not mean that no literature exists examining the impact of standards-based reform on special educators and the students that they teach. Research on the applicability of educational standards for students with disabilities is emerging. Three general trends in the research are identified:

1. General descriptive material about the "nuts and bolts" of standards (Bechard, 2000; Elliot & Thurlow, 1997).
2. Descriptive exemplars of ways in which students with disabilities, particularly significant cognitive disabilities, access standards-based instruction or an earlier version of inclusive instruction (Ford, Schnorr, Meyer, Davern, Black, & Dempsey, 1989; Jorgensen, Fisher, & Roach, 1997; Kearns, Kleinert, Clayton, Burdge, & Williams, 1998; Kearns, Kleinert, & Kennedy, 1999; Kleinert & Kearns, 2001).
3. Perceptions and attitudes related to standards-based instruction for students with disabilities (McLaughlin, Henderson, & Rhim, 1998; Raber, Roach, & Fraser, 1998; Thompson, Thurlow, Parson, & Barrow, 2000). An important aspect of the literature regarding special education's access to standards-based reform is an emerging

literature on the assessment component of standards-based instruction for students with significant cognitive disabilities (Kampfer, Horvath, Kleinert, & Kearns, 2001; Kleinert, Kearns, & Kennedy, 1997; Kleinert & Kearns, 1999). How appropriate will participation in such instruction be for students with special needs? What will the impact of including such students in school accountability systems be?

In research conducted prior to the reauthorization of IDEA 97, McLaughlin et al. (1998) use a case study approach to study policies, programs, and reform initiatives implemented in a diverse cross-section of five school districts. Each of the districts differed in terms of size, economics, location, and degree of state versus local control. The authors analyzed teachers' and administrators' perceptions of observed reforms regarding the impact of those reforms on students with disabilities. Data were collected from participants in various roles in each district, using a variety of qualitative techniques, including in-depth interviews, focus groups, classroom observations, and document review.

Mclaughlin et al. (1998) discovered that the most prominent reform initiatives in the districts studied were the implementation of standards-based reforms and the resulting changes in assessment practices. They documented a dichotomy in response patterns regarding access to content standards for students with high-incidence and low-incidence disabilities. Participants often noted questions about including students with high incidence disabilities such as specific learning disabilities, mild developmental disability, and behavior disorders. However, administrators and teachers expressed few worries regarding including students with low incidence disabilities such as significant cognitive disabilities and multiple handicaps; it was generally felt that students with significant cognitive disabilities required a set of individualized standards.

Overall, the study indicated that moving toward standards-based instruction had several positive effects. Participants expressed a belief that standards were directly changing the ways teachers instructed students. Teachers and administrators noted a move to a more process-oriented, project-based instruction. They expressed concern with how "all" students would meet designated performance standards. Teachers believed students with disabilities were receiving increased access to a wider variety of subject matter. They also believed the standards provided an impetus for setting more challenging goals for learners.

Despite this optimism regarding the impact of standards on curriculum, special education personnel expressed worries about how they would find the time and the opportunity to help students with disabilities learn content-related standards and acquire more functional skills. While teachers and administrators could identify potential benefits associated with including students with disabilities in standards-based instruction, they were more skeptical about including them in assessments. School personnel were concerned that the inclusion of such students would potentially impact school scores negatively.

Raber et al. (1998) study the manner in which four states were responding to standards-based reform. They employed qualitative methods to document states' responses to standards-based reform. They noted, "variability surrounding the education of students with disabilities is particularly acute" (p. 12). They further noted great variability in inclusion practices among the states and districts studied. Among the districts studied, students with high-incidence disabilities, such as specific learning disabilities, mild developmental delay, and behavior disorder, were more likely to be targeted for inclusion, resulting in greater access to academic content. This finding is consistent with the dichotomy regarding the inclusion of students with high-incidence disabilities and low-incidence disabilities as reported by McLaughlin et al. (1998). With regard to students with significant cognitive disabilities, Raber et al. (1998) concluded the districts studied were "struggling with the problem of inclusion."

In one of the few studies focusing on the responses of special education teachers directly, Thompson et al. (2000) conducted an investigation of the perceptions of educators as they worked toward including students with disabilities in instruction using Minnesota's new educational standards. They surveyed a group of 90 educators in ten schools across all grade levels in a large suburban school district in Minnesota. The majority of their respondents were special education teachers. Thompson et al. (2000) present their data in a "pre-statistical percentage analysis," stating that their sample was too small to support statistical analysis.

Thompson et al.'s (2000) results indicate that the expectations for meeting the standards are higher for students with disabilities who have increased time in general education classrooms than for those served primarily in special education resource rooms. This finding is consistent with findings in both the McLaughlin et al. (1998) and Raber et al. (1998) studies. Thompson et al.'s teachers also had higher expectations regarding participation in standards-based instruction for students with high incidence disabilities and lower expectations for students with low incidence disabilities or more significant disabilities.

The researchers also noted that the majority of the teachers surveyed expressed the belief that most students with developmental disabilities were not expected to meet Minnesota's High Standards. This finding is somewhat consistent with the McLaughlin et al. (1998) finding that teachers had lower expectations for students who were more cognitively involved. However, this cannot be accurately determined from the manner in which the conclusion is expressed. In this study, Thompson et al. (2000) do not indicate the levels of functioning of the students with disabilities.

The three preceding studies provide useful information regarding students with disabilities accessing standards-based instruction. The studies do not address how students with significant cognitive disabilities might also address standards-based instruction. The literature regarding alternate portfolio assessment provides some understanding of standards-based reform for students with significant cognitive disabilities.

Literature on Participation in Standards-Based Reform for Students with Significant Disabilities in Standards-Based Reform

Researchers have argued that a state or district assessment process for students with moderate and severe disabilities is key to ensuring high expectations for all children (Kleinert, Kearns, & Kennedy, 1997). Some researchers suggest that the inclusion of students with moderate and severe disabilities in the assessment process, through an alternate assessment, will improve instruction and enhance learning for these students (Elliot, 1997; Kleinert, Kennedy, & Kearns, 1999; Sailor, 1997). Preliminary research in the area of alternate assessment indicates that these assertions of positive impacts from participation in the assessment process have merit. In a survey study, using a Likert-scale response format, special education teachers cautiously indicated that they perceived general benefits for their students from inclusion in a portfolio assessment process. They noted some positive changes in instructional programming that resulted from their students' participation in the process. These changes included greater independence in certain areas of performance and increased opportunities for self-determination for students as a result of meeting the requirements of an alternate assessment (Kleinert, Kennedy, & Kearns, 1999).

While teachers perceive certain benefits from participation in the assessment process, the literature also indicates important concerns with that participation. Several factors influenced teachers' perception of and acceptance of the alternate assessment process. Such factors appeared as general problems associated with the alternate assessment process or as variables that influence the production of a portfolio. Teachers noted multiple problems with the alternate assessment process. These problems included time lost from teaching, a focus on teacher assessment rather than on student assessment, subjectivity in portfolio scoring, the need for evidence not natural to typical learning environments, and the need for more scoring training (Kleinert et al., 1999). Kleinert et al. (1999) also noted as problematic some teachers' pre-determined negative opinion regarding the final score of the portfolio in relation to the amount of time required to create a student portfolio. In actual practice, no matter how much time and effort was involved in the portfolio, students with disabilities still could not achieve a passing score in high stakes testing situations.

Extending the work of Kleinert et al. (1999), Kampfer et al. (2001) look at variables influencing teachers' responses to alternate assessment and the relationship between the amount of time and effort required to complete an alternate assessment portfolio and the portfolio score. They noted five items requiring moderate to extreme teacher effort in portfolio production. The items were (1) deciding what to include in a portfolio entry, (2) facilitating social relationships, (3) documenting student progress, (4) developing natural supports for instruction, and (5) accessing multiple settings for instruction. Regression analysis was conducted using teacher time spent on the portfolio and portfolio score as the outcome variable. Correlation coefficients indicated minimal correlations between time spent on the portfolio and the portfolio score. Results further indicated that teacher hours invested in completing the portfolio were only minimally related to portfolio scores. Instead, instructional variables such as (1) the degree of student involvement in the portfolio, (2) the extent to which portfolio items were embedded into daily instruction, and (3) teachers' perceptions of benefits of the portfolio to the student had a greater impact on portfolio scores. Kampfer et al. (2001), in particular, indicated a range of response in the perceived benefits of a portfolio assessment process. Teacher comments illustrating the extent of response in the perceptions of the alternate assessment process range from "the portfolio assessment is of little or no value" to "the portfolio provided wonderful evidence of student performance." Some teachers have positive perceptions of the alternate assessment process but other teachers find little or no value in the process.

Research in the area of alternate portfolio assessment focuses more on quantitative than qualitative analysis of the assessment process. Current literature in this area includes surveys regarding teacher perceptions of the alternate portfolio assessment and a study of the technical adequacy of the Kentucky model for alternate portfolio assessment. Although Kleinert et al. (1999) and Kampfer et al. (2000) analyzed teacher comments that were optionally included on their surveys, neither study explicitly sought to elicit teacher comments regarding the impact of the alternate assessment on teacher practice.

As states have further developed their standards-based instruction and alternate assessment processes, literature addressing these areas continues to appear. New literature has focused on the uses of assessment in special education classrooms. In a study that can be placed in the category of special education teacher practice, Siegel and Allinder (2005) examine the use of assessment practices for students with moderate and severe disabilities. The researchers surveyed 22 teachers in an urban Midwest school district regarding their use of different types of assessment. Diagnostic assessment came closest to meeting best practice standards. They found a pattern of mixed results on the teachers' uses of evaluative types of assessment. Some, but not all, teachers made use of the recommended practices of anecdotal recording, task analytic assessment, discrete trial, curriculum-based assessment or time-based assessment. Anecdotal data received the greatest amount of teacher use. However, this study focuses on assessment and not necessarily daily practice.

The results of the literature review reported here suggest that there is a need to further examine special education teachers' classroom practice. There is clearly an absence of information addressing the classroom practice of special education teachers. Taken as a whole, the research literature presented reveals the necessity to look more formally at teacher practice regarding accessing standards-based instruction for students with special needs and particularly at the practice of special education teachers.

Studying Special Education Teachers

This study is further grounded in research on teacher development as well as research on teachers' interactions with reforms. Educators respond differently to reform efforts and policies. Their responses include the creation of hybrids of old and new practices or adaptation of the elements of a reform effort in ways to address the practical issues of its implementation (Cuban, 1993; Mayrowetz, 1999; Weatherly & Lipsky, 1977). These responses become elements of teachers' practical knowledge. It is this practical knowledge that helps shape and dictate daily practice. Existing literature on teacher development and teacher interaction with standards-based teaching reform efforts, as well as the study of the contexts of teaching knowledge are briefly reviewed as they relate to developing the methodology for this study.

Literature on Studying Teacher Development

Research on the practice of teaching indicates the factors that comprise teaching include teacher knowledge and learning, teacher attitudes and beliefs, and teaching context (Clandinin & Connelly, 1986; Elbaz, 1981; Malouf & Schiller, 1995; Pajares, 1992; Peterson, et al. 1996; Richardson, 1990; Richardson, 1994; Swanson-Owens, 1986). However, teaching is more challenging than has previously been recognized (Evans, 1991). According to Evans (1991), the complexity of teaching is under-estimated and there is often little assistance provided to teachers to help them more fully understand their practice. Understanding the complexity of teacher practice involves knowledge of teacher development. The literature traces how teachers develop professionally (Holly, 1989; Johnson, Bowman, & Hall, 1990; Kelchtermas & Vanderberghe, 1993; Kelsay, 1989).

A variety of research methods have been employed to understand teacher development and practice. Clandinin and Connelly (1986) and Elbaz (1981) used case study methods to document the nature of individual teacher knowledge. These studies indicate that teacher knowledge consists of subject matter knowledge, personal knowledge, interaction knowledge, and practical knowledge (Elbaz, 1981). Such works also demonstrate that teachers carry out the business of teaching in a rhythmic cycle that is generally linked to the cycle of their lives; these rhythms become better defined as teachers' experience in the classroom develops (Clandinin & Connelly, 1986).

Kelchtermas and Vanderberghe (1993) used a biographical approach to study the professional development of teachers. They looked at teachers' career stories, that is, stories influenced by critical incidents, concepts, phrases, or people that teachers encountered. The critical incidents identified by the teachers influenced their development as teachers. Information obtained from the interviews of several teachers was analyzed vertically and horizontally. Vertical analysis referred to the teachers telling their career stories. Horizontal analysis consisted of comparing the teachers' stories with the intent of discovering the patterns, commonalities, and differences among the teachers. Kennedy and

Wyrick (1995) employed a similar methodology—a retrospective autobiographical approach to look at teachers-in-training. Their methodology was supplemented by the use of reflective assessment to examine critical incidents occurring during teacher training opportunities. The pre-service teachers in this study used retrospective autobiography to reflect on and examine their educational pasts and what influence those educational pasts had on their present teaching activities.

Other qualitative research has also made use of interviews and the development of case studies to look at the components of teacher knowledge and how teacher perceptions affect practice (Clandinin & Connelly, 1986; Elbaz, 1981; Hunsaker & Johnston, 1992; Janney et al., 1995; Lieber et al., 1998; Lipman, 1997; Mclaughlin et al., 1998; Peterson et al. 1996; Raber et al., 1998). The quantitative research on teacher practice used survey methods to explore topic-specific perceptions of several different educational reforms (Kampfer et al., 2001; Kleinert et al., 1999; Scruggs & Mastropieri, 1996; Soodak et al., 1998; Thompson et al., 2000).

In summary, this research emphasizes the importance of the teaching situation in the development of teacher practice. Teacher development occurs under situation-specific conditions. Teacher development is influenced by the situations in which teachers find themselves. Teachers develop their practice in a manner consistent with their unique personal histories of teaching and their beliefs. That is, teaching practice is impacted by the teacher's belief system. The third important factor in the development of teaching practice is the teacher's experience in the context of teaching, that is, the interaction of the teacher within the act of teaching students.

Literature on the Context of Teaching

A review of the theory addressing teacher knowledge suggests there are varied school-specific elements that influence teachers' practices (Bruner, 1977; Tyler, 1949). These elements include the development of curricula, appropriate learning experiences, evaluation, learning style, and student learning capacity. They become important as they are incorporated into a normative model of teaching. This normative model of teaching is a plan for teaching. Teachers take the elements of the teaching model into account as they practice in classrooms. These elements of teaching became the context for teaching in the study.

Tyler (1949) named three areas important to teaching—the development of curricula, appropriate learning experiences, and the use of evaluation. He stressed the importance of creating curricula that included objectives developed from studying learners' needs and interests, the community, the knowledge of subject specialists, and the broader culture. The organization of curricular content reflects a relationship among its elements over time and a relationship from one curricular area to another. Successive learning experiences build upon the experiences that preceded them but also emphasize a deeper understanding of the original material (Tyler, 1949). Evaluation of learning experiences was strongly recommended since it allowed teachers to determine the effectiveness of instruction. Evaluation allowed teachers to modify and improve both the learning experiences of the student and the curriculum.

Writing several years later, Bruner (1977) presented a similar view of curriculum. Curriculum should be organized in such a way that basic ideas are revisited repeatedly until a student's full formal thinking capacity is achieved. He placed emphasis on the role of the learner to the context of teaching. At each stage of development, a child has a characteristic way of viewing and explaining the world. A teacher must be able to represent the structure of the subject in terms of the child's way of knowing (Bruner, 1977). Together, the components of teaching described by Tyler (1949) and Bruner (1977) constitute the elements of teaching that were used in this study.

Further, each of the components of teaching mentioned so far—curriculum, learning experiences, evaluation, and learning style and stage can be incorporated into a normative model of teaching applicable to both general and special education.

In special education, the elements of such a teaching model are most commonly found in the Individual Education Plan (IEP) document. The IEP serves as the blueprint for a student's education for a year. It addresses areas of student need, including accommodations to be made in a general education class and the services and supports provided in that setting. The IEP process was recently revised as a result of the move toward standards-based education in general education and the reauthorization of the Individuals with Disabilities Education Act (IDEA 97). IDEA 97 mandated that students in special education also participate in and be evaluated through local and state assessments. The most recent reauthorization of IDEA, in 2004, has maintained the earlier mandate that students with special needs be included in local and state accountability efforts. For many states, this evaluation continues to encompass the idea of standards-based education. And, as stated previously, the impact of standards-based instruction on special education teacher practice bears examination. These literatures provided the necessary elements for studying the practice of special education teachers. The next chapter presents an initial self-study that came about as I applied this literature to my personal experiences.

Chapter Two
Evolution of the Study

"People have 'always' known that there were 'Others' living just beyond their territories: human beings who spoke in strange tongues and practiced unusual customs..." (Bohannan & van der Elst, 1998, p.3).

Students with special needs display an extensive range of abilities that impact the practice of education. The history of special education is a tale of two separate educational systems (Lipsky & Gartner, 1997; Winzer, 1993). Winzer (1993) noted that the earlier history of special education indicated that teacher practice and student experiences were not well documented. This remains true—neither special education teacher practice nor student experience is well documented especially when compared to the documentation that exists for general education teacher practice and student experience. Often such experiences are only indirectly documented. The concepts important in the history of education—teacher practice, curriculum, mainstreaming, integration, and inclusion are just as significant now as earlier. Their impact on the education that students receive remains vital. While there is an abundance of literature on the experiences of teachers in general education, there is a very limited literature on the experiences of teachers in special education, though special education must exist in the general education world. While special education has been historically discussed in terms of being a separate system, in fact, its services are typically delivered in the broader settings of general education environments. Given that special education is a world that is underrepresented in the literature on the practice of schooling in relation to its position in the general education world I was motivated to examine my own practice as a teacher of students with moderate and significant cognitive disabilities in that broader general education world.

My career in special education began in July 1981 with the acceptance of a position in a residential home for moderately handicapped adults. I had no background in special education and no real experience being with adults with disabilities. One of my more vivid memories of this time occurred during my actual interview. I found myself sitting at the picnic table with one of the more handicapped residents. No one else was in sight; the individual was having a very emotional moment (i.e. he was crying). It seemed that he remembered the people who were visiting that evening as former service providers. I somehow managed to cheer him up and redirect him to another activity. The significance of this event lies in the fact that I would never have guessed that I would be able to work productively with individuals as handicapped as this young man was. I had always hidden behind shyness in the few experiences that I had had with such individuals. I stayed at the residence for five years. During this period, I returned to school to take an introductory special education class. I knew that I wanted to learn more.

In 1987, I changed positions, relocating to the Center, a residential school for children with severe and profound developmental disabilities. My first position there was as a residential coordinator in the residential component of the program. In 1988, an opportunity to go into a classroom presented itself and I found myself in the classroom under a certification waiver and enrolled in a teacher certification program. This afforded me an opportunity to learn about teaching while I was teaching. It was during this time that I acquired a variety of beliefs and supporting skills that have stayed with me through my subsequent teaching career. Foremost among these beliefs and skills was exposure to the concept of the principle of "partial participation." The essential premise of partial participation is the belief that all students with severe cognitive disabilities can acquire many skills that will allow them to function, at least to some degree, in a variety of chronologically age-appropriate activities in a variety of school and non-school settings (Baumgart, Brown, Pumpian, Nisbet, Ford, Sweet, Messina, & Schroeder, 1982). The chief benefit of partial participation lies in the belief that students with severe handicaps might be perceived as "a more valuable, contributing, striving, and productive members of society" (Baumgart et al., 1982, p.19).

I also learned a considerable amount about behavior management, organizational skills, program modification, and data collection and its management. Data collection and its management were important foci of the program at the Center. The school's educational delivery model was built around precision teaching methodology. Instructional activities were time-based and charted on specialized time-based charts known as standard celeration charts. Students' performance of tasks over time was considered to be the key factor in their acquisition of skills; the celeration charts provided the information on that performance. This data was then analyzed in terms of trends and changes in instructional programming were made as needed. I learned the importance of collecting and analyzing student performance data for the purpose of modifying instruction on a regular basis. One very prominent skill acquired during this time was the ability to use Boardmaker (Mayer-Johnson, 1981), a picture/line drawing communication program. Use of pictures from this program became a ubiquitous feature of my subsequent classroom organizations. The use of these pictures became instrumental in allowing my students to grow both academically and physically. For example, they could participate in "written work" by using pictures to represent written responses and they could read and follow personal schedules.

I remained at the Center until 1995. The impetus to move on came in the form of the reaction to a proposal outlining an increase in the amount of community-referenced instruction that occurred in the residence in which I was then the teacher. (The organizational structure of the Center linked classrooms to residences so that a self-contained educational and residential unit was created. The students lived and also went to school as a group.) The management chose to reject the proposal not on the basis of any potential flaws or trial implementation but rather on an unspecified basis that was not communicated to those of us who had spent long hours working to create the proposal. School had ceased to be school and instead had become little more than an understaffed babysitting service.

I next accepted a position as the teacher in a public school self-contained resource room in September 1995. I entered the public school expecting to see what I had come to understand from my teacher education program as "inclusion" in action. That is, I expected to see students with significant disabilities taking part meaningfully in the daily life of school. I also began keeping a journal in which I recorded daily teaching experience around this time.

The period from 1995 to the present has been one of considerable evolution. As I said, I had entered the school expecting to see inclusion in action. This turned out to be inaccurate. Instead, I found myself constantly trying to figure out exactly where my students and I fit into the larger picture of school life. I learned that I was functioning in a structure with two parallel and not completely integrated systems, despite district rhetoric to the contrary. We often talked of integration but we never quite managed to get past the initial discussion stage. In 1998, my school experimented with the idea of creating schools within the larger school. The experiment involved creating teams of classrooms that would work together to create a feeling of a small neighborhood school. I had hoped that there would be some way for my classroom and students to become linked to one such team. My thinking at this time was that I could assist in creating a team of teachers who would actively link with my special education students, helping to alleviate pressures with learning multiple teachers' methods of practice, scheduling issues, and curriculum issues. However, the school-within-a-school plan was short-lived, its demise coinciding with the movement to link our instruction to the newly developed State Curriculum Frameworks. Grade level curriculum leaders replaced the school within a school concept. These curriculum leaders would assist their respective grades in the development of standards-based instruction. There was no mention of any plan for special education in these plans despite our IDEA '97 mandate to access the general education curriculum. I began trying to figure out how I would create my own "standards-based" classroom.

Then in 2000, I became involved in the state Alternate Portfolio Assessment Program. I was quite excited by the process since the state was now talking specifically about students with whom I was very familiar. Teachers at the assessment trainings were given a thoroughly organized resource guide that addressed ways in which students like mine could participate in their school experience. Students and activities with possible adaptations were described in detail. These activities and students were topics I knew well. My involvement in portfolio training has been ongoing. That participation has been an eye-opening experience. I discovered that other teachers in positions similar to my own often held negative opinions of the need for students with significant handicaps to participate in academic-oriented instruction and an assessment program. I began to wonder how other teachers working with students like mine could hold opinions that were so different from those that I had been taught. At the same time that this was occurring, I also became involved in advanced graduate studies, specifically, enrollment in a Ph.D. program (September, 2000). Here I began to learn a great deal about the nature of schools and about teachers in general. It was an eye-opening experience. At that time, understanding the differences in teacher reactions to the portfolio experience became a major interest.

My first years in the public school have been interesting, an important learning experience, frustrating, at times, and enlightening. I vividly remember my panicked reaction to the information, "This is George and Kenny. You're doing their reading this year!" Being in the position to sometimes work with students that were mildly handicapped led me back to the academic arena to build my knowledge of teaching academics and of general education curriculum. My participation in these classes led me to seek elementary education certification as well. At the same time that I have been fascinated by my experiences in public school, I have often felt that my primary position—being the teacher who deals mostly with the students with the greatest disabilities—kept my students and I outside the life of my school. The school's philosophy and position seemed undefined in my case. Co-workers and peers seemed at a loss as to how to integrate my students. I seemed at a loss to know how to communicate that my students could be meaningfully integrated into the life of the school. There were viable techniques to achieve goals related to such integration. I continually hoped for an opportunity to share my knowledge of these techniques. There was no time to invest in the use of such techniques. I constantly struggled with gaining greater understanding of curriculum, academic and functional skills, teaching methodology, and inclusion. Navigating through this complicated world of special education in the public school became my new objective.

My examination of my own practice continued with the exploration of my thinking regarding my activities at school. I did this by analyzing the journals that I had been keeping since my entry into public school. I conducted a survey of several of the entries that I had made from the beginning of this journal to roughly the time at which I became involved in my advanced graduate studies. I searched for journal entries related to school, beliefs, and practice. I then categorized these entries for themes that were prominent. This review, though simple in nature, indicated that the school figured significantly in my regular writing.

Initially, themes noted most frequently included daily events, and getting the work done. Many entries addressed my attempts to understand exactly what the requirements of my position were and just trying to fit in with the life of my school. They reflected a desire for guidance and support. Many other entries addressed constant concerns regarding the sheer amount of work with which I was faced. So much time needed to be spent on generating ideas for adaptation, on creating materials, and on just managing daily events, such as staff and student scheduling. Little time was left over for interacting with peers. I was becoming increasingly aware of a significant sense of isolation from those peers, both in general education and in special education. Many individuals in general education were often unresponsive to the notion of my students participating in classroom activities; the students would not be able to do the work and might be disruptive. The sense of isolation also applied to my special education peers as well. Peers in special education sometimes displayed similar reactions. In addition, the students had to learn a variety of prerequisite skills before they could do grade-level curriculum. Neither position adequately incorporated the knowledge that schools and practitioners possess regarding inclusion.

I also frequently wondered in my journal if I was "doing the right thing." At issue was the definition of "the right thing". I was somewhat disturbed by the thought that the idea of "doing the right thing" was open to a number of interpretations. Closely related to these types of journal entries, were several entries documenting what I consider to be a struggle for control of my classroom. Would the classroom take a more chronological and functional academic approach—more consistent with best practice—or would we take a more developmental age approach generated from students' test results?

While questions of understanding what best practice in the context of my school were considered, most often these entries were flavored by a significant amount of frustration over the issues of personal control arising out of the behavior of certain peers. The understanding of the majority of my peers seemed to reflect a desire to follow the developmental approach. At one point, many daily entries began to reflect a desire to exit special education altogether. I was beginning to feel very disengaged. However, these issues point to a much larger concern regarding my own self-efficacy, my sense of effectiveness.

The entries addressing self-efficacy can be broken down into two distinct types. There is a general type reflecting the previously mentioned "doing the right thing." There is also a more specific type that situates issues of best practice within a student context. Best practice for students with significant disabilities involves more than an understanding of placement in a school curriculum. It also involves understanding the meaning of being severely developmentally disabled and that teaching these students is both similar in some ways and very different to teaching general education students.

There seemed to be a very distinct contrast between a functional participatory approach and a more traditional developmental age approach. My students were often seen more as a function of their developmental age rather than their chronological age. The question that the school seemed to be asking of inclusion for my students was how appropriate were they really for anything more than social inclusion—attending lunch, recess, and occasional specials (i.e. classes such as art, music, computer, gym, and library)?

It became clear to me that I had a very different understanding of my role and what I was supposed to accomplish with my students than the understanding that others had of my students. I somehow was not able to adequately communicate my concerns and ideas to my peers. They did not seem to be able to follow my teaching philosophy. I could not always follow their teaching philosophies. These entries were characterized by thoughts, questions, and concerns regarding the development of a balanced special education curriculum—one that incorporated the need to address functional skills and academic skills, and that could also meet the needs of my students regarding school participation. The principle of partial participation is evident as an underlying belief in these entries. I held onto the belief that my students could participate in the life of school with the appropriate adaptations despite what I considered to be the frequent stumbling blocks placed in our path. Yet, at the same time, the sense of isolation and separateness remained.

The focus of my entries began to change as I became actively involved in alternate assessment procedures. My journal writing in general began to take on a more structured approach. There is a distinct shift in what I chose to record—from an emphasis on daily events to an emphasis on curriculum. How would I meet the requirements mandated by IDEA '97? How would I access the required Curriculum Frameworks? What were my perceptions of our experiences? I was actively hoping that the mandated requirement of accessing the general education curriculum would increase my opportunity to include my students in their general education classrooms. However, this did not turn out to be the case. Peers still tended to look at my students in terms of what they could not do rather than in terms of what they could do. My concerns regarding my place in elementary education continued as I began my graduate studies.

I next looked at several papers that I had written for the courses focusing on the nature of education and schooling that I had taken during my first two years as a doctoral student (September 2000—May 2002). These papers could easily have fit into the types of reflections that I was then recording and that I continue to record. In fact, they often performed the function of being my journal. Themes included experiences in the classroom, thoughts on accessing the curriculum, reflections on teacher knowledge and behavior, effect of different educational variables on my special education experience, student development, and alternate portfolio assessment. I actively tried to apply the literature offered in the courses to my own teaching experiences. The writings were more formal treatments of many of the topics that I wrote about regularly in the journal. They provided a vehicle for more formal examination of my experience in special education.

My initial exploration (October 2000) into the formal investigation of my experience consisted of describing experiences from my own substantially separate classroom. In this paper, I came to the conclusion that my classroom had often been thought of as a resource pool for achieving the smooth operation of the rest of the school. My classroom assistants were frequently pulled to fill openings elsewhere in the school regardless of the impact their loss would have on our classroom routines. There appeared to be a somewhat rigid social system based on student ability. My students experienced limited entry into the overall life of our school on the basis of the fact that they often did not have the necessary skills for participation in the general education curriculum. The classroom was often more of a respite setting for child-care than an educational setting.

Next (November, 2000) I addressed the concept of accessing the curriculum in greater detail. Here, I was interested in examining topics related to special education curriculum and instruction and the move toward the alternate portfolio assessment. I concluded that there was a difficult political context that surrounded my teaching. That political context took the form of the previously mentioned conflict between a functional participatory approach and the more traditional developmental age approach. This context was influenced by the general culture of teaching in the school as well as the move toward educational reform. I began to really become aware of the fact that I possessed truly different knowledge than my general education peers. At times, it even appeared as if I had acquired more knowledge than they had. For example, when I was initially informed on my first day in public school that I was going to be teaching reading, I immediately headed back to school to learn how to teach reading. This attitude of curiosity, of opening oneself to acquiring new knowledge did not always seem to be prominent in my teaching community. I knew of very few, perhaps no other teachers in my school, who headed for the local inclusion seminar.

Following that (April, 2001), I examined my thoughts on student development. The paper that resulted addressed two questions: 1) why were my students able to participate successfully in activities that would seem to be beyond their developmental level (a common concern in many of the curriculum discussions in which I took part; it seemed that others often did not have high expectations for my students performance)? and 2) how did the notion of developmental level affect the education that my students received? As a result of my work, I came to the conclusion that students with moderate and severe disabilities mastered skills outside a tested or "actual level" of development as a result of appropriate assistance from teachers and peers. This idea of appropriate assistance is, for me, a key element in all my conceptions of participating in the general education curriculum.

Finally, I began developing the paper (February, 2002) that attempted to integrate all of the information that I had acquired regarding my students, developmental theory, curriculum, teacher knowledge, and alternate assessment during these studies. Initially, I conceived of my dissertation research topic as heading in the direction of understanding special education teachers' level of acceptance of alternate assessment reform. However, in some ways this was a non-question since teachers did not have the choice to participate in portfolio assessment. My interest was evolving into looking at the practice of special education teachers and how changes in such practice might occur as a result of participation in alternate portfolio assessment. What might my daily practice reveal about my portfolio perceptions and my own beliefs about special education? How would I accomplish finding an answer to such questions?

As I continued journaling and writing, I also kept a daily practice log for a short period of time. This log served as the mechanism to "observe' my own teaching actions as I taught and began developing a research methodology to further examine my questions. This daily practice log yielded information regarding the events that occurred on a regular basis in the classroom. The log information was sorted into broad categories that included daily activities, routines, classroom comments, and portfolio activities. Data was also analyzed for prominent themes. As I worked through this self-study I discovered that I was beginning to think in terms of an ethnographic study of special education teachers.

The information on the daily life of the classroom revealed much about the way the classroom operates. My daily activities covered a broad range of activities to be accomplished. These were best related to the journal theme of getting the job done. Typical activities included a range of different items. I had a standard settling-in for the day routine. During this time, I got ready for the day both physically and mentally. I organized the variety of things that I would have to accomplish during the day. I had regularly occurring organizational activities—I planned for the creation of materials. This often included creating picture adaptations with Boardmaker, the picture communication software. Such adaptations typically included making communication boards, adapting worksheets and activities or creating new materials altogether. For example, I adapted our reading series to Boardmaker phrases. I placed the necessary clerical items to be completed and tagged them with directions for completion in the general work bucket. My paraprofessionals then completed them as time permitted. I attended to planning for the classroom. I logged progress information and reviewed student work. I had brief meetings with "host" teachers (those teachers who provided a degree of general education exposure for my students). I engaged in frequent alternate assessment portfolio activities. I had weekly bus duty. I also did laundry and organized cooking activities. Each week we did a social lunch/language group that involved meal preparation and using associated language. I participated in student personal care. This generally consisted of assisting in toileting the students. I went to lunch with the students.

The log additionally indicated the daily instructional routines of the classroom. These, of course, had some degree of similarity with those that occur in general education classrooms. We had daily jobs, reading and math periods, and lunch and recess just like any other classroom. These routines were often completed using highly adapted materials. Though we used many of the same materials and strategies as can be found in other classrooms, it was entirely possible to see a variety of different academic aids in use at any given time. We had picture aids, communication boards, and an adapted math program. In my opinion, we tended to carry out the business of school in much the same way as all the other classrooms in our building. We might do things a little differently, perhaps less conventionally, but the students were held to expectations of independence and participation to the best of their ability. The students were held to expectations of performing to the best of their academic ability as well. The classroom always had an academic element because it was my belief that academics were the business of school.

However, we also had routines that are not characteristic of general education classes. These included our community walks and our weekly social lunch. The students had a daily language group. They participated in a daily personal care routine that involved learning to wash themselves and brush their teeth. As with any other classroom, these routines occurred daily, weekly, and on an as-needed basis.

It was perhaps in the idea of "on an as-needed basis" that possible distinctions between the special education classroom and the general education classroom were most likely to be evident. Issues came and went. One major theme of the practice log was that of classroom discussion. This was generally a staff related activity; students were often not involved as a result of their functioning levels. It tended to often occur within the context of the day since there was little or no common planning time for the paraprofessionals and myself to be had outside of the special education classroom. The content of these discussions could generally be categorized along several recurring topics. These included acquiring and using needed assistive technology, inclusion concerns related to both the means and ends of the process (i.e. getting into general education classrooms and once there, determining our purpose), creation of materials, personal care issues, and behavior management. One notable example of the inclusion theme occurred around a fourth grade biography project. The students were to choose a historical figure and plan a short multi-media presentation about that person. This was an activity that my students would have some degree of difficulty with. Questions centered on what my students would get from the project as well as how they might access the materials needed to complete the project.

Discussion often focused on the overall sense of marginalization that we frequently felt as a result of being associated with this classroom. We were often last on lists if we are remembered at all. We were frequently neglected in professional development topic planning. The paraprofessionals were often moved about as if they were substitute staff. Outsiders did not generally have a positive perception of the classroom. Outsiders did not understand that the students learn in much the same way as anyone else, although their learning often takes much more time and repetition than that required by general education students. They had difficulty with the fact that the majority of our class work was adapted in some way that is beyond the conventional. The class was often viewed as non-academic in nature.

Also prominent in the daily practice log was my work on portfolio activities. Items related to portfolios occurred on a regular basis in the classroom. These included things such as charting student results, student evaluation of work completed, and reviewing portfolio entries. There was frequent talk about what would be needed for the portfolios. I found myself thinking of the portfolios often—what would be a suitable portfolio activity, what else would I need to complete my portfolios etc. A review of the items selected for my portfolios supported both an academic orientation to our daily routines and an attempt at providing a range of academic activities. For example, literacy activities have included text innovations, adapted story maps, and making words work. Composition activities have included writing parent notes, seasonal letters and notes, and sequencing an art activity related to ancient Egypt. Math activities have included computation, geometry, and simple data collection. Portfolio production was a time consuming process and involved the institution of several new organizational schemes and routines. Potential portfolio evidence was collected from the start of the school year. It soon became necessary to create an evidence collection system, and a monitoring system for tracking student progress. A student self-evaluation plan had to be developed. Many of our portfolio activities would also involve the students charting and interpreting their own results. It was necessary to become re-acquainted with regular data collection, something that I had not been actively involved in since my time at the Center and something that is typically not naturally occurring to a general education setting.

Other issues that came up during the three week period recorded in the log were staff placements for the next school year, the cycle of the school year, and beginning to think of host teachers for next year as we entered the final third of the school year. One paraprofessional expressed this last topic in terms of who was "our student friendly" (i.e. someone who would be open to addressing the unique behavioral, learning, instructional and curricular challenges that working with these students often provides).

My journal revealed a sense of growth as a teacher. I moved from multiple entries of just getting through the day to entries characterized by thoughts, questions, and concerns regarding the development of what I saw as a "balanced curriculum"—one that incorporated the need to address both functional and academic skills and that could also meet the needs of my students for school participation. Through all of my writing, I held on to my belief in the principle of partial participation. My course writings offered more formal treatments of many of the topics that I wrote about regularly in the journal. The tone of many of these writings generally reflected a sense of separateness from the events of the school, for both my students and myself. We remain distanced from being a true part of the conversation of school. There was little sense of any attempt to establish true dialogue between general education and special education in this instance.

The foregoing provides a sampling of teacher practice in a special education classroom. It is a personal account, quite subjective in nature. This analysis of my personal experience was both disturbing and constructive. It represents one teacher's experience and voice. As such, the use of structured and unstructured journals proved to be a useful research tool. The story of personal practice recorded here provided an opportunity to explore the nature of my development and practice as a special education teacher working with students who demonstrate moderate and significant cognitive disabilities. I could feel myself becoming disconnected with so much of the work that I had valued for so many despite the time and energy invested over the last 22 years. But as I examined that experience I also began to remember my purpose as a special educator. My reflections on my practice and my analyses of the situation in which I taught contributed strongly to my re-engagement in teaching students with significant disabilities.

Conclusion: "Managed Chaos"

The observations described here are important because they continue to hold true, even as I write this introduction on a hot summer day in July 2006. Few people have come to me truly wanting to understand what goes on in the classroom in which I continue to teach. The tone of the conversation still seems to reflect an attitude of separate understanding, or perhaps misunderstanding. We seldom think in terms of what students with special needs can do; rather, we think in terms of what they cannot do. Trying to navigate the tensions that arise in these interactions often leads to a sense of chaos. But that chaos must become a managed chaos. How does managing that chaos come about?

The significance of my self-study is twofold. I became reengaged in my role as a special education teacher. As I examined my experience in light of educational literature I began to see the importance of giving voice to teachers. I also noticed that the special education teacher was seldom heard from. *My personal study provides a voice to a segment of the teaching population that is often left quietly on the sidelines. Added to what the literature tells us, the work presented opens a door into the investigation of other special education teachers' experiences—to provide them with voices as well.* With my re-engagement in teaching in special education came the desire to share my story as well as the desire to move beyond my own profound experiences and document those of other special education teachers. The overarching question of interest became—how does being a special educator manifest itself in the broader world of elementary general education? Several secondary questions contribute to answering this broad question. What will the experiences and the resulting practice for these teachers look like? What factors will be similar or different in other special education teachers' experiences? How do these experiences affect the practice of these teachers on a daily basis? Have current reform initiatives in standards-based education and accountability affected that practice? How do special education teachers see themselves in the broader world dominated by general education curricula?

The study that follows uses ethnographic methods (e.g. interviews and observation) to examine the practice of six special education teachers. In it, I seek to identify the elements of such practice for each individual teacher, to describe their experiences as special education teachers, to provide insight into the meaning of being a special education teacher based upon an analysis of those elements of practice and teaching experience, and finally to offer a description and interpretation of being a special education teacher in the broader world of elementary education.

Now, why select ethnography as the methodology to examine my research question? On the simplest level, I was an anthropology major before I became a special education teacher. I have always had an interest in describing the experiences of special education that I have had in the schools in which I have taught. Ethnography is well-suited to that task of description, to providing a picture of the way of life of some identifiable group of people, to understanding that way of life (Ayers, 1989; Wolcott, 1997). Ethnographic methods are clearly appropriate to telling the story of teacher practice in special education settings.

Finally, answering this overarching question brings me back to the quote that opens this chapter. Special education is a separate world filled with others, who "live just beyond the territories of general education" and who speak "in strange tongues and practice unusual customs (Bohannan & van der Elst, 1998)." Its workings are somewhat obscure to those not well versed in its nature or practice. The work presented here will contribute to correcting the lack of information that exists regarding the practice of special education teachers.

A reading of literature addressing curriculum and teaching (Bruner, 1977; Tyler, 1949) led to the development of a normative model of teaching—a plan to structure the description of teaching. The story begins with the use of that normative model of teaching in a pilot study of general education teachers. This provided a set of interview question categories in four areas: 1) curriculum, 2) teacher actions, 3) instruction and learning, and 4) assessment and evaluation. A fifth category, the Individual Education Plan (IEP), was added to focus the study on special education teachers.

The participating teachers provided information on their teaching in a series of open-ended interviews and allowed me to observe them, from twenty to forty hours, as they went about their teaching duties. These individuals were professionals whose acquaintance I made as I searched for teachers interested in participating in the study. They were individuals with whom I share a common knowledge base related to special education but with whom I did not interact regularly. Kristie Barren teaches in an inclusive setting and works primarily with students diagnosed as learning disabled. Charlotte Cannon describes her experience in a substantially separate setting. She also works primarily with students identified as learning disabled. Marie Konners works with students in a substantially separate program she describes as specifically designed for students with low-incidence disabilities. Low incidence refers to any of the less common disabilities; among the disabilities that might be seen are multiple disabilities, hearing or visual impairments, orthopedic impairments, deaf-blindness, autism, or traumatic brain injury. Significant cognitive disabilities can also be listed here. Carlene Erlich teaches in a substantially separate setting and works with students who have a greater degree of learning disability than the students that Kristie or Charlotte works with. Both Betty Larson and Jeri Palmer work with students typically described as significantly or moderately cognitively handicapped in substantially separate settings. These students make up the smallest category of students with special needs.

The teachers' stories are presented in Part II. With the information that they have graciously provided, I hope to offer illumination to a research community that has often missed their experiences, and to describe what being a special educator in the larger world of elementary general education entails.

Part II
Chapter Three
Methodology Employed in the Study

"Participants in research provide us with something of great value, their stories and perspectives on their world (Quinn, 2002, p. 415).

This study is fundamentally ethnographic in nature. The trials that I have experienced as a special education teacher led me to the brink of exiting special education as my teaching specialty. A careful examination of my own professional practice and education in general using the tools presented as part of my graduate studies contributed to my re-engagement in what I do. As I became reengaged in my practice, I better understood that special education exists peripherally in the world of general education. As we now know from the historical overview and review of the literature presented here, special education teachers and their experiences of their students are underrepresented in the general literature on education. With my re-engagement in teaching in special education came the desire to move beyond my own profound experiences and document those of other special education teachers. This led to the question that framed the study. The overarching question of this work is—how does being a special educator manifest itself in the broader world of elementary general education? Several secondary questions contribute to answering the broad question of the study. These questions are listed below.

- What are the elements of special education teachers' daily practice?
- What will the experiences and the resulting practice for these special education teachers look like?

- What influences in teacher development over time contribute to special education teacher practice?
- How do special education teachers see themselves in relation to the dominant general education setting?

Closely related to these important questions is the question--

- Have current reform initiatives in standards-based education and accountability affected special education teacher practice? In what ways?

These questions were examined in a pilot study (May-October, 2003) that focused on developing an interview protocol that would be used as the major tool in this work. The pilot study involved two general education teachers who had worked with students in my classroom in the past. That is, they provided inclusion opportunities, both academic and social, for students that the district considered to be severely handicapped. The setting for the study consisted of the classrooms belonging to these teachers.

This pilot study provided an opportunity to gain insight into the larger plan of studying special education teachers. Each element of that work provided useful information for developing the plan to study special education teachers. From it, a framework with which to examine their practice was created. As previously stated, what teachers know, think, and do in general education classrooms is well represented and often eloquently stated in the literature of American education. The complex world of general education is brought to life. At the same time, what teachers know, think, and do in special education classrooms is far less evident in that literature. The unique challenges that these teachers face are left unreported. The broad conceptual structure created by the intersection of the research on knowledge regarding teacher practice, teachers' responses to change, and the lack of research addressing special education teachers have led to the need to explore several of the questions noted in the pilot study with special education teachers. In the study that follows, the practice of special education teachers in the context of general education and educational reform is examined.

District administrators referred the teachers who participated in the study to me. Teachers were selected for inclusion in the study on the basis of their interest in participating. Six special education teachers provided information on their teaching and allowed me to observe them as they went about their teaching duties. Five of the six teachers worked in elementary schools in southeastern New England; one teacher worked in an elementary school in central New England. School sizes ranged from a low enrollment of approximately 95 students to a mid-high enrollment of approximately 500 students. Each teacher generally worked with students in a specific disability category (e.g. learning disabled, low-incidence, or significantly cognitively handicapped); all of the teachers indicated that their students displayed a range of ability level. Each teacher participated in five to six interview sessions. Each teacher also allowed me to observe her in her classrooms for periods of twenty hours to forty hours. All names and places included in the study are pseudonyms. Table 3.1 summarizes the length of interview and classroom observation time for each teacher.

Table 3.1 Summary of Interview and Observation Time

Teacher	Hours of Interview	Hours of Observation
Kristie Barren	5	29 over 2 weeks
Charlotte Kannon	5	43 over 2 weeks
Marie Konners	5	28 over 2 weeks
Carlene Erlich	5.5	26 over 1 week
Betty Larsen	4.5	44 over 2 weeks
Jeri Palmer	4.5	21 over 2 weeks

- Carlene's observation time occurred as my sabbatical time was ending.
- Jeri's observation time occurred as my sabbatical time was ending. The observation ended abruptly as it was felt that my presence as an unfamiliar person/researcher may have contributed to student behaviors.

Ethical Considerations and Committee on the Use of Human Participants in Research Review

The power of this study lies in its ethnographic methodology—what does it mean to be a special education teacher? Quinn notes, "Participants in research provide us with something of great value, their stories and perspectives on their world (2002, p. 415). Ethnographic methods of research typically rely on information provided by cultural participants. This information may come in the form of answers to open-ended interview questions or observed actions. In either case, collecting this information requires the researcher to delve into the lives of those would act as participants, to lay open participants' thoughts, feelings, and knowledge (Quinn, 2002; Spradley, 1980). In this study, the participants include both teachers and students. Ethical considerations are of particular importance here. The data consist of information provided by teachers about students who present special vulnerabilities. Further, the students and their actions are clearly present in the observation phase of this work. They are doubly vulnerable both as children and as a result of having special needs. Several key steps were taken to protect the thoughts, feelings, and actions of both the teachers and the students who participated in the study.

Approval to conduct the study was granted by the Committee on the Use of Human Participants in Research for the doctoral program in October 2004. I met with each teacher as she was recruited to participate in the study in order to share research goals, any potential risks and benefits from the study, the interview protocol, and the disposition of the information that resulted from the data collected. This information was incorporated into an Informed Consent document. Teachers were told that they could elect not to answer specific questions and were not pressed for information that they did not wish to share. Teachers were also told that only my study advisor and myself would see the interview videotapes and that the interview tapes would be destroyed upon word from the study advisor. As the observation phase of the study approached, I provided the students' parents with Informed Consent documents that addressed the same issues as those included in the teacher document. Finally, as previously noted, all teachers, students, and places have been protected by the promise of anonymity.

Settings and Participants

Kristie Barren came to teaching as the career that she had always planned on. She has a Bachelor's degree in elementary education and a Master's degree in special education; she has been in the classroom for approximately six years. Experiences with a child with special needs contributed to her decision to enter special education. She teaches in an inclusive school setting located in southeastern New England. She worked primarily with students diagnosed as learning disabled. The school's grade configuration consisted of kindergarten through grade five. Approximately 300 students attended the school in which she taught. The school has met some of its adequate yearly progress goals as specified by the No Child Left Behind Act (though the available information for its progress goals was not complete). Further, the school had been involved in a number of efforts to improve its ability to provide inclusive education. Students with special needs switched classes for their math and reading in an effort to effectively utilize the available special education staff. This means that Kristie's students leave their homeroom and switch to a different class for math. They then return to their homeroom for reading.

Kristie's current caseload consists of nine students—seven boys and two girls. When she described her students, she spoke of working with grades two and four. She followed her second grade students to the next grade. Zeb, Adam, Ellie, and Timmy were in fourth grade during the observation phase of the study. Tom, Vincent, Chrissie, Allen, and Adam were in third grade during the observations. The majority of this group of students blended quietly into their classes. This was less true for Zeb. He frequently managed to require being spoken to by the classroom teacher, especially when he was in his reading class.

Charlotte Kannon came to teaching as a career choice after having been counseled in that direction by college advisors. She has a Bachelor's degree in special education and a Master's degree in reading. She has been in the classroom for approximately three years. Experiences with a teenager with special needs contributed to her decision to enter special education. She described her experience in a substantially separate classroom setting. She left this position as the interviews were completed; observations took place in her new teaching setting. In September 2004, Charlotte began teaching in an elementary school located in southeastern New England. The school's grade configuration consisted of kindergarten through grade five. Approximately 500 students attended the school in which she taught. The school has been consistently meeting its adequate yearly progress goals as specified by the No Child Left Behind Act.

Charlotte's teaching assignment consists of working both in the inclusive setting and also in a substantially separate setting. She worked primarily with students identified as learning disabled. Her grade assignment consisted of grades 1 and 2. She stated in passing that it would be her guess that she will follow these students as they move to the next grade. Her caseload consisted of five boys, three in first grade and two in second grade. Her first graders were in an inclusive setting, while her second graders were seen separately in Charlotte's substantially separate space. Two of her three first grade students blended into the classroom very quietly. The third boy, Aaron, was frequently a source of disruption to his group and to the classroom in general. Paul and Jake, her second graders, were both easily distracted. Paul could display behavioral issues such as non-compliance to teacher requests. Jake, on the other hand, was a talker. Every statement Charlotte made could be an excuse for him to initiate a tangential conversation.

Marie Konners also came to teaching as a career choice after having been counseled in that direction by college advisors. She has both a Bachelor's degree and a Master's degree in special education and has been in the classroom for approximately 19 years. Marie has held a variety of special education positions throughout her career, including a vocational position and a position working with significantly cognitively handicapped children. She currently works with students in a substantially separate classroom program she describes as specifically designed for students with low-incidence disabilities. The term "low incidence" is used to refer to any of the less common disabilities; among the disabilities that might be seen are multiple disabilities, hearing or visual impairments, orthopedic impairments, deaf-blindness, autism, or traumatic brain injury. Significant cognitive disabilities can also be listed here. She has been with this program for the majority of her years in teaching. As with both Kristie and Charlotte, Marie also indicated that her decision to consider special education as a profession was influenced by an experience with a student with special needs.

Marie indicated that her program is a separate program currently located in a school in central New England. The school's grade configuration consisted of kindergarten through grade 6. Approximately 95 students attended this school. The school has been consistently meeting its adequate yearly progress goals as specified by the No Child Left Behind Act. Her caseload consisted of four boys and three girls. Three of the boys and two of the girls were diagnosed as learning disabled to some degree. The fourth boy and the third girl both demonstrated greater degrees of disability. The boy was paraplegic, with limited movement and cognitive ability. In addition, he demonstrated behavioral issues that typically took the form of non-compliance to teacher requests. He was semi-verbal and frequently difficult to understand as he spoke. The girl was also of limited cognitive ability. Her academic skills were somewhere in the preschool range. Like the boy, she was semi-verbal and frequently difficult to understand as she spoke. All Marie's students completed the state assessments by means of portfolios. Marie was actively engaged in creating activities that would be useful for completing her state assessment portfolios.

Carlene Erlich noted that she couldn't remember a time when she didn't want to be a teacher. She has a Bachelor's degree in elementary education and a Master's degree in special education. Unlike the other teachers in the study, she originally started off in general education. After taking time off to start raising her family, she returned to work as a special education paraprofessional. She then returned to school to get her Master's degree in special education. She started out as an inclusion specialist but moved to her present position when it became available. She has been in the classroom for approximately 15 years throughout her teaching career. Carlene teaches in a substantially separate classroom setting in a school located in southeastern New England. She worked with students who have a greater degree of learning disability than the students that Kristie or Charlotte worked with. The school's grade configuration consisted of kindergarten through grade three. Approximately 500 students attended the school. The school has been consistently meeting its adequate yearly progress goals as specified by the No Child Left Behind Act.

Carlene's caseload consisted of eight students—six boys and two girls. Of these students—one was in the third grade, five were second graders, and two were first graders. Cary, the third grader, was autistic. He was essentially nonverbal, though he could say a few isolated words. He was reluctant to participate in group activities and could read some simple texts and solve simple calculation problems in math. He participated in the class' spelling program. Kyle and Zeb were both quiet and blended into the classroom easily. Roland was diagnosed as being on the autism spectrum but demonstrated characteristics typically seen with students having language processing disorders—he frequently demonstrated word finding problems; however, his language issues were possibly more a result of his family being bi-lingual than his disability. Blending quietly into the classroom was also true for the girls, Noreen and Marissa. Marissa was the younger of the two girls, a first grader and had very low academic skills. Dennis and Rich were also first graders, both generally learning disabled. Both boys demonstrated behavioral difficulties in the form of non-compliance and some verbal aggression. The aggression was typically directed toward each other. They often had trouble interacting with their peers and most frequently with each other. Carlene's students had some, though limited contact, with their general education peers. She has had some experience with the state assessment portfolios.

Both Betty Larson and Jeri Palmer work with students typically described as significantly or moderately cognitively handicapped, the lowest functioning of the students, in substantially separate settings. These students make up the smallest category of students with special needs.

Betty Larsen entered college with the intent of becoming a teacher. She has a Bachelor's degree in elementary education with a concentration in special education. She later completed her Master's degree in special education with a concentration in students with severe and profound disabilities. She has worked in the field, in various positions, for approximately 22 years. Over the years, a nephew with autism has influenced her career choices. She teaches in a substantially separate alternative learning program located in a school in southeastern New England. The school's grade configuration was kindergarten through grade five. Approximately 400 students attended the school. The school was consistently meeting its adequate yearly progress goals as specified by the No Child Left Behind Act.

Betty's caseload consisted of seven students—three boys and four girls. All of her students had a 1:1 paraprofessional assigned to them. All of the students were non-verbal and all functioned below the one-year level as measured by diagnostic testing. Further, six of the seven students demonstrated different behavioral issues. David M. could be aggressive toward other students in the room. David S. engaged in inappropriate vocalization (e.g. whining) when expected to participate in activities. Nate and Celine could both be non-compliant to teacher requests. Katie had Down's Syndrome and could be both non-compliant to teacher's requests and was frequently aggressive to others—both peers and teachers. Last, Tanya had significant medical issues. These included a chronic seizure disorder and the need for a feeding tube. She had a nurse with her throughout her day in school. The students all used a variety of switches and other augmentative/adaptive devices to participate in classroom activities. Two of the students, Celine and Nate, spent some extended time in their general education classrooms. The other students had limited opportunity to go to general education classrooms. Betty had some experience with the state assessment portfolios. Of the teachers in the study, her group probably presented the greatest difficulty with participating in standards-based instruction.

Jeri Palmer credits her entrance into teaching to her mother who once made her return to a church-initiated community service experience in a school for severely disabled individuals. She began her career with an Associate's degree in child development. After working in a collaborative program for children with special needs, she returned to school to get a Bachelor's degree and then a Master's degree in special education with a concentration on students with severe and profound disabilities. Jeri teaches in a substantially separate classroom setting located in a school in southeastern New England. The grade configuration in the school was grade four and grade five. Approximately 270 students attended the school. The school has experienced some difficulty with meeting its adequate yearly progress goals as specified by the No Child Left Behind Act.

Jeri's caseload consisted of four students—three boys and one girl. All four students functioned below the one-two year level as measured by diagnostic testing. All of the students were essentially non-verbal, though Adam and Ned could say some isolated words and sentences. Three of the students demonstrated behavioral issues. One boy, Normand, had Down's Syndrome. He had the most significant behavioral issues—engaging in non-compliance to teacher's request, control issues, aggression, and lengthy tantrums. Ned was autistic and could become aggressive if he became uncomfortable in the environment he was currently in. Keely had Angelman's Syndrome and often engaged in non-compliance to teacher requests. She could also be aggressive. Normand and Andrew had some extended contact with their general education peers. Keely and Ned had some, though less, contact with their general education peers. Jeri was actively engaged in creating activities that would be useful for completing her state assessment portfolios.

Table 3.2 summarizes the teachers' broad student assignments and teaching settings.

Table 3.2 Summary of Teacher Assignments and Teaching Settings

Teacher	School Enroll.	Grade Config.	Disability Category	Teaching Setting	Caseload (# students)
Kristie	Approx. 300	K-5	Learning Disabled	Inclusive	9
Charlotte	Approx 500	K-5	Learning Disabled	Inclusive Substantially Separate	5
Marie	Approx. 95	K-6	Low Incidence	Substantially Separate	7
Carlene	Approx. 525	K-3	Learning Disabled	Substantially Separate	8
Betty	Approx. 400	K-5	Significant Cognitive	Substantially Separate	7
Jeri	Approx. 270	4-5	Significant Cognitive	Substantially Separate	4

Key:
- Learning disabilities—students with learning disabilities have dysfunction in processing information typically fond in language based activities
- Substantially separate setting—students in such settings receive the majority of their education in a setting other than the general education classroom
- Low-incidence disabilities—students have disabilities that are considered to be of low occurrence, typically includes disabilities such as multiple disabilities, significant cognitive disabilities, or traumatic brain injury.
- Significant/moderate cognitive disabilities—students with such disabilities typically have an IQ of 55 or lower and require substantial modifications in order to access grade level content

Data Collection and Analysis

Qualitative ethnographic methods were appropriate to conduct the study given that desire was to "tell the story of being a special education teacher." According to Quinn (2002), interviews add depth and provide an entry into understanding the perceptions, feelings, and knowledge of people in a setting. Observations allow the reader to become a part of the setting that has been observed and described (Quinn, 2002). The study used interviews and observation to investigate the components of the normative model of teaching previously described in the section addressing the literature on studying teacher actions. The elements of this model include: (1) curriculum, (2) teaching actions, (3) instruction and learning, (4) assessment and evaluation, and (5) the Individual Education Plan (IEP). Participants' words and actions were used to examine the practice of teachers of students with special needs and cognitive disabilities of differing levels as they negotiated access to general education curriculum. The ethnographic data consisted of interview and observation content and classroom cultural artifacts when appropriate (Spradley, 1979, 1980).

The study included multiple sets of data. Data consisted of six sets of multiple interviews as well as six sets of multiple observations. These interviews and observations yielded 800 pages of transcribed data. The data sets that resulted could be compared to each other. There were two teachers in each teaching specialty. Therefore, each teaching specialty could also be compared to the other. In addition, there was an advantage to having two teachers in each category. Each set of teachers could be compared to each other. The verbatim interview transcriptions insured accuracy in the recording of the teachers' words. The observation fieldnotes were used to check the teachers' words. These multiple sources of data illuminated the practice of these special education teachers and allowed for a triangulation of data. The triangulation of data provided by these multiple data sources and checks increased the reliability and validity of the results of this study and were central to ensuring an accuracy of data interpretation of a study using qualitative methodology (Patton, 2002).

The reliability and validity of the interpretations that were developed as part of this study was further enhanced by the use of outside reviewers who checked the interpretations of the data as they emerged. These outside reviewers consisted of special education teacher peers as well as individuals who worked within both special education and general education. These individuals had appropriate access to interview transcriptions and observation field notes. The triangulation of data is modeled in Figure 3.1.

The initial interview phase occurred during fall 2004. The observation phase occurred between September 2004 and January 2005, following the completion, transcription, and interpretation of the initial interviews. The interviews conducted with each teacher participating in the study were both formal and informal in structure. The formal interviews were structured by an interview protocol developed as part of the 2003 pilot study (Gorden, 1975). (See Appendix A.) Each interview was videotaped and then transcribed.

The participant's interview transcripts expanded the formal interviews. That is, each participant's experience sometimes led to specific questions based on that experience. In the analysis of the interviews, the participants' understanding of their professional development as teachers was investigated. The teachers identified critical incidents that were significant in their development as teachers. The teachers' critical incidents and their responses to other interview questions provided an explanation of the teachers' understanding of what makes them teachers and illustrated the activities that they do on a daily basis. During the interviews, I was specifically interested in teachers' ideas about their daily practice and the influences of standards-based instruction on their practice.

Figure 3.1: Triangulation of Data Sources

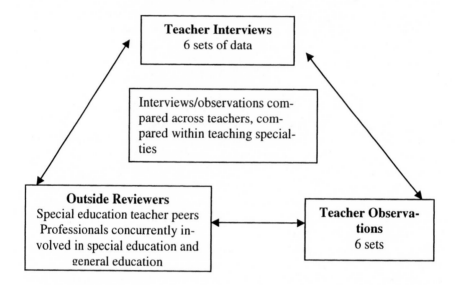

Electronic media (e.g. videotape) to record the interviews was selected as the primary means of data collection because it is supported as good practice in the literature (Gorden, 1975; Patton, 2002; Spradley, 1979). Taping of interviews is suggested when dealing with large quantities of complex information and when unsure of what categories of information of are relevant to the questions under study (Gorden, 1975). Taping the interview omits nothing from the record, provides the most complete expanded account of what occurs during the interview process and allows the researcher to devote full attention to the individual speaking (Gorden, 1975; Patton, 2002: Spradley, 1979). This thorough and complete account of events is invaluable for conducting an ethnographic analysis (Spradley, 1979, 1980).

Classroom observations of the participating teachers supplemented the interviews. The observations allowed me to gain a better sense of the experiences, events, and activities that the teacher was describing. Within the observations, classroom activities that occurred as a result of standards-based initiatives were of particular interest. I typically acted as an on-looker during my observation periods (Spradley, 1980). That is, I selected an observation point that allowed me visual and auditory access to the teacher and staff in the classrooms as they went about their teaching. I interacted with various staff and students during periods of unstructured time or when the students initiated interactions with me. The observation process was documented in fieldnotes. All material collected was analyzed on an on-going basis, using methods of ethnographic analysis that allow for an analysis of the meaning the participants make of their classrooms. Specific techniques of analysis used included domain analysis, taxonomic analysis, and componential analysis to identify components of the participants' educational cultures and belief systems (Spradley, 1979,1980). Each of these techniques provides methods of organizing participant knowledge. Domain analysis was used to identify participants' categories of knowledge. Domains are the categories of cultural knowledge possessed by participants in a setting. While researchers have an understanding of the categories (e.g. content areas, curriculum, students, teaching methodologies etc.) that are present in teaching, what new information might special educators add to the common categories of school? Taxonomic analysis and componential were used to determine the structure of and attributes of the categories identified by the participants.

Interpreting the Data

The interview process illustrated the teachers' practice/belief system. The participants' words described what they think and do. The classroom observations illustrated the belief system in action. The interview transcripts were analyzed for categories, domains, patterns and themes illustrating teacher beliefs about practice, standards-based instruction, and accessing the general education curriculum. Fieldnotes were analyzed to match the patterns observed in teaching actions to the descriptions provided in the interview transcripts.

The analysis of these patterns and themes proceeded on several levels of interpretation. These interpretations included: 1) determining prominent codes and themes in the data, 2) describing the properties (e.g. the contents and structures of the categories) that may be present in the observed themes and 3) making an attempt at developing a model that explains the ways in which special education teachers practice in settings dominated by general education curricula. In the first level of analysis, participants' actions as they are described in the interviews were interpreted.

The descriptions of teaching offered by the participants were compared to the actions observed in the classrooms to determine the match between the interview data and classroom actions. Patterns in teacher actions in the classroom were identified and then matched to the expressed topics in the interview data. This formed a second level of analysis. This second level of analysis allowed for the potential development of individual theories of each teacher's practice and educational setting.

In a third level of analysis, the information provided by each teacher was compared to the information provided by the other teachers. Similarities and differences in teacher development and practice were identified and interpreted. These comparisons allowed for the generation of a more global theory that describes teachers' beliefs regarding the meaning of standards-based instruction and their development as special education teachers, alternate assessment, and their development as teachers of students with a variety of cognitive disabilities as well as an explanation of the ways in which special education teachers practice in settings dominated by general education curricula.

I expected such theory building would be driven by the special education teachers' responses to their students, as was the case in the pilot study. I anticipated that elements of both the teaching environment and teaching context would have greater influence on the practice of special education teachers than indicated in the pilot study, where the data demonstrated that teaching environment and certain elements of the teaching context had less influence on the practice of the teachers than their teaching actions with the students. And finally, I expected that I would see some sense of separateness from the everyday life of the school for these special education teachers. My findings, conclusions, and recommendations are presented in the remaining chapters of this book.

Chapter Four
Special Education Teacher Practice Described

"All teachers who enter: Be prepared to tell your story..." (Paley in Ayers, 1989, p.vii).

Introduction

Anthropology has been beneficial to the study of education, as its methods provide instruments with which to identify, classify, compare, and explain aspects of human behavior. Specific tools, devised by Spradley and McCurdy (1972)—domain analysis, taxonomic analysis, and componential analysis—and the ethnographic accounts that result from their use allow researchers to discover and describe the cultural knowledge of specific settings and the individuals that participate in them. The purpose of this study is twofold—to identify and describe special education teacher practice and to reveal specific cultural knowledge possessed by special education teachers. What is it that special education teachers know and do as they work with their students on a daily basis?

The knowledge that special education teachers possess is incorporated into what I have identified in Chapter Three as the "normative model of teaching"— a term that came about as I considered what teachers know and what they must do in their classrooms. Identifying such knowledge required the collection of data that addressed the components of that normative model structure— curriculum, teacher actions, instruction and learning, evaluation and assessment, and the Individual Education Plan (IEP). This model provided a framework for organizing the data that resulted. The components of the model were treated equally in the presentation that follows.

The interviews and observations of the data set were analyzed with the overarching question of the study in mind—how does being a special education teacher manifest itself in the larger world of elementary general education? Stated more practically, the major question being considered is—how do special education teachers function in a world dominated by elementary general education practice? This chapter presents excerpts from the interview data that address the components of the normative model and focus on the secondary study questions embedded in the larger study question. What are the elements of special education teacher practice? Have current reform initiatives in standards-based education and accountability affected special education teacher practice? The initial step in describing special education teacher practice consisted of sorting the interview questions into sections related to the four major study questions. Questions that yielded the richest descriptive data were then selected for further analysis. This task involved examining the data for categories and then codes— the basic elements of cultural knowledge.

Setting the Stage: The Business of Schooling

The business of schooling is educating our children. We know that elementary schools are complex settings where teachers seek to educate a diverse group of students. Within that diverse group of students is a population of students who are eligible for special education services. General education teachers and special educators work to educate their students, sometimes side by side, sometimes separately. Special education teachers have specific roles that they must play in schools and in general education classrooms. These roles may include support teacher, classroom teacher, student advocate, and coach. Special education teachers provide in-class support; in such situations, they work with small groups of students, assisting them through lessons primarily taught by the classroom teacher. Special education teachers may function as classroom teachers in their own right; that is, they may have their own self-contained classrooms where all students there have needs requiring "specially designed" instruction. As advocates, special education teachers provide voice for their students in an effort to insure that student needs are met. They potentially provide voice for making sure that schools incorporate best practice for learners with special needs into their daily teaching and school improvement efforts. Special education teachers are further faced with the task of meeting a complex arrangement of student curricular needs brought about by student variability, school structures, and reform initiatives.

The physical sites where the tasks of education are carried out are easily identified. Education takes place in classrooms. These classrooms include such items as student desks, technology stations, a variety of educational materials, and perhaps instructional postings adorning the classroom walls. Classrooms also include, generally, a standard teaching arrangement—that is, there is a single teacher assigned to a group of students. While the class size can vary, presently a typical classroom in the schools of the participating teachers holds 20-25 students. This becomes the first and most basic difference between general education and special education teachers' practice. A general education teacher has a full classroom, while special education teachers often have a "caseload," consisting, on average, of 6-12 students. Certain classrooms may have paraprofessional assistants assigned to them. Such arrangements tend to occur in situations where student learning issues or behavior issues are known or are anticipated. A variety of service arrangements exist to carry out the tasks of special education. These general features suggest the first categories comprising the knowledge held by special education teachers.

These initial categories include service delivery arrangements, staffing arrangements, and the general actions of teachers as well as the general actions of students. Typical special education service arrangements are arranged along a continuum of services that ranges from inclusive general education classroom support for the majority of students who receive services to substantially separate educational settings where students with greater learning needs are typically educated. There are myriad structural arrangements answering to the description of inclusion. Each school or district often has an arrangement specific to its individual setting and students. The typical arrangement for many schools is a combination of inclusive services with a smaller degree of "pull-out" services (e.g. removal for a short period of instruction in a given subject area) and a very small substantially separate group. A student who continues to struggle academically or behaviorally may be a candidate for "pull-out" services. This type of arrangement generally involves a student leaving the general education classroom to go the special education teacher's workspace. Such space may be a separate classroom or part of a classroom shared with other special educators. Teachers in both general education and special education usually refer to a student receiving services outside of the classroom as a "pull-out" student.

Kristie and Charlotte work in generally inclusive arrangements. While both spend the majority of their time in general education classrooms, they also share their resource room space with at least one other additional special education teacher. In addition, both have done some "pull-out" service for students. At her own discretion, Kristie has done "pull-out" teaching with some of her students. She determined that taking the students from the general education classroom was the most appropriate course of action. Charlotte's situation is more of a standardized combination of inclusive and "pull-out" arrangements—she spends the majority of her time in the "first grade inclusion classroom" and a much smaller amount of time in her own separate space providing "pull-out" services for two second grade students.

District specific varieties in structure concerning substantially separate educational arrangements also exist. These settings typically involve groups of students who are assigned to a special education classroom for the majority of their day. Substantially separate settings can exist for students having similar diagnoses, similar cognitive levels, or behaviors or any combination of these categories. These classrooms can also have different levels within these categories. For example, Carlene and Marie work with students diagnosed as learning disabled, as do Kristie and Charlotte. Yet, their students are educated in separate classrooms and join their general education peers only for lunch, special curricular subjects, and sometimes recess. The majority of both Kristie's and Charlotte's students do not leave their general education classrooms. Marie's program is defined as the "low-incidence" program. This means that she is likely to be assigned any struggling student that has a diagnosis that fits into the low-incidence category of disability. This also means that she has times where she has students who display significant cognitive disability along with her more typical group of students with learning disabilities.

Then there are substantially separate programs where the chief organizing criteria are more cognitive in nature—as is the case with both Betty and Jeri. Both their classrooms serve students who are diagnosed with significant cognitive disabilities. Even in these situations, the students served show great variety. Both classrooms have students that primarily work on skills considered to be "access skills", skills that are related to communication or movement. At the same time, this is in some degree of contrast to my own substantially separate classroom. In my classroom, the students are also diagnosed as having significant/moderate cognitive disabilities, though technically, they are moderately disabled in terms of an IQ-based diagnosis. They spend the majority of their school day addressing academic kinds of skills at the "entry point" level.

These different service arrangements bring us to a second broad descriptive category for thinking about special education practice—types of skills. With the requirement that all students, regardless of disability level, participate in local district and state assessments, all states have developed assessment programs for students with special needs. States are now required to demonstrate how students with disabilities are participating and progressing in the standards-based general education curriculum. Standards may be addressed as written. That is, the students address all standards as written, but display that knowledge in alternative forms. For example, students may complete a project rather than take a test that demonstrates what they have learned in a given unit. Students may also address the standards as written but focus on only a narrow range of those standards. Still other students may address standards through the "entry point." At this level, students address academic standards noted in curriculum documents but do so in a substantially modified manner. These are the students that typically receive their education in more substantially separate classrooms, such as those belonging to Marie, Carlene, Betty, and Jeri, and also my own classroom. Finally, there are the students who are working on "access" skills. Students working on access skills are typically working on communication and physical skills but within the context of standards-based academic activities (Resource Guide to Massachusetts Curriculum Frameworks, 2006). Accomplishing standards-based instruction (or any instruction in general) for such students often requires additional staffing arrangements beyond the academic paraprofessional often assigned to the general education classroom. The most typical of these arrangements is the provision of a 1:1 paraprofessional assigned to a specific student.

The Interviews

The Students and the Classrooms

Teacher practice goes beyond the obvious categories first suggested. This assertion is clearly evident in the words of Kristie, Charlotte, Marie, Carlene, Betty, and Jeri. To complete the in-depth examination of the data, I summarized the teachers' responses to specific interview questions. Each participant provided rich and detailed answers to the questions asked of her. Understanding the teachers' practice begins with their descriptions of their students and their classrooms.

In describing her students and current schedule, Kristie spoke of students who were "pretty much high functioning...with basically Language-Based Learning Disabilities." Her students' disabilities often played out in instruction as problems with decoding at the beginning of the year and became problems with comprehension as the year progressed. But, the reverse could also be true. Kristie's most challenging student was a boy who "comprehended well but who still couldn't decode...he couldn't read 'I' from one page to another if the text wasn't patterned." Of his progress, she said, "He started at Level A [using the Differential Reading Assessment (DRA) program and is now a Level 6. We don't make a ton of progress...but we make a little progress. He doesn't make huge leaps...[but] progress is progress, so that's good." When she described her fourth grade students, Kristie said, "They could decode a newspaper but they had no idea of what they read...and [I] kept on using simple texts that had problem-solution in them until I read an article [stating] that is was wrong to keep them on a low-level. They're not really learning anything...there's not a lot of meat in those books..." Finally, she talked of having "the big behavior problem of the school." This boy "was just so angry...he didn't let anybody in." She added, "I'm used to difficult kids and I can usually break them by at least November. This boy was unbreakable. He had skills but just didn't do any of the work."

Kristie generally spent her mornings teaching math and reading in fourth grade classrooms where "sometimes the students were integrated and sometimes they were not." She implied that the degree to which her students were integrated was directly related to the actions of the general education teachers. Her afternoons were spent teaching math in both second and fourth grade classrooms in environments where "we were totally integrated...the children didn't look any different than any other student...in fourth grade, it was the same...We basically co-taught for math in both situations...I could be up there teaching or she could be...either of us could be helping students or taking groups, but it was very seamless in math...I had wished always that the reading part of the day would be more like the math part of the day, because I really felt as if the kids felt good about it...."

Of her students' feelings regarding being in special education, she noted, "The kids here that are on IEPs, most of them are not your low-functioning child so they have an awareness of what's going on...so...they get resentful and I don't blame them." She also spoke of difficulties with returning to the instruction of the general education classroom, "And then when they return to their home classroom...sometimes they're welcomed back and sometimes they're not...they're just, like, shoved off to a corner . . . it's not, like, the teacher would transition them to something that would make it easier for them to transition into the classroom...she throws them back into the back of the classroom and continues on with whatever she's doing..." She went on to add, "And then it's like...what are you going to give them to do when they come back into my classroom? So, I think...like...well you are their teacher...so that was difficult...usually I'm a little bit more aggressive...but I didn't want to step on people's toes."

Charlotte worked with students in the first, second, and third grades. The children and the classroom she described were those in a district she was soon to be leaving. She often experienced difficulties with scheduling because of having all three grade levels as well as having her paraprofessional removed to assist with other duties in the school. Issues of student behaviors characterized her descriptions of her students. Her students were children "falling a year or two years below reading, writing, and math expectations, tending to be ADHD (Attention Deficit Hyperactivity Disorder)... and having behavioral difficulties." The behavioral difficulties that she noted included "not being able to follow class routines and expectations, refusing to do work, hiding under their desks, banging etc." Her students were not moderately disabled in terms of their academic ability but they were so in terms of the "[behavior] supports they need." She added, "The students showed "a huge split, ability-level wise." As Charlotte talked of her issues with the students' behaviors and her difficulties with trying to manage them, it was clear that she felt that administrative support was lacking. She spoke of not receiving enough behavioral training to effectively teach her students.

Marie described her classroom as a "substantially separate, self-contained, 502.4 classroom." This designation, 502.4, is the state code for a classroom in which the students are substantially separate from their general education peers for the majority of their academic program. Currently, her students go to a fourth grade gym class as a result of class sizes. They also go to lunch and recess with their grade level peers.

Marie's students ranged between the ages of ten to twelve. Some had behavioral issues; she qualified these issues as "social behavioral kinds of skills." Most were diagnosed with non-verbal learning disabilities, "compounded by other problems." Among the students in her classroom were two students with substantially limited skills. Of both students, Marie says, "We're still trying to figure out what they can do…It's hard to determine what each is really capable of doing…lots of times it's a fifty-fifty chance. We know [the girl] can count to three, we're working on counting to four…[but] she wants to be doing what everybody else is doing—we try to make it easy for her to do that…typically though, the conversations seem to be over her head…I don't know if this is the most appropriate place for her, but this is where her mom wants her. We make it as meaningful and significant as we can." The second student was low academically and displayed behavioral issues. Marie noted that she was particularly unsure of whether this second student belonged in her classroom. His behavior and substantial cognitive disability complicated his placement in her classroom.

As Marie discussed her class, she stated that her current class of students is much higher than those she has had in the past. Previously, she has had students that were working on pre-academic skills. Some of her current students, like the two described above, were still working on that sort of content but the others were not. Marie noted, "This creates a challenge…[especially] when you have others doing third and fourth grade work."

Issues in diagnosing several of her students also heavily influenced Carlene's description of her current class. She noted, "[One] first grader doesn't have a diagnosis…we're guessing ADHD. His behaviors were very, very severe…to the point where he couldn't be in the classroom [and] he was in my room on a trial basis…there really wasn't any other place to put him." Other students also had severe learning disabilities. These students were with her because "they have difficulty functioning in a large group."

Of special interest in her description was her account of her "severely autistic boy." Carlene noted, "[He's] considered non-verbal…he was just toilet-trained this year. He's actually very bright. He reads, does math, but appears to be extremely low functioning and in some areas he is low functioning. Sometimes, he is my top student, which is really surprising…He came in kindergarten, flapping and vocalizing constantly…" She was pleased by the fact that this boy was now toilet trained, was using some speech, and was initiating contact with adults. Carlene attributed the range of variety in her classroom to the fact that there was "no real criteria [for placement] in the room…there used to be one…a very academic criteria—but as the population changed, that criteria didn't fit. They never designed a new one…my room is a catch-all, a room of last resort."

Carlene indicated that she currently had nine students but her count can "change daily." She noted that she was pretty well set with supplies, meaning that she had materials ranging from kindergarten up to grade three but stressed that having such materials has not always been the case. She said, "When I first came to this job, there was a high turnover of teachers. There was not a lot of materials here…[the teacher] came, brought her own materials…the teacher left and took the materials with her. Everybody just kind of invented their own [programs] for these kids."

When asked to describe her students, Betty responded, "It's a range...they run the gamut as far as their skills go." All of the students worked on access skills. Several of the students worked on beginning academics. Two of the students had inclusion opportunities in general education classrooms. She added a dimension of physicality not seen with the other teachers to her descriptions. The majority of her students were ambulatory though there was a degree to the amount of assistance that they needed. Some could ambulate without assistance; some used gait belts (a device with handles held by the teacher that a student wears while walking; its use prevents the student from falling.) Two of her students used wheelchairs. Both could weight bear or had the ability to stand with assistance, one was up and out of the chair quite a bit and could walk from his locker to the classroom, a "good stretch" of a distance. In fact, this distance was approximately 15 feet. She noted, "The second student was extremely spastic (stiff)...it took two people to get his feet to the floor to ambulate or to get him up and out of his chair to engage in physical activity...but that was not the priority...other things were." All of Betty's students had 1:1 paraprofessionals, resulting in a complicated staffing schedule. The management of this complicated staffing schedule often made keeping the class engaged in its designated activities stressful.

Betty described her classroom as a "program" rather than a class. Her program was initially known as the Early Learning Center but was now the Elementary Alternative Program. Her classroom stood out among the six classrooms in the study as a result of the large amount of specialized equipment that was present. The preponderance of this equipment shows the variety of specialized therapeutic devices that can be necessary for students with special needs and, at the same time, calls attention to this classroom.

Jeri's students were chronologically in the fifth grade. She, too, offers a description of a range of students. Two of her boys worked at the pre-primer or primer level of reading—that is they were able to read a few sight words and they continued to work on letter recognition. They displayed beginning math skills such as 1:1 correspondence—matching objects to the correct number and the ability to match objects according to specific attributes. Jeri noted, "Even though [these] are some of my higher level students, the skills are still at the kindergarten level. The other students in the class were currently working on access skills, that is, on ways to participate in their environments more independently. She added, "You reach a point where you say, okay, he's 11, do we still continue doing letter recognition...if they don't have the skill at this point in time, then you move onto sight words and maybe they see the connection...some of the students just can't see the connection...but, I have to work with what the IEP says." The IEPs were written at the end of the previous year . . . that's kind of a bummer...it's too bad we didn't have them at the beginning of the year...I could have rewritten them to what I would typically be doing in the classroom. They [the administration] said, think about it in a way that it was a new teacher that didn't know how to write IEPs and didn't know the kids." Jeri was uncomfortable and unhappy with this idea.

Three of her four students had 1:1 paraprofessionals. Many of these paraprofessionals had been with their students since the student was in preschool. Throughout the interviews, Jeri frequently commented that sometimes it seemed that the paraprofessionals behaved as if they were "second mothers" to their students and she was somewhat displeased by this fact.

She began her classroom description by noting the major changes that she had made in the classroom. These changes encompassed both physical and curricular aspects of her classroom. She noted, "The classroom is very different from [when you first saw it]. All those partitions that were used for ABA and discrete trials have disappeared." Jeri saw them as interfering with what she saw as one of her major educational goals, "Each student had an individual area but socialization and inclusion were also part of their goals, so why were they secluded within their secluded classroom?" She also stated, "Classroom visitors come in and say…wow, it looks like a regular classroom now!"

Curriculum and Standards

There is significant debate concerning the topic of curriculum in public education. Curriculum, the tool by which knowledge is acquired in school, must be defined in terms of its purpose and what it teaches. At the most basic level, curriculum is composed of topics to be taught and in many cases specific methodologies and materials used to teach them. A curriculum is typically a formal document that is intended as a plan for what educators want to happen in classrooms. Content is often categorized within subjects and subject fields. Teachers consciously organize, plan and deliver this material to students. The subject matter is frequently identified through studying and understanding the content-related needs of learners, community or societal needs, and expert knowledge (Tyler, 1949). Defined in this manner, a curriculum leads to the academic education of students in school.

At the same time, a curriculum has important social functions. These social functions result in students acquiring behavioral repertoires that enable them to interact successfully in the various social settings they encounter. Such settings include, but are not limited to, behavior in the cafeteria, at recess, in classes, and in social interactions in the community. The social functions of a curriculum are generally not so consciously planned. Defined in this manner, curriculum leads to the social education of students in school. The academic and social functions of the curriculum work together to help prepare students for the roles they will ultimately play in society. Both the formal academic curriculum and the social curriculum have long been the subject of debate in general education as well as in special education (Kliebard, 1995; Nietupski, Hamre-Nietupski, Curtin, & Shrikanth, 1997). The central question in either discipline is what exactly should schools teach?

In his historical study of the curriculum, Kliebard (1995) identified several interest groups that have sought to determine what schools should teach. The Humanists advocated a traditional approach to knowledge and teaching. The Developmentalists reacted to the Humanists by advocating the importance of the student in the educative process. Dewey argued that education must lead the child from his or her present interests to intellectual command of subject matter. To make knowledge accessible, one started where the learner was and whenever that learner was ready to begin a career as a learner (Bruner, 1977). Meanwhile, the Social Efficiency movement advocated a strict skill oriented approach to teaching. Education became a matter of extensive task analyses, goals, and objectives. Schools had a factory-like quality to them. Students were expected to meet the predetermined goals set for them. The emphasis on precise measurement advocated by educators subscribing to this position ultimately tracked students into a specific position in life. The present context of schooling continues to be very much aligned with a Social Efficiency perspective. The No Child Left Behind act has brought a massive emphasis on skill instruction and standardized testing to schools in the effort to monitor school accountability.

Similar curriculum study exists for special education. In a study examining the various trends in special education curriculum research, Nietupski et al. (1997) identified the major topics of curricular emphasis as functional life skills, social relationships development, and academic skills. The question of interest is which components of these three areas should receive the greatest emphasis in determining what to teach students with special needs? This question is of particular importance when students with more significant cognitive disabilities are considered. Teaching academic skills to all students is reflected in the literature under the term "access to the general curriculum." The teaching of such skills is currently a primary focus of research attention as schools operate within the requirements of NCLB and the recent reauthorizations of IDEA in 1997 and in 2004 (Downing, 2006; Spooner, Dymond, Smith, & Kennedy, 2006; Wehmeyer, 2006). But, just as debate continues with determining the general education curriculum, there remain questions as to what exactly the term "access to the general education curriculum" means (Spooner, et al., 2006). This debate was also reflected in the teachers' words.

Kristie described curriculum as the "framework you use" and "a guide that you have to plug into." She said that for her the school's curriculum is a guide to her teaching." At the same time, she did not see that curriculum as a "set step-by-step way of teaching." She noted that the curriculum does not define her teaching. For her, the curriculum is the guide to what she needs to be teaching and to where her children need to be at the end of the year. She added, "[Curriculum] is just not off the cuff for me. I take the important things from the curriculum and I adapt them to the books and the writing that my students are doing." When asked what assistance regarding curriculum she receives from the general education teachers that she works with, Kristie said that she received very little.

Kristie attributed difficulties encountered in delivering curriculum to her assigned grades to herself. In the case of her second grade assignment, she had a good understanding of the necessary reading and writing because she pulled her students out of the classroom. She associated her difficulties with fourth grade curriculum clarity to a lack of communication. She further noted that she needed "to be more on top of that." She stated, "In fourth grade, I tried to follow along with what the [general education] teacher was doing as best as I could, but things were just a little bit 'hodge podge'. Sometimes, I just didn't know where we were going with things in the general education classroom."

Kristie closed her description of curriculum by contrasting her experience with her present school district to her former district. In her former district, she spent some time as the teacher for a self-contained classroom. While there, she was in charge of determining the curriculum topics that were presented, especially with regard to social studies and science. There, she was more likely to speak up regarding what was working or not working with her students. She described this as being "more aggressive" regarding student needs. At the same time though, she stated that she "worked really well with her general education teachers. There was always a sense of back and forth between herself and her teachers. In her current district, she noted that she was the "new kid on the block" and so she was concerned about being too forceful." In her words, she did not want "to step on anyone else's toes" as she advocated for her students.

Kristie equated the topic of standards with curriculum. She described the standards as "a blueprint for what you're supposed to be teaching." She added that she tends to use the terms interchangeably, though she also noted that there were differences between the two terms. She said, "Standards are about meeting the standard and standards-based assessment. Kids will be up to the standard. Curriculum kind of gets you to the standard." She saw the standards as being embedded within each grade level. Additionally, she commented that she has been in her present district for a year and had yet to see a complete list of standards. In the absence of this list of standards, she said, "I just go by the curriculum." She noted, "Standards basically constitute the curriculum."

When asked to address the topic of training in standards-based education, she pointed out that the standards movement was firmly established when she began teaching. As a result, her lesson planning has always been driven by the standards. She further added that once she entered either school district, the standards were a document that she was given. It is of note that she received no district training on the standards or the curriculum.

Charlotte also equated curriculum with standards. She spoke of both as "frameworks of what the children need to learn" and "what the state thinks is appropriate for children at a given grade level." She defined standards as "just really the major points that the children need to know." When she spoke of curriculum, she noted that she had the opportunity to do a lot of training with curriculum mapping. She said, "the curriculum is kind of roped into the standards and the standards help you to know what it is that you need to be teaching."

Charlotte described several different purchased programs that she typically used. These programs included such items as the Edmark Reading Program, Telian Lively Letters, and Lexia Reading software—all programs designed to assist students in building literacy skills. She distinguished subject areas as core subject areas and noted that she typically taught language arts or math in her self-contained setting and supported science or social studies in the general education classroom. As she described these different programs she used, she commented that there may be overlap within areas of special education but that there was no overlap with general education. For example, there was no overlap between special education and general education in the use of the Telian Lively Letters phonetics program.

When Charlotte spoke of curriculum, she also spoke of differentiated tasks. She briefly noted that in general, general education teachers have better materials. She often found herself scrambling to get access to the necessary curriculum materials. Her brief mention of differentiation became more elaborate as she talked about the concept of "access to the curriculum." She noted that while her math students could "pretty much stay with the math series" difficulties were created by having to jump around in the textbook. She shook her head and added with a degree of lament, "Students didn't have a great deal of time to become comfortable with the topics taught. The pace was just too quick." Charlotte said, "I like to make sure that I'm on the same page as the classroom teacher as far as presented skills to make sure that I'm not missing anything." She saw her role in presenting curriculum to her students as "trying to mirror where the general education teachers are." As she moved further into the school year, she noted that instruction often became "finding ways to meet the goals." At the same time, she stated that mirroring where the general education teachers were could be problematic. Some of the teachers she worked with were inviting, while others were much less so. Feeling wanted in the classroom made her day run "just a little bit smoother."

Charlotte also spoke of the uniqueness of being a special education teacher as she discussed curriculum. She said, "Being a special education teacher gives you some degree of flexibility or creativity." The ideas in the general education curriculum "have access points in the classroom." She elaborated, "I might not have been teaching exactly what other classes were learning or doing but I was doing those topics in some way." She added, "With special education, you can take points in the curriculum and teach them...but they definitely have to be modified. There are a lot of ways that you can modify the curriculum if you have the resources and if it's allowed in your district. There are a lot of little access points to help the children learn certain standards." For Charlotte, curriculum and ultimately her instruction was a "combination of looking at the standards and at the students' IEP goals." She noted, "The IEP goals need to be addressed but they're just a piece of the educational puzzle."

Unlike Kristie, Charlotte stated that she's had "lots of training in standards." This statement was then qualified in terms of the state's alternate assessment program. She added, "I guess I'm lucky to have had an alternate assessment [for a student] in my first year. I started realizing that regardless of whether I agreed with the process or not, I think I was understanding why it was important that these children were reaching some of those standards." She went on to say, " A child may not be making a standard at grade four but there's a section of the standard that's at grade three—the student is accessing this point of the standard. This is just a great way to show how to create instruction based on the standard." At the same time, Charlotte commented that her training in standards was also lacking. She stated, "I didn't get a whole lot of training on standards from the school. There was perhaps one workshop but that workshop was to emphasize 'these are your books, they're important for the state test." After a moment, she added, "A lot of this [the training aspects of standards] may also have been addressed during grade level meetings...but I didn't go to these!"

Of the teachers participating in this study, Marie's experience with curriculum may be the most varied. She has been working with a range of students of varying disabilities for the longest period of time and has seen many changes in state and district policy. These changes in how schools think of educating students were clearly reflected in her comments regarding curriculum and standards. Her immediate answer to the question of defining curriculum was "state-mandated." It was important for her to be focused on what the state says the curriculum is. Here, she was referring to the state's Curriculum Framework publications. She noted that her Curriculum Resource Guide was "like a bible." She further linked her definition of curriculum to those items that she needed to document for her students' alternate assessment portfolios. She commented, "I have leeway...significant leeway...in what I have to teach. I have to teach English language arts, math, science, and social studies. Within those four subjects, I have to teach to specific strands and within those strands, I have specific standards that I have to address. All of these are modified as the Curriculum Resource Guide suggests." She added, "All of my lessons are geared toward something that the portfolio needs or wants. My activities vary depending on what I see or hear and what I have access to or what I already have."

Marie also spoke about the issues she encountered as she taught in the various subject areas. She noted that social studies were easy for her to teach because it was essentially the world around us. Math and reading were also easy because she had specific purchased programs or materials that she could use—items such as "Explode the Code"—a phonetically based reading series, or "Touchmath"—a multisensory computation strategy that has great utility for students with special needs. She described her math and reading as "more traditionally structured." Science, however, was difficult because she had to get it out of the science book. She noted that she did not always have resource kits for science and often had to create her own. She then related how she brought the school's science and math texts home to review with the thought that "we could follow these." She stated, "But we can't. We're not all in the same place. So, instead, I say, well we're doing number sense today and tomorrow we're going to do patterns, then geometry after that and then some data. And next week, we'll do composition, language arts, and the solar system. It all applies to the curriculum, but it's not in nice concise plan where you can flip through the pages and say, 'I'll do this.'"

Of special note in Marie's understanding of curriculum was the current events focus that she used to structure a great deal of what she teaches. She explained that this focus came about as a result of working originally with really young students and implementing a morning classroom meeting such as that found in many elementary classrooms. Marie said, "We'd discuss the weather, set up the calendar, talk about what we had done the night before—basically, lots of language stuff." Because the students were with her for more and more years, sometimes as many as seven consecutive years as a result of their continued need for a separate educational program as defined by her school district, it became obvious that she couldn't do the same thing year after year. A second major impact on her curriculum occurred when her program began growing as a result of being assigned students who were more academically capable but who were not "making it in the mainstream". These students did not need to continue practice on identifying days of the week or months of the year—common elements in a calendar routine. The question became, How do we adjust what is happening in the classroom so that everybody's needs are met? Marie said, "So I thought—the newspaper! The newspaper has the calendar, the weather, and all sorts of things of interest. So the topics suggested by the newspaper became the basis for the skills that we did." She added, "I try to make the units and topics flow. So, for example, we had a lot of hurricanes, so hurricanes led to a study of the weather, which led to a study of clouds, and about rain and water." She further noted, "The kids can drive what is presented if they bring in topics of interest."

Like Kristie and Charlotte, Marie emphasized the close relationship between curriculum and standards. Standards were the difference between what she did in the past and what she does now. Standards have made her more accountable and as a result more organized in her teaching. Standards "provide more of a purpose to what gets done in the classroom." She finally noted that the students enjoy the standards-based approach. She said, "Knowing the technical terms and properties for things makes the kids feel smarter."

And again, as with Kristie and Charlotte, Marie said, "School training was not really provided. We were given the manual and told to align our curriculum." She is the only teacher in the study to have been told that she had to align curriculum for her students. When she spoke of the task of aligning curriculum, Marie stressed the value of the Curriculum Resource Guide. She said, "The resource guide should be available to all general education teachers as well so that they can understand that it [standards-based instruction for all] is not as scary as it appears, that they're really doing it already." Yet, at the same time as she made these comments, Marie also lamented, "But we don't share it with the general education teachers until they come to borrow mine..."

Carlene defined curriculum as "the subjects you teach and also the skills that are at each level." To this definition, she added the qualifier that such subjects and skills were "sometimes dictated by the school and sometimes dictated on your own." Carlene said that she had considerable flexibility when selecting units to teach, "especially in my room." She noted, "I think that general education teachers have a stricter guide that they have to follow." When describing her classroom, she said, "My classroom can be more flexible. General education classrooms are given—this is what you use for math, reading...you can supplement, but you have to use 'the program.' I can basically use any curriculum that I feel comfortable with—if I feel it's beneficial for my students." She added, "I'm pretty lucky that way. Carlene then listed a number of the different programs that she has available to her. These programs included the Telian Sight Word Program, Project Read, a variety of computer software, Explode the Code phonics program, Touchmath, and a new math series that she encountered through a workshop.

Carlene said that she had put a good portion of her math program together herself. She noted, "The school uses the "Trailblazers" math program. The program is very difficult for my students—it moves very quickly and does a lot of spiraling. The program is not always doing the same thing two days in a row which is difficult for the students that I work with." Her writing curriculum was also self-created. She said, "I look at what the [state] Frameworks that the state wants the students to cover at their grade level, and if they're capable of that, then I modify from there." When teaching science and social studies, Carlene was able to use the same curriculum that the rest of the school uses. However, she must "greatly modify the material" for her students. She added that she typically had to borrow the materials that she needed to do this.

Carlene stated, "There's a lot of making up your own curriculum when you're working in a classroom like this. You have to adapt and take bits and pieces from different places." She added, "But, you're making up everything! You don't have a scope and sequence to follow. That's one thing about a series—a scope and sequence is provided; you can make sure that you cover all the skills." She emphasized, "That was always my worry—did I miss something? Was there something that I didn't think of or that was changed from one grade to another?" She concluded, "But my preference is to adapt and to take bits and pieces from a lot of places rather than to access the existing curriculum. I like the flexibility of being able to adjust my curriculum to the students."

Turning to the topic of standards, Carlene said, "Standards are the expectations that you're expected to teach...or aim for, if not reach." She noted that her district provided some minimal training to all teachers once the standards movement acquired prominence in the state. She added, "I think in the beginning, we might have had more training; it would be nice to have a refresher now and then...or even time just to sit with your grade level people and say, 'alright, what's different?'" Carlene pointed out that she felt that the standards have been helpful because they provide a "structure for the content that gets taught." At the same time though, she lamented, "As a special educator—I thought, 'Oh my gosh! I've got kids who don't recognize all their letters yet...how are they ever going to do different genres in literature?" She further stated, "I like the Frameworks and now that we have to do alternate assessments, the fact that they give us the Curriculum Resource Guide that shows how you can address standards at a lower level is really helpful. You can go back and use an entry point to work on the standard. I particularly like the concept of 'Essence of the Standard'; it puts things in English so that we all understand it." Carlene stated, "I really do like the standards and the Frameworks. I think they're very helpful. But the state assessments—now those are a different matter! The Frameworks are something to aim for. Certainly, I'm not working on the same grade level but I can talk to my kids about the content of the standard." Carlene concluded, "Standards have changed my teaching in some ways. Standards didn't so much change the way I taught reading though they have made me make sure that I touch on some things that I might not previously have thought of touching on."

Betty immediately equated the concept of curriculum with the development of her students' IEPs—their Individual Education Plans. She noted, "One of the first things that I do is to go to the giant Frameworks book [The Curriculum Resource Guide] and just sort of pore through it. This helps me to see what a student needs to work on." She continued with the idea that curriculum is very individualized for her students; she was teaching students that were working primarily on access-oriented skills. Access skills for her students included such skills as using a switch to activate a communication device, grasping and releasing items, and making eye contact when spoken to. The ideal was for such skills to be taught within an academic context. She made it clear that her first curriculum thoughts were related to social, physical, or communication skills that the students needed to acquire rather than academic content skills. Her starting question was, "How can the access skills that the students need to acquire be incorporated into a content activity?

When planning activities for her students, Betty also stressed that she had to spend time trying to match students with possible routines that currently exist in general education classrooms. She noted that she often asks herself, "Is the student appropriate for the activity?" As several of the other teachers did, Betty also spoke of purchased programs to provide curriculum. In her case, this material was a program called "The Hands On Reading Curriculum." This program addressed literature that was included in the district's kindergarten and first grade general education curriculums. It provided "tons of follow up activities to do with a classroom of multi-need students."

Betty next related her thoughts concerning her experiences with public school curriculum. She said, "When I came into the school system, I worried a lot about curriculum. There's just so much...there was probably material that I wasn't even aware that I needed to be addressing. It was difficult to stay on top of that." Her experience with standards was closely related to these comments. She defined standards as "something you just gotta do!" She found herself asking how am I going to do it? She noted, "When I first realized that I have to do this [the standards], it was difficult to look through them and say how am I going to do this? Is this going to make sense to any of these students? But I realized that the standards have helped me to consider areas that I might not have previously considered." She further noted, "The alternate assessment has made me view standards so much differently than I did originally. The idea of access skills was helpful. I felt a little reassured in knowing that they're not going to understand something like Greek folktales but that you can take an activity and incorporate other skills into that and those skills might be the access skills." She noted that she hasn't received much training with standards, "I don't know if [the lack of training with standards] is the special education department or the school district. I'm not always in the loop."

Jeri defined curriculum as a "framework…people just kind of decided what was really important for individuals to know and to learn to become functional and independent adults in society." She went on to add, "There's a fine line between the functional and with what the powers that be say that we need to know." She noted that her classroom was considered by her district to be a "life skills" classroom. This meant that the students were engaged in learning "functional skills"—meal preparation, money, and community use, etc." She continued, "People can find out that it isn't all that difficult to mesh life skills and what students need to know academically. They're seeing here [in this classroom] that doing this just kind of makes sense. For example, when we're doing cooking, we're bringing in the food from different places. So while we're making pizza we're learning about Italy. Jeri further related a description of theme-based curriculum; she created themes of modified academic activities based on district identified curriculum topics.

As with the other teachers, curriculum and standards were closely linked. Jeri used the same terminology to define both curriculum and standards. Standards were also "what children are supposed to know so that they can become functional independent adults." She said that standards determined her teaching; she added, "the standards are definitely where my themes come from." But determining her themes was tough because she was not always looking at just one grade level. She also commented, "I had to look at a couple of grades though, at what the other classrooms were doing. I wanted to make what I was doing fit [in with the overall curriculum of the school]." As she said this, she noted, "standards are very important but there's so much on the standards that it's taking away some of the quality teaching time. We've had to focus so much on the standards that other stuff such as character education stuff and learning to respect each other…there's no time for that. And that's a shame."

Jeri's curriculum activities were additionally dictated by her students' IEPs. These IEPs have created problems for her classroom in determining, creating, and scheduling activities. For example, one student had music class four times a week in her IEP. Fifth grade did not have music scheduled that frequently. Jeri next noted that she often lost her preparation time because of meeting this service schedule. Further, much of her school day often had to be given to completing unconnected activities identified in individual IEPs. These activities generally consisted of providing the ABA discrete trial training opportunities noted in the individual IEPs. She pointed out that each student had an individual work bucket that contained tasks and materials that address isolated academic skills. These skills included such things as letter-sound correspondence tasks, number identification, color identification, following one step directions, and sight words and safety signs. These IEP requirements impacted her ability to devote time to creating opportunities to access the general education curriculum. She finally noted that she changed some tasks, most notably her "following directions" activities; the directions being taught were unrelated to the educational context and not functional in nature. She said, "I felt that it was time to move on to at least more functional types of directions…things like touch, take, give…things that you can use in a lot of activities."

Alternate Assessments

Closely related to the topic of standards and participation in standards-based instruction is the mandate to have students with special needs participate in district and state assessment programs either through taking the regular test or through completing alternate assessments. Such alternate assessments often take the form of assembling a portfolio of work rather than taking the on-demand test that many states require. These alternate assessments are typically reserved for students with the most significant cognitive special needs. Of the six teachers participating in the study, Charlotte, Marie, Carlene, Betty, and Jeri all had students who are alternately assessed. Kristie did not have experience with the alternate assessment process.

Charlotte cast her limited alternate assessment experience in terms of the training that her district provided. She considered herself lucky to have had early experience with the alternate assessment and added that without such district professional development she would have been "lost." She said, "I think that the state did a relatively good job with the training…with showing examples of student work and how it met standard. It was interesting because if you first looked at the work you might say, 'well, that doesn't meet the standard' but it's also a way to justify to other professionals in your building the importance of finding ways to show how children are meeting their goals and their standards. I wouldn't necessarily have known the process for determining what to include in the portfolio or what made an acceptable piece of work."

Charlotte's thoughts concerning the effectiveness of the alternate assessment process were of special importance. She made note of the state's concept of the entry point. She said, "The process can be effective, if it's something that you're already implementing into your classroom; but if it's something that you're doing just because the state says so then it doesn't necessarily reflect what the student is doing. The portfolio process is good in that it really did make me think about whether or not my students were meeting standards and about finding ways that I could modify work so that it met different entry points for the students. At the same time, Charlotte also stressed that she felt that the portfolio process had significant problems. Such problems were created by the manner in which portfolios were scored. She was concerned that issues related to student scores were the result of teacher errors in portfolio production rather than a true indication of what students might be doing with regard to standards-based instruction.

While Charlotte related limited experience with the portfolio process, Marie related just the opposite—extensive experience with portfolio production as well as having been trained to be a Portfolio Training Specialist—a teacher who is available to train other special education teachers in the portfolio process. Her initial comments regarding the portfolio process were positive. She opened with the statement, "Portfolios are a lot of work but they're worth it. People in other places think that they're not." After a moment of thought, she qualified her statement to say, "I shouldn't say they're worth it but they have made me a better teacher. The portfolios have made me less scattered in terms of what my curriculum needs to be. Portfolios have made me more focused on things other than math and reading because that's all that we used to do—math, reading, and cooking. And we'd read the newspaper...but we never applied it to anything. Now, we apply it!"

Marie's next comments provided greater context for her initial statements. "In the past, IEPs basically dealt with reading and math...you taught a kid how to read, how to count money, how to tell time...but you also have to teach kids about history and science. This may not be in the education plan (IEP). History and science are in my education plans because I figure that if I'm doing it for the portfolios, then it should be there." She added, "I did science and social studies according to the newspaper but I didn't have to be accountable, didn't have to keep data on it." She continued, "The portfolios have also made me organized. I know that I have to teach something from earth and space, something from biology, physics, or chemistry...I have to get at least three separate science strands. In the past, I used to do some of these topics but it was more for the fun of it. Now, I have to have evidence; I have to have things that show what the kids are doing." Marie contrasted these thoughts with those of an acquaintance who works with students who are more significantly handicapped than those that she usually works with. She said, "It's difficult for him to see the sense in a third grade reading portfolio for kids that he just basically changes diapers for." She further noted, "I can definitely understand where he's coming from; he would like to see a life skills curriculum as I would for some of the kids in my class...but not for all."

Carlene opened her discussion concerning portfolios by noting that the portfolio was "valuable for some students. It shows what they know." At the same time, she added, "But I think it's horrible that they ask us to do all this work and the students don't have a chance of passing. It's bad that these kids who work the best that they can will never get a high school diploma because they're never going to be able to work at a tenth grade level. While the state says 'Yes, alternate assessment is a way that students can show their competency,' they still have to be able to do tenth grade work to pass and graduate." She continued, "The portfolios are creating a two-tiered system, kids that can't function [academically] and can't get diplomas and other kids." Carlene concluded, "The portfolio is only valuable for students who can't take the regular test as a result of non-intellectual reasons. It's great that these students have an alternate way to prove what they know."

Carlene next focused on the amount of work required to create a portfolio. She said, " It's a lot of work to get a piece of paper back—you get a little checklist back with three items checked off; that tells you very little. The student is working at the level of progressing or emerging. Well, I knew that before I sent the portfolio in!" She added, "The state is supposed to give back all this valuable information that you can use for your teaching. I don't find that the information that they give you is valuable; I don't find that I learn anything that I didn't know about the student already." She emphasized, "I know that the student is really making progress. I also know that the student is always going to be emerging when compared to kids working at grade level because the grade level skills that he is expected to know just go up higher."

Betty's experience with the alternate assessment provided yet a different example of the role that the assessment process played in her teaching practice. She described this process in terms of finding ways that her students can match the standards. She said that her first task in considering student portfolios is "going through the state Frameworks to try to see where the students fall in them and if there's a standard that we can do—not at grade level but a little below grade level and have it make sense to them and have them get something out of it, yet still meet the requirement of the alternate assessment." She continued, "The alternate assessment is a challenge but it has definitely made me look at things a little differently. I have to be a little more creative. The good thing about the state assessment is that it brings in the technology." Betty provided the example of one of her students using an adaptive switch to tell jokes to peers and staff at the school. He used the switch to activate a tape player with a previously recorded joke. In this way, he was able to demonstrate that he had met identified language standards in the Curriculum Frameworks.

Betty continued, "With the whole involvement in alternate assessment, although it was grueling and at times, tortuous, I think I view the standards so much differently than I did originally. The alternate assessment made me look at things differently; it made me see that I can take a lot of those standards and either do them below grade level or through access skills." She added, "When you have an end product and you can see it, that's the good part of the alternate assessment. The process is hard work but my attitude is positive. One student enjoyed portfolio activities so much that it forced me to create more opportunities for this kid!"

In a situation similar to Betty's, Jeri provided examples of the difficulties that are associated with portfolios. She said, "My biggest challenge is my lowest kids. They did good with patterning and with sorting but those are not some of the standards. The state wanted them to do stuff with fractions. I'm having a tough time with that—no matter how much I try, it's just not getting there." She noted that her students sometimes take control of the teaching situation—"the kids may not want to do a task twice; it's like they're saying, 'I realize it's work and I won't do it again.'"

Jeri pointed out that some portfolios are easier to do than others. "Whether a portfolio is easy or not is usually a function of the fact that some students can do more than others. Some students can do work samples (the primary type of evidence required for a portfolio) but you know, Keely rips up her work samples and so we have to rely on videotape. Can she do a task? Yes. Will she do a task? I don't know; it all depends on how she feels at the moment." Jeri closed with the statement that standards and the alternate assessment do not drive her teaching.

The Individual Education Plan (IEP)

An important component of teaching in special education is the individual education plan. Created annually, the IEP describes and delineates the specialized instruction and services that schools will provide to students with special needs. It consists of a listing of the goals and objectives that will be addressed during a yearly cycle. One of the more recent reform initiatives related to IEP development was that of mandating standards based instruction and progress in the general education curriculum into education for students with special needs. IEPs are often typical documents. This is to say that an average IEP has goals in reading and math. There may also be goals for social studies and science, depending on the district. Finally, there may be goals for daily living or personal care and communication depending on the student's level of ability.

Kristie began her process of IEP development by simultaneously examining the school curriculum and then the state standards. But she pointed out that she based her goals and objectives on the students themselves. She added that she also thought about the test scores and any student observations that she might have done. Such information was especially important to her when she didn't know a student. She noted, "With a student that I know, I look at any type of progress that we've made and at their strengths and weaknesses. I always do the strengths and weaknesses first. This helps me to determine what I choose for goals and objectives." She continued, "I think about the student and the goal. Like, if someone is struggling with basic mathematics, I go into the standards and say...okay...what are the basic computation skills that they need; so then, I break that down and think about [the needed skills] within our own math program...what do they need to know?" She further noted, "If I perceive the problem as being one of not having the basic concepts in place, I go back into the curriculum and standards and look and see what they're going to be facing for the next grade or setting. This helps me to determine what we should focus on."

Kristie said that her IEPs usually have three goals—reading, writing, and math. Each goal typically has four objectives—items that a student should be able to accomplish in a school year. After determining her goals and objectives, Kristie moved on to considering how a student's work needs to be modified. She continued, "A lot of the kids we have demonstrate a lot of the same issues—academically and behaviorally. Typically, I can select topics from across the curriculum, but with lower functioning children, I do have to focus on certain standards."

Charlotte noted that she prioritized the standards that she worked on based on her students' IEP goals. She said, "But my goals are also based on what I think they are capable of doing and what I think would be most meaningful to them, especially when it comes to math." She continued, "Math can get pretty technical—so finding standards that I think would be appropriate for them and really sort of looking at life skills and things you really need to know in order to succeed is important." At the same time, Charlotte stated, "IEP goals need to be addressed but they're just a piece of the puzzle." She continued, "I think about what points of the curriculum are necessary for them to be functioning when they leave school. I think about what assistive technology can be provided to students and I think about how they will need to be assessed—do they need an alternate assessment or can they pass the state test with accommodations for their testing. I look at the goals from the previous year and whether the student has reached them. Then I think about where they're going from there."

Charlotte's IEPs typically included reading, writing, and math goals. There was usually a "mainstreaming" objective—an objective that focuses on social studies or science and is a district practice. She also had goals for how the students can be successful when they were in the general education classroom.

Marie cited recent portfolio training as important to IEP development. That training stressed the necessity of including social studies and science goals in IEP development and she again stressed the presence of such goals in her IEPs. She stated, "My goals for history and science are usually not specific. In social studies, I talk about becoming aware of the world around them. This encompasses history, civil government, and your job. For social studies, they have to understand chronological order in terms of historical significance. It's patriotism at their level. Science goals are all about inquiry and recording that information. The goal just says that kids will be able to investigate, to compare, form hypotheses, or identify similarities and differences in a variety of subject areas. I don't write down that they'll master specific information, but rather that they'll be able to recall some of the information presented."

As the other teachers did, Carlene started her IEP development with thinking of what the students were capable of. She said, "Starting with thinking of what they're capable of is a good reflective piece. Sometimes, I'm not really sure just how much the students know. Then I think about what areas I want them to focus on. What do I consider to be the most critical among the need areas?" She added, "I also have to think of how I will break the needed skills down so that you can see the progression. What is the most critical piece?"

Betty began her IEP development by thinking about what was happening in the classroom and about what's worked and what hasn't worked with the students. She said, "I think of where we need to go from where we are. I also think of areas throughout the day that students might be having difficulty with. I try to achieve a balance between functional goals and standards-based goals." Because of the students with whom she worked, Betty also developed social-communication and life-skills goals. She noted, "Those areas are usually pretty clear cut."

Betty continued, "For academics—I'd go back to the standards and see what we were addressing the past year and how we could build upon that. She noted, "My IEPs probably have five or six goals. These goal areas don't change a lot—I have a social goal, a communication goal, a life skills goal, and an academics goal. Then there are also fine and gross motor goals; such goals may be incorporated into the life skills goals."

A typical life skill goal might consist of eating. Here, the student might be working on picking up a spoon, bringing a spoon to his or her mouth, holding a cup, or drinking from a cup. A typical social-communication goal might consist of completing an appropriate greeting, making requests, responding, turn-taking, accepting, or sharing. Finally, a typical academics goal might consist of sight vocabulary (functional sight words or community sight words), number sense, money skills, reading a simple story, making predictions or conclusions, or answering questions about the stories read.

Jeri provided limited information on the topic of IEP development as a result of the constraints placed upon her by her school district. She believed that "there is a fine line between a functional goal and what the powers that be say we need to know and to learn." She went on to add, "This is a life skills classroom." With this, she began an explanation that illustrates the difficulties achieving balance between life skills and academics. Her students have a history of working on skills appropriate to discrete trial training. These skills have their basis in pre-school oriented school readiness skills such as following directions and mimicking actions made by an adult. One of Jeri's first actions in the classroom was to change the content of such objectives from the non-functional "touch you nose" to directions that are functional to a school setting—directions that can be used in a lot of different activities. Such directions might include "take," "give," or "touch."

Interaction with General Education

The teachers have offered rich descriptive information regarding their daily practice. The information shared addressed the components of being a special education teacher. This next section addresses their interaction with the general education teachers in their schools. Here, the teachers offer insight into the overarching topic of the study—existing in the world of elementary general education curriculum.

Kristie's experience with her general education teachers was somewhat variable. She described her situation with, "Some teachers are very open. The math teacher was very open. Other teachers are not as open. The fourth grade reading teacher is a lovely person who thought she was doing the right thing." She noted, "[This teacher] always kept me abreast of things but then she would kind of go off the schedule…and, she wouldn't always include my kids."

Kristie's primary means of keeping in contact with the general education teachers with whom she worked was informal conversations. She got information about what would be occurring in quick conversations in the halls, at lunch, or during other brief periods where she might run into the teachers. She had some common planning time with her fourth grade teachers but not with her second grade teachers because of scheduling issues. This informal conversation system worked especially well with her second grade teachers. She said, "We were just always on the same page. If they noticed something they would come to me and if I noticed something I could go to them." She added, "The kids felt that they had access to the room, which made me feel like I had access too. Anything that the other kids had, my kids also had." She implied that these informal conversations were less of an option with her some of her fourth grade teachers, "It wasn't necessarily like that in my other classrooms." She pointed out, "When the kids felt relaxed, I felt relaxed; when they were tense, I was tense." She continued, "In the other classroom, the class would usually be doing one lesson and we'd be doing another lesson in the back of the classroom."

As she considered the interactions that she had with the teachers with whom she worked, Kristie said, "It's personalities and I think teaching styles and what you're used to. You do something that's so effective for so many years and then you know, it works for you and it works for the kids…then all of a sudden, someone throws a wrench at you and it's like, okay, we're going to bring all these kids back that you don't know how to teach and you're uncomfortable. They might think, 'I don't know how to teach this kid.' And it's not that they don't want to but they might be a little bit intimidated by it all—accommodations, modifications and such…"

Kristie regarded the issues that she experienced in her classrooms as an indication that she needed to present a stronger case for inclusion. She emphatically stated of her own role, "You need to be an advocate for the students." As she reflected on the situation with the reading teacher that she just mentioned, she said, "I didn't feel comfortable telling her, 'this is not the way that we're supposed to be doing things.' You feel uncomfortable because it's the general education teacher's classroom." She further noted, "I'm very leery of next year's teacher. I think that she just doesn't want the students with special needs in her classroom. I've just got to put my foot down at the beginning of next year and say 'this is how we need to do it. I have to think—what can I do different, what can I say to do better for the kids?" She added, "It's not that this year was bad, it's just that I want next year to be better. I just want the philosophy to be followed by fourth grade. Inclusion should look like you shouldn't be able to say what kids go with what teacher."

Charlotte's experience with her general education teachers was similar to Kristie's. She noted that the first grade teacher with whom she worked was "wonderful." This first grade teacher was really "open to having the students in the classroom." These teachers "make it a better experience for the children as well as the teacher." Other teachers were much less so. Charlotte noted, "Some teachers wanted the students with special needs back in my room as soon as attendance and lunch count was over. Some teachers took service minutes noted in the IEP verbatim. The IEP says that the student only has to be in the general education classroom for two hours per day, so he's yours now." With that statement, Charlotte was referring to the fact that the general education teacher released responsibility for the students with special needs as soon as she was able to. She added, "My second grade teacher thought of the situation as 'these are your kids and these are my kids.' I was really taken aback by this—she had taught special education in the past. She did open up a little but it was kind of picking and choosing who she wanted to be in the classroom."

Charlotte continued, "One teacher was just more rigid than the other teacher. She hadn't been in the school as long as the more open teacher. She was worried about feedback that she was getting regarding disruptive children preventing others from learning and also was afraid that she was falling behind in the curriculum. She would say that she was able to move faster through the curriculum when the students with special needs were not in the classroom." Charlotte added, "When the teachers are more open, the experience is more enjoyable for everybody. There's an extra pair of hands in the classroom, the kids are more positive. The students with special needs see more positive role models. The kids in the classroom seem to take on a nurturing role." She closed with, "The nurturing role is a life skill that we can all benefit from."

On the subject of interaction with her teachers, Charlotte noted, "There is common planning time but I didn't get to go because of duties. Not getting to go to common planning time was a big problem—the teachers talked a lot about the different assessments that we needed to do. I had to chase everybody around to find out what needed to be done." Charlotte continued, "The teachers got to meet together but I was the person who really had the kids with the most intense needs and I had little idea of what was going on at each grade level." She emphasized, "Special education teachers are the first ones to not be included in grade level trainings geared toward cumulative assessments."

As she considered her interactions with the general education teachers in her building, Marie talked first of the perceptions that these teachers have of what occurs in her classroom. She said, "My program is well-recognized in the district. Teachers know that once the student is placed in this class they don't have to worry about those kids anymore." At the same time, she notes, "I'm not so sure that they know exactly what happens in this class though. They just know that I work with those kids that they can't work with. They know that I accomplish things with these kids." She added, "I think they think that I have the patience of Job. They can't imagine how I do it every day, all day. There's a lot of activity and there's a lot of movement, and there's never a time where it's twenty-five minutes of sitting there looking at your social studies book and answering the questions at the end of the lesson." Marie also noted, "There is never any quiet learning, it's always me feeding the students information and asking them to feed it back to me and then practicing things where in general education classrooms, the kids just need a little bit of practice. In the general education classroom, they have ten minutes of instruction and then twenty minutes of practice. We have twenty-five minutes of instruction, five minutes of practice, five minutes of instruction, ten minutes of practice and then repeat. Then there is the fact that the activity is different for each student."

Of her interaction with the general education teachers in her building, Marie said, "I have lots of interaction, but it's usually conversational during break time or maybe a planning period or at the end of the day." Topics of conversation can include perceptions of what the kids can and cannot do or perhaps behavioral issues. Marie stated, "There's not a lot of curricular conversation unless it's someone from the lower grades coming to ask if I have some materials...and I usually do." She added, "I don't really like this because I'd rather be able to consult with people and say, 'what do you do for this?' She continued, I do go to staff meetings but as soon as they start talking about curriculum I'm allowed to leave because that doesn't really apply to me since I'm in the special education department. I think, okay, that's fine with me...but I'd like to learn about differentiated instruction; I'd like to learn about the new spelling program that they're going to use...but, on the other hand, I've got other things that I can be doing during that time so there's a part of me that doesn't mind."

On the topic of inclusion for her students, Marie noted, "The team chairperson was previously an inclusion specialist so she'd like to see us get out of the room more, as would I. It just has to be done correctly; otherwise it's just one more thing to add to the day and in the age of portfolios, our days are busy!" She continued, "There are one or two teachers in the building who think inclusion would be great. But we're a small, veteran staff. The general education teachers are always up to try new things but they don't want it to be any more work than they already have." She noted, "The fifth and sixth grade classes are combined due to numbers in the district. So it would be a burden to include my fifth and sixth grade students. I'm sure the teacher already feels that she's doing two jobs. So we could be included with the fourth grade teacher who's a little younger and thinks it's great; that probably wouldn't be a problem. That's not to say that the fifth/sixth grade teacher wouldn't be more willing if this was a different year."

Of all the teachers in the study, Carlene characterized the degree of interaction with general education teachers most bluntly. She said, "Our interaction with the general education classroom depends on the teachers' willingness to have us in. With some classrooms, it's just sort of a touching base—maybe once a week or every couple of weeks on whether there are any issues. That's not usually a problem because if there are issues, I usually hear about them fairly soon." She added, "Then we have teachers who will constantly invite us to their classrooms. Some teachers are just more open and accepting of having us there. The general education teachers can also be good about adapting—they'll talk to me abut how to modify activities…that's more of a third grade thing because in third grade they tend to get more projects." She noted, "Usually, getting a sense of who is or isn't open to inclusion opportunities is pretty easy. If you start getting complaints early in the year…then there are going to be issues. If you get people that say, 'I was amazed that the student could do the activity', that usually means greater openness. If the student doesn't have behavior problems then that's a huge thing. You're much more welcome in the general education classroom if the students don't have behavior problems."

She continued, "I tend to work with the same teachers because they are the inclusion classrooms and those are the classrooms that I usually work with." She stated, "I tell teachers that I haven't typically worked with that I'm available for suggestions, if they would like them—for the time that one of my students may be in their general education classroom." She concluded, "There are some teachers who get inclusion classes every year, there are some teachers who get inclusion classes for a few years and then say, 'I need a break, give it to somebody else.' There are some teachers who never get an inclusion class here because it's quite well known that they would not work well in that situation."

Carlene next noted, "We encourage the general education teachers to have the students come back into the room as much as possible. We stress that we'd like to have them go back for parties or any other special activities; we consider that pretty important and we will make it work with our schedule."

Carlene cited lack of time as her biggest problem in interacting with general education teachers. She said, "I try to do the student pick-ups so that I have some kind of contact with home-room teachers. That's the time we'll get invited to parties. If they don't see me, they don't think to say it." She added, "I don't have prep times…and I have three grade levels…so if I don't get to talk to teachers at lunch, I'm usually catching them before or after school." She continued, "I don't get to sit down and say, 'Oh, what are you doing in the classroom this week that maybe they could come to.' If they don't tell me or I don't hear it through the grapevine, I don't know. They really have to approach me."

As the other teachers have done, Betty also pointed out that there are teachers who are wide open, "They're wide open and willing to go above and beyond. That's a lot given what they need to accomplish for their own students given the state assessment. It's big that someone would take the extra time and work with me and some of our students."

On the topic of inclusion, Betty added, "Inclusion as a philosophy is not something that's really been discussed in a formal way like at a teachers' meeting. I think it's encouraged but I would say that's it's up to me to go out there and more or less pound the pavement. If I want it, I have to get out there and make those opportunities happen. Once they do happen though, everybody is very supportive."

As most of the other teachers did, Jeri also spoke of the concept of invitation into general education classrooms. She stated, "I wish that the general education teachers would invite us in more often." She said, "I don't feel like I see them enough just because we're so busy. I am still amazed at how fast the day goes by!" She added, " I never turn down an opportunity to go to a classroom. As long as it fits into my schedule, we'll be there." In her district, the teachers were required to actually make note of the amount of time that they spend on specific activities and so she qualifies her statement with, "I guess I understand that they have this on-task time and that they already have classrooms filled up with a lot of other kids who are also special needs that are already included so that they have their 25 students…but you can see the different mentalities. You can see that some people are more accepting than others."

Jeri continued, "Some people go out of their way and I've had some people who have just laughed." She pointed out that the art period that I observed was not the common period that the students usually receive. Jeri bluntly said, "The art period was better that time because you were there watching." She added, "At one point in time, the art teacher came to me and said, 'I don't know what to do with your class. I don't know if I should make the lessons for the assistants or for the kids.' I said, "Make the lessons for the kids. He then said, 'Well, I make something and the assistants complain.' This is not surprising!" Here again, Jeri expressed great concern with the fact that her assistants often treat the students according to their developmental age rather than their chronological age. She said, "Such treatment often resulted in the students being seen as generally helpless. They get treated as if they were toddlers rather than the young adults that they are becoming."

Professional Development

The issue of professional development for the special education teacher can be closely related to their interactions with general education teachers.

Kristie was pleased with the amount of professional development that occurred in her district. She said, "There is always something coming up that you can go to. Lots of times, the district uses its own teachers." She added, "I think that using the teachers is awesome because there are a lot of resources in your building or district and we don't use them a lot." Finally, she noted that her district provides its teachers with the opportunity to do "grade-level days." These are days where the whole district got together by grade to discuss curriculum and any problems that had arisen regarding implementing it. It was important to note that she had to choose which day she would like to attend. She was unable to attend the days for all the grades that she is associated with.

Charlotte's district was similar to other school districts—there were whole staff professional development days. She pointed out that the district days are often divided along department lines. She said, "General education might do curriculum mapping whereas special education might do the Autism spectrum." However, she also noted though that her school would often host district professional development days for all staff focusing on special education topics. Charlotte stated, "It's really kind of good to get the general education teachers involved in special education topics." The down side though is also prominent; Charlotte added, "Sometimes though, you really need the special education teacher to go into the classroom and say, 'We're going to use this." She also said that she would rather be at the special education workshops because they provide her with "more information that applies to what I'm doing at the time."

Finally, she spoke of her frustrations with not being able to attend the most frequent source of professional development in her district—the weekly grade level meetings. She was unable to attend such meetings because she either had duties or she had to stay with the students because her paraprofessionals were used to cover for the general education teachers. She said, "I really wanted to go to these meetings. The teachers would talk about their programming and what they were doing in the classroom. I always felt that I was really missing out because I had to stop by and always ask the teachers, 'what are you doing this week?'

Marie's professional development opportunities ran a close second to those reported by Kristie. She was able to access her district's professional development but was also able to supplement that training with other activities that she has sought out. As several of the other teachers noted, there was some discrepancy between the usefulness of professional development opportunities offered to general education teachers and those offered to special education teachers. Marie said, "Right now, there is a guided reading program going on for training. But I'm not participating in it. I kind of do guided reading anyway and what they want me to do is probably not something that would be conducive to the class that I have now." The district typically offered professional development days as half-day options; the students come in for the morning and the teachers do professional development in the afternoon. Marie noted, " The last time I stayed in my room and worked on modifying material for my [more involved] student. That was good professional development for me...now I have blocks underneath his desk that we needed."

Regarding professional development, Carlene noted that it has been some time since her district did professional development regarding standards. She reflected, "It would be nice to have a refresher course to say what's new and different. Sometimes you get into a rut with teaching the same topics. So, you might not realize when things are updated or changed or when new approaches are discussed. Most of us do not have time to cruise the Department of Education website very often." As an example of some of the recent topics that she has had to manage, Carlene cited the Individual Professional development Plan. She said, "You're supposed to line up your goals to the school's and the district's goals. Well, the professional development that I am looking for is mostly related to special education. Then there's also the fact that if you look at the district goals—there's nothing related to special education included there.

Finally, Carlene spoke of the survey addressing professional development needs that her district recently completed. She noted, "I won't be surprised if math shows up as a professional development theme this year. The district has wanted to revisit the new math series for several years now. There are several new teachers who did not have the original training. There are also big questions that remain with the series. For example, we were told at the beginning that there was almost too much material to cover and that we would probably not finish it all. Some guidance for how to deal with this would be very helpful."

Carlene's comments about this professional development led her to her final comments regarding the topic. She said, "Lots of the professional development topics don't really apply to special education. The topics don't often apply to what I'm necessarily doing in the classroom." This is a feeling echoed by several of the teachers. Such feelings may be the best indicator of the separation between special education and general education.

Betty categorized district professional development as appropriate to her classroom or not appropriate. Among the appropriate trainings were applied behavior analysis techniques and the use of assistive technology. She further commented that there's not much out there that pertains to situations such as hers. While the district naturally focuses on curriculum, Betty noted, "I've always worked with students where you're talking about basic academics…if that. Most of the work that I've done is in the area of life skills.

Jeri noted, "There are not many professional development opportunities. The current professional development initiative is for the new report card." She added, "I have to go to all the trainings, which I think is an important thing. Other teachers need to see me as being part of their grade level. That's where they schedule me, that's where they expect me to be, that's where I expect to be! The only thing that would change this is if the training were something like learning new IEP software!" She is only one of the six teachers who stresses that general education training is where she needs to be.

Concluding Remarks

The teachers have shared their stories. They have offered compelling thoughts about the experiences that they have had. What will their daily experiences look like? Will their words be reflected in their daily activities? These questions and daily life in the classroom is the subject of Chapter Five.

Chapter Five
A Day in the Life:
Special Education Teacher Practice Observed

"Curriculum is a framework...people just kind of decided what was really important for individuals to know and learn to become functional and independent adults in society." (J. Palmer, data collection interview, 2005)

To this point, teachers have offered descriptions of the students, classrooms, curriculum development, their understanding of standards, IEP formulation, and their interaction with other teachers in their teaching environment. Their words clearly provide insights into their individual teaching experiences and the current state of special education practice. The data begin to show that there are a number of different potential points of concern between what the teachers know and do. This chapter presents the observational data collected as part of the study. Such data allowed for a deeper understanding of the teachers' experiences as well as the opportunity to see the their beliefs in action. The descriptions that follow present summaries of the time spent in each classroom. A vignette that illustrates typical classroom activity is provided for each of the six teachers.

Classroom Observations
Kristie
Kristie described herself as an inclusion teacher. She had followed her second grade students to third grade with the new school year's teaching schedule. Her third grade students included Tom, Vincent, Chrissie, Allen, and Adam. Her fourth grade students included Zeb, Adam, Ellie, and Timmy. Her

teaching day typically began with several minutes in her resource room space. During this time, she had the opportunity to touch base with the other special education teachers in the school.

In her fourth grade math class, Kristie began by getting her students organized for the day. She assisted them with their work planners and then with getting positioned for the lesson. Sometimes they worked as a group at a table in the classroom but the desired place to work was as part of the larger class group. Her students began most lessons as add-ons to groups that had already formed. During some observations, Kristie opened the whole class. She positioned herself in the center of the room so that she could offer encouragement to various students. Much of the encouragement offered to her specific students took the form of successive approximations to the stated direction; she told them that she liked the way that they were almost ready to proceed to the next component of the activity. For other students, the encouragement was more general in nature. As she got ready to distribute paper on one occasion, she asked, "Who is my paper passer?" but quickly corrected her question to, "Who is the paper passer?" The general education teacher did not notice either Kristie's statement or her correction of that statement. Kristie, however, was very aware of her slip in communication.

As the homework assignment was completed, the math specialist arrived to teach the lesson. Both Kristie and the general education teacher took on roles of "teacher assistant" to the math specialist. As the math specialist taught, Kristie and the general education teacher circulated throughout the classroom, observing, monitoring, and assisting different students. The level of assistance varied—for some students, Kristie listened to their explanations of their work, and for others she sat and talked them through the presented problem. The general education teacher performed similar actions, stopping to oversee the work of all the students in the classroom.

One student kept putting his head on his desk and Kristie made frequent stops by him in an effort to motivate him. A second student was seated at a desk that was positioned directly up against the blackboard. The student who sat here was the boy that Kristie referred to as "the behavior problem of the school." At the moment, he was reasonably engaged in the activities of the classroom. His engagement was short-lived though—soon, he was bouncing and fidgeting in his seat. This behavior caused some disruption to the flow of activity. Many students stopped working to watch this boy's actions. When he finally managed to tip his seat over, he received reactions from the general education teacher and Kristie. The general education teacher sharply reprimanded him with, "There's no need for that behavior." Kristie quickly visually checked to make sure that he was unhurt and then immediately redirected him to his work. She successfully managed to get him reengaged in the lesson.

During the independent practice component of the lesson, Kristie suggested that the students complete their practice in their math journals. Zeb promptly raised his hand to say that he could not find his math journal. As Kristie moved to assist him, he grinned and announced that he had found his journal. The general education teacher caught Kristie's attention and rolled her eyes. The student seemed pleased with the attention and the response that he had received from both Kristie and the general education teacher. By the end of the lesson, Kristie's students were more active members of the class activity, even though this was not their homeroom. They raised their hands and offered explanations of their work. The math specialist occasionally called on them; the classroom teacher attended to them. As the lesson concluded, Kristie again took the lead, complimenting all the students for doing "nice jobs." She later noted that she also often taught the math lesson. She commented that this helped "to blur our roles." Kristie saw herself as a teacher in the classroom, not just the special education teacher for a few identified students.

Following math, Kristie and her group moved to the other fourth grade classroom for reading. She began her time in this classroom by helping her students, as well as others, get situated. During the period of observation, the class was focused on reading Judy Blume's, *Tales of a Fourth Grade Nothing*. It was also time to complete the first DRA reading assessment of the school year, so, some of the lesson time was spent working with various students as they completed their assessments. The teacher was reading the book aloud and the class was responsible for completing response journals related to the day's reading. After getting the students situated, Kristie began circulating between the two rows where her students were seated. She assisted three of her four students with getting their journal entries onto paper. She spent the majority of her time with Zeb. He often spent a good deal of his time during lessons fidgeting with his materials or his clothing.

Once the response journals were completed, the students moved to a partner activity for retelling the material read to them as a comprehension check. Kristie's students showed a greater degree of motivation during these types of activities than they did for the read aloud portion of the period. However, they were also often apt to get reprimanded by the general education teacher for "bothering other students" as they transitioned between activities. Yet, there was often no discernible sign that anyone had been bothered as the students moved about the room. The general education teacher had limited interaction with Kristie's students throughout the period of observation. In addition, what contact she did have with them was often of a punitive nature, despite the fact that this was their homeroom. Kristie remained on the periphery of activities in this classroom throughout the observation period. It was only toward the end of the entire observation period that she was allowed to read aloud.

Kristie next went to her third grade reading class. As she arrived, the general education teacher was giving the class instructions for the literature circle block. As she talked, she referred to the chart that held the directions. The classroom teacher was new to the general education classroom; she was previously a special education teacher in another school in the district. The students were to complete their assigned literature circle roles, review their previous reading, and move onto new material. The students read, discussed, and wrote about the story being read during these activities. There were four literature circles, with one circle made up of Kristie's students. Her students completed the same roles as other students in the classroom, though they were using a text that was at their reading level. Other than their lower level text, there was no noticeable difference between them and the other literature circle groups. Although, she monitored this group closely while they worked, Kristie also circulated throughout the other three groups, assisting them as needed.

The class finished their literature circles and moved onto writing. Again, Kristie often acted as the second voice to remind the student that the general education teacher had given them directions. Her role during these actions was one of an "enforcer". As the students worked on their writing activities, both Kristie and the general education teacher took students aside to complete their DRA assessments. The general education teacher frequently consulted Kristie for advice on the use of the assessment tool.

Charlotte

Charlotte also described herself as an "inclusion teacher." She defined this as spending the majority of her teaching day in the general education inclusion classroom. As the observations began, Charlotte noted that her new school district considered her students as "severely handicapped." She commented that in her opinion, the students were actually "more moderately handicapped."

Her students included Paul, Jake, Tim, Colin, and Aaron. Paul and Jake were second grade students that she sees outside their classroom for "pull-out" instruction. They were students that "it was decided that they could not be in the classroom." As she worked with them, one could readily see how their distractibility might cause a degree of disruption to standard academic activities. Both boys needed frequent encouragement, reinforcement, and redirection to their assigned tasks. One boy, Jake, was especially observant of what others said and did. He was quick to comment on his observations, often, with an almost adult sense of humor.

Charlotte's classroom was a typical first grade classroom. All the usual furnishings and materials of a classroom —teaching tools, a meeting area, student work displays, pocket charts, academic stations—were present. Charlotte had a study carrel of her own positioned next to her students and space in a resource room down the hall. Her desk and the majority of her teaching materials were located in the resource room. The student desks were arranged in groups. On each group of desks, were two or three "I need help" pictures. Students held up one of these pictures to get assistance from the general education teacher or from Charlotte. Charlotte's students were divided among two of the classroom groups. Two of her three students did not stand out from the other students in the classroom. They were able to follow directions, interact appropriately with their peers, and generally complete their work with only occasional guidance from either Charlotte or the general education teacher. The third boy, Aaron, was far more noticeable. He was older and bigger than many of the students in the class and had a very limited attention span. He was also repeating first grade.

Aaron frequently engaged in behaviors that were disruptive to the group and that appeared to be motivated by a desire to get attention from the adults in the classroom. His group mates attended to him on occasion, though their usual response was to remind him that he was not doing what he was supposed to be doing. He usually laughed and continued with whatever he was doing. He always seemed very aware of his actions; reprimands were often responded to with the hint of a smile or a smirk. Two of his more interesting interactions with his tablemates included an episode of wanting to share his snack by offering a finger coated in canned frosting to each of the other students at the table and leading a burping contest during an academic activity. While both Charlotte and the general education teacher ignored his inappropriate behavior as much as possible, he could be very successful at gaining more than his share of attention from them. If the first attempt to gain attention failed, he would often increase the intensity of his action. Throughout the observation period, he did very little classroom work. When he did complete work, it was generally done according to what he perceived as correct rather than what the work actually required.

Charlotte generally began her school day with a short session with Paul in the resource room. Here, they worked briefly on math. Throughout the observed sessions, Paul was frequently off task. His lack of ability to focus on his schoolwork stood out throughout each of the observations. Charlotte often spent a substantial proportion of their time together redirecting and refocusing him on their work.

Upon arrival in the first grade classroom, Charlotte placed a teacher-made necklace consisting of behaviorally oriented pictures made from the Boardmaker computer program around her neck. The pictures on the necklace included pictures for "my turn," "quiet," "stop," "hands down," "wait a minute" and "walk" and were intended to assist students with remembering classroom rules.

The general education teacher generally led the class through their activities. Charlotte contributed small additions to certain activities, but for the most part, was in the position of an observer or an assistant to instruction presented by the general education teacher. She spent a significant amount of her time circulating through the classroom assisting different students and checking on their work. This occasionally changed as the class worked on center activities during the reading period. During the reading period, both Charlotte and the general education teacher took reading groups while the rest of the class completed center activities. Charlotte typically took her students while the general education teacher took the other groups. The general education teacher took Charlotte's group from time to time. On certain activities, Charlotte acted as a scribe for Colin. He often had the answer to questions but needed help with the physical act of getting that answer on paper.

When Charlotte was not with her first graders, she was working in her resource room space with Paul and Jake. She described Paul as having the greatest needs among her group of students. She noted that he had an IQ "somewhere in the low 70's. In addition to his low IQ, he was also easily distracted and often displayed a variety of off-task behaviors. Paul and Jake did not work well together. Most of the time, they were more interested in irritating each other. Charlotte described them as being "like an old married couple...they have little use for each other." Getting Paul ready to work was a matter of having him determine where he would like to work—the quiet desk or the round table. Such a choice was necessary because another special education teacher would soon be arriving with her group of students. At these times, that teacher was in the room working on her own activities while Charlotte was there attempting to focus Paul and Jake on their reading. The classroom atmosphere often became very hectic.

During several of the observed lessons, Paul displayed his off-task behaviors. These behaviors typically took the form of responding to teaching instructions in a sing-song voice. Charlotte initially dealt with this by asking him to respond in "his best reading voice." When he did not respond appropriately, she increased the firmness of her tone and used a command such as "I need you to say this in your school voice." If he continued to behave inappropriately, she withdrew her attention by moving away from him. She told him to tell her when he was ready; he was always ready quickly and usually resumed working appropriately. Throughout any lesson, he would also attempt to engage Charlotte in conversations unrelated to the lesson or play silly little jokes on her. Her task at these times was to get him refocused, keep him focused, and provide him encouragement in order to keep working.

Marie

Marie described her classroom as one serving students with multiple needs, needs that are both social and academic. Her students included Greg, Mike, Asia, Clarice, Tina, Marshall, and James. Four of the students were working on academics within the third to fourth grade range, though they were chronologically in the fifth grade. The other two students were working on their academics at a much lower level. Her students had limited contact with their general education peers. The classroom was full of student-made projects that will ultimately have a place in the students' state assessment portfolios.

There were two paraprofessionals assigned to the classroom. One actively assisted Marie as she taught, while the other focused more on collating the work that the students produced for their alternate assessment portfolios. A major component of her job was to record data that would be used for these portfolios.

Her secondary function in the classroom was to provide some 1:1 assistance to Greg, who needed such supervision, both as a result of his physical disabilities and his disinterest in participating in the classroom. Marie often noted that she did not believe that he was properly placed in her classroom.

The daily schedule for the classroom was a combination of traditional academic skills and current events. For current events, Marie examined the newspaper for events that might be of interest to the students. As she did this, the students were also free to begin discussions related to her reading. One such discussion referenced a local bus accident. Mike said that it was his sister's bus that had been involved. One of the paraprofessionals questioned the veracity of his comment on the basis that his sister would have commented on the accident if there had been an accident. After some discussion, the group decided that the bus in question could have been Mike's sister's bus because the accident happened on the bus' late day. His sister could have been dropped off before the accident occurred. Such discussions were always brought back to classroom activities. For example, a later discussion on the topic of snow led to a measurement demonstration. Marshall was directed to get a ruler to model typical snow amounts.

Other current events discussed during this period included a hostage situation in Greece, notable because the class had recently done a unit on the Athens Olympics. Such interactions clearly showed the students' abilities to make connections to things they have heard and to their own lives. Their connections ranged from the preferred color of Christmas lights to some understanding of the Molly Bish abduction. As they discussed different topics, the students tried to shift the focus to their preferred topics. Marie was always quick to remind them that they needed to stay on the class topic.

The students moved onto writing sentences in their journal. The sentences that they wrote included sentences with their spelling words for the week and a personal sentence. The major criterion for this activity was that the sentences make some sense more than the actual spelling. All students except Greg began working appropriately. As soon as Marie positioned his Alphasmart keyboard, he began to display behaviors. In one instance, he started pulling at the device. As she worked, Marie offered comments such as, "If you wait until I get everything set up, I will be very happy. If you get your work done, I will dance a jig. But, if you pull the Alphasmart, it will fall and break and I won't be very happy about that." She then sat down with him and worked for several minutes trying to get him to finish his work. Greg eventually produced a small amount of work. Asia participated in this activity with one of the paraprofessionals sitting next to her. The paraprofessional assisted her by helping her to frame a sentence. She was given choices between activities that they knew she had recently done. If she got stuck on a word, she was directed to get her communication book to help her to remember selected words. This book consisted of a selection of

Boardmaker pictures that assisted Asia in requesting, commenting, or offering information to conversation partners.

Throughout the journal routine, the students brought their work to Marie for correction and recognition. The students were well aware that all the work must pass her inspection. But with each inspection, Marie was also waiting to offer encouragement and support as she did when she told Clarice that she would expect nothing less when Clarice told her that a given assignment was completed. After spelling, the students moved on to a more formal writing lesson. These lessons typically involved the students generating a list of items appropriate to the given topic and then the completion of a group generated paragraph. Once again, Asia participated in this activity with her communication book and a partner. She selected items to contribute to the discussion and her partner provided the sentence that got written. Greg produced no contribution for the paragraph. As the students worked, Marie reminded them that she was getting a little bored with them starting their sentences with "We can ___." She expected them to be more creative as they developed their sentences.

As they worked on writing, Mike became very interested in the length of the sentences that the students were producing. In one instance, he commented that Marshall had so far produced the longest sentence. When Marie stopped to check this fact out and then correct him, Mike became upset and lowered his head over the correction. His upset passed quickly but soon returned when he was not called on to do the next sentence.

Math and reading came next. During the observation period, the students were working on place value. The majority of the class practiced creating and naming numbers with values beyond a million. Greg and Asia participated, with Asia participating more reliably than Greg. They named numbers that were smaller or identified individual digits within the larger numbers that the other students were creating. Much of the math instruction was presented in game format. For example, the place value concept was practiced as the students used several dice to create numbers. They then placed these numbers on place value period charts that Marie had created. Reading was generally straightforward in nature. The majority of students worked in phonics readers at their reading level.

The students were always aware of the assistance that Greg and Asia might require. They often moved to provide the necessary assistance without being asked to do so. Marie or one of the paraprofessionals was always ready to praise such behavior. It was interesting to note that when Mike provided such assistance to either Greg or Asia, there was no hint of the "tough guy" in his attitude. However, the "tough guy" was apparent in the majority of his other interactions in the class. He was a boy who had a well-developed sense of confidence in himself. Marie had expressed a concern that his attitude will one day get him into trouble. She felt that he was "just getting too interested in students who have too great a disregard for school rules."

Following lunch, the students typically returned to the classroom to attend specials or to work on other curriculum related projects. Despite being written into the schedule, these specials did not always happen as they were supposed to. One such incident occurred with chorus. The majority of the class headed out to chorus one afternoon; only to return within a few minutes with the news that chorus had been cancelled for that period. Asia expressed the students' feelings about this best when she made eye contact with Marie, raised her hands, shook her head, and said with sadness, "No chorus today!" Marie and one of the paraprofessionals exchanged a mildly unhappy look. She said that they had planned the remainder of that afternoon around the fact that the students were going to chorus. Its cancellation created a void in what was supposed to occur. They had been told that the students could still go to the chorus room to "hang out" if Marie would like them to. Marie shook her head and said, "I'm not going to send them down there to sit and do nothing."

To adjust for this void in the schedule, Marie directed the students to play a game for the remainder of the afternoon. It was during such less structured game activities that the students' social difficulties began to show. They had not been playing long before many of them were bickering amongst themselves. Marie soon found herself in the position of mediator. She reminded them that, "Santa is watching you grumpies…" This was only marginally effective. They quieted briefly but soon started arguing again. It was a frequent pattern in the students' interactions with one another if activities were less structured.

Marie's lessons typically ended with a comment related to how the students should hand in their work. At the end of math, she told them, "Remember to hand in your math pages if you are a math portfolio person." The directions on how to hand in their class work were important because Marie was currently working on a number of different portfolio configurations. She had some students working on portfolios in English language arts and math, on portfolios in reading and math, and finally on portfolios in reading and science. This was so because the state has specified different tests for different grade levels. Marie's classroom incorporated a number of grade levels determined by the students' chronological ages.

Carlene

Carlene described her teaching assignment as students with severe learning disabilities. She defined "severe learning disabilities" as disabilities that made it very difficult for the students to be included full time in their classrooms. Her students might be functioning far below grade level and have difficulty with paying attention to whole class instruction. Their difficulties in the general education classroom typically led to behavioral episodes in their general education classrooms. There were currently eight students—Dennis, Cary, Kyle, Zeb, Rich, Noreen, Roland, and Marissa—in the class.

Cary was the autistic student that she spoke of during the interviews. Marissa is the newest student, the one that the district is having difficulty with diagnosing. Dennis and Rich constantly sniped at one another. Five of her students were second graders, all assigned to the same general education classroom. Cary was in third grade. Marissa and Rich were both first graders and were assigned to different general education classrooms. The students went to lunch but not recess and to specials with their general education peers. Instruction in the classroom addressed first and second grade skills. Grouping was generally arranged according to chronological grade level. The students were well aware of who was a first grader or a second grader and so grouping had to address this.

The classroom was somewhat typical of a special education classroom. The furniture was arranged in small group work areas. There was a meeting area in one corner and a technology station on the wall next to it. The group area held calendar and daily schedule tools. The schedule tools included Boardmaker pictures of the regular routines that the students took part in. A typical day's schedule included the following—spelling, the school counselor, snack, recess, circle, math, reading, lunch, and therapy. After their therapy sessions, students went to special curricular activities with their class, back to their general education classroom activities, or returned to the classroom with Carlene to finish any uncompleted work.

The first few minutes of any morning in the classroom were hectic. Students arrived in the classroom, put things away and got their homework out to be checked. Cary was often distracted during this routine. Carlene usually stopped to greet him but he often did not respond. On one occasion, she repeated her greeting twice and then positioned herself directly in front of him. He finally noticed and responded to her greeting. Cary next moved to turn in his homework. He went directly up to the paraprofessional, cutting in front of the other students who were also waiting. He was reminded that he had to wait his turn and quietly got in line. Both actions were typical for him. He frequently needed to be reminded to follow the established social routines of the classroom.

Of all the students in the room, Cary had the most difficulty with transitioning between and interacting within routines. A personal schedule book and picture communication system built around making choices assisted him in participating in classroom routines appropriately. Despite options to participate and these aids, he often hovered on the periphery of the familiar classroom routines. He was able to address academics but often in a very specialized way. Much of his instruction was delivered using an Applied Behavior Analysis (ABA) discrete trial format. If he became observably upset, he was allowed to go to the leisure area to calm down. While in this area, he typically engaged in self-stimulatory behavior. He used the area often but was generally quick to return to his work at every instance.

Once homework was turned in, the students began their spelling program. A standard lesson started with sight words practice. The students wrote their sight words on individual white boards, checked their work with each other, and then spelled the word aloud as a group. Carlene often had to refocus the students back to the spelling activity. She moved onto the new sound for the spelling lesson. As she opened this segment of the lesson, she reminded the students that every word that she gave them would have the focus sound in it. After they practiced these words, they moved onto to "chunk words." Chunk words were multi-syllabic words that contained familiar word chunks in them. The students enjoyed working on these words and worked very hard to spell them correctly. Their reward for spelling a given chunk word correctly was the opportunity to go to the other adult in the classroom and show her what they had just spelled. Some of the words that they had worked on included "location," "visitation," "vacation," and "superstition." They displayed an obvious sense of accomplishment at spelling such lengthy words.

Shortly following spelling, the students moved onto snack and then recess. The classroom normally did a separate recess. They had this separate recess because of the variety of different schedules and frequent student behavior difficulties. One snack and recess period stood out among the observations. On this day, Cary was slow to finish snack. As he ate, his ABA therapist arrived. While Cary finished eating, the therapist took a moment to confer with Carlene. They discussed recent behaviors and Carlene noted possible causes for them. This was just one more instance of having to gather and share information on the run. As recess continued, the students played together in small groups. But, they grew increasingly irritated with one another. Carlene gently reminded them about the importance of being kind to one another. Feelings were settled and the student resumed playing. However, despite Carlene's intervention, it wasn't long before a new episode occurred.

Recess ended and the class got ready for their meeting routine. The students were seated on the floor, many using adapted cushions that help them to sit still. The majority of them were fidgety throughout the session. This was especially true of Dennis. He was often out of his seat and off his cushion in the attempt to see what others were doing or to provide assistance to them if he thought that it was necessary. Carlene had to stop frequently to remind him to return to and remain in his seat. The meeting routine consisted of formulaic calendar and time-related activities. That is, students supplied answers to questions in question frames such as "What day is today? Today is ____." Boardmaker pictures supported all the reading involved in the routine. Throughout this routine and others, the students were eager to assist one another when someone got stuck. Carlene often had to remind them that they first had to give each other the chance to answer a question without help. The group completed the calendar routine and then discussed the specials for the day. They concluded with a language activity and a read aloud. After calendar, they moved on to math and reading.

For both subjects, the students worked in small groups and with small components of larger concepts. The students were not as able to work as independently with these subjects as had been the case with the spelling. As Carlene led the different parts of any lesson, she also supported each student individually as they worked on a skill at their level. She noted that they were just learning to use a new math program. She described the program as one that provided a greater degree of actual practice for important concepts as opposed to an investigative approach. Her students had difficulty with understanding the reasoning behind the concepts but that they could effectively learn the more concrete components of those concepts. Reading was more straightforward in nature. The students read their texts together and then moved onto comprehension activities that involved writing and drawing. Students frequently had a sentence frame that they used to complete their responses. When the students finished with these academics they got ready to go to lunch.

After lunch, the students regrouped in Carlene's classroom. They went to their therapy session as a group. The session included both occupational therapy and physical therapy and was primarily conducted in a hallway by the therapy room. A few students worked with each therapist for a short period of time and then rotated. Therapy lasted until most of the students left for a special curricular activity with their class.

Carlene returned to the classroom with Dennis and Cary. Dennis spent the time completing activities that he hadn't gotten done earlier while Cary did some individual work with Carlene. Together Carlene and Cary worked on choice making and leisure skills as he selected and participated in singing and doing finger play songs that had been adapted with Boardmaker pictures. Cary had considerable control over the activity as he made choices regarding songs. As he worked, he watched Carlene carefully in order to get her to sing along with him. They continued these activities until Cary ended the session by exiting the area in which they were sitting. As Carlene and Cary finished singing, the other students began returning from their specials. They finished their day with a read aloud and then got ready to return to their general education classrooms for the remaining few minutes of the school day.

Betty

Betty taught students diagnosed as significantly cognitively disabled. Her students included David M., David S., Nate, Celine, Katie, Ellen, and Tanya. Six of the eight students were non-verbal. They often used negative behaviors to reject unwanted or less desirable routines. Such behaviors included whining, crying, silliness, and aggression. Two of the students, David M. and Katie, displayed frequent aggressive behaviors. Both might hit, kick, and pull hair when they became agitated. Katie was the more aggressive of the two—she generally did not participate in group activities unless she was wearing arm splints—devices that prevented her from hitting her neighbors or unless she was belted into a chair so that she could not get up to go hit or kick another student. Both Nate and Celine had inclusion opportunities in their respective grades.

Each student had a 1:1 paraprofessional assistance unless someone had called out sick. In those instances the classroom worked short-staffed. Betty noted that it was very difficult to arrange substitutes for her classroom. She occupied a dual role in the staffing arrangement—she was both the classroom teacher and was also assigned directly to a specific student. Tanya had a feeding tube and attended school with a paraprofessional who was also a nurse. Nate and Celine used communication books consisting of line drawings. Others used individual pictures. Such devices assisted the students in communicating their wants and needs.

An array of excess physical equipment in the hallway marked the location of the classroom. Upon arrival, each student worked through a locker routine. The students participated in removing their coats and then placing them into the locker. Next, they removed their lunch and snack materials as well as their school folders from their backpacks. Backpacks were then placed in the lockers. The students entered the classroom and placed the items they had removed from their backpacks into a storage unit. This unit also created a wall that formed part of one of the students' individual work areas.

The perimeter of the classroom was organized into individual work areas. Work materials were stored in buckets that stayed on the tables. Within each work area was the student's daily schedule. These schedules were individualized according to the student's needs and consisted of a variety of materials. Several of the students primarily used line drawings for these schedules. Others used a combination of line drawings, actual photographs of the routine, and representational objects—objects that were chosen to symbolize the scheduled routine. Such objects could be items such as a small spoon to represent an eating routine or a number card to represent a work routine. Still other schedules consisted totally of the representational objects. All schedules were made with Velcro attachments so that the students could participate in noting the current routine and the end of a routine. A student removed a picture from the schedule and placed it in a spot that showed the current routine. Once a routine was finished, the student removed the picture from the current work location and put it into a finish bin. All of the students were very much aware of their schedules and demonstrated an understanding of their use, though all had significantly different levels of independence in that use.

The paraprofessionals were assigned to a specific student for the morning period and then switched to a different student for the afternoon. The schedule was further arranged so that as a given week progressed, the paraprofessionals were assigned to all the students. This arrangement gave all the staff the opportunity to be familiar with all the students in the classroom. Tanya was an exception to this rule because of her need to have a nurse present, though she did have more than one nurse who worked regularly with her.

Toward the back of the classroom was a group meeting area. A variety of different seating equipment was arranged on the back wall. This equipment included seating bolsters, a prone stander, an adapted bench, and a couple of specialized Rifton chairs. This equipment provided the students with support as they developed bodily strength for sitting more independently. It came into constant use as the students went through their group meeting and the group game portion of the school day. The classroom contained a leisure area. The students took breaks from their work periods here. They typically "earned" time in the area as a reward for engaging in their work appropriately. Students got a toy once they used the appropriate line drawing to request that item.

As with their seating, many of the students used adapted eating utensils. These items included such things as scoop dishes, dishes with built-up edges that assisted students in being able to scoop food themselves, utensils with built-up or weighted handles to assist students in holding their own utensils, and universal cuffs, a cuff that the student wore that actually held the utensil. The students used photographs to communicate their choices during the meal. Finally, there was a second larger group area that did double duty as the meal area and on occasion, the therapy group area.

Once in the classroom, the students began with an exercise routine. This consisted of spending several minutes engaging in a variety of different movement activities including the use of a textured therapy ball that the students were rolled on, an adapted trampoline, a mat, and a bolster. Students were also allowed to make use of a variety of toys. These toys tended to be items that are typically selected for younger children and included items such as large Lego blocks, Fisher-Price toys, or Disney themed toys. The exercise routine was a transitional routine and was in place to get the students oriented to being in school and to effectively utilize the time that it took for all the students to arrive at school.

After the exercise routine, the students began the first of their individual work sessions for the day. During one observation, Betty worked with Celine. As they worked, Betty conversed with her about her currently messy work area. Celine quickly agreed with her but then complained that she was tired. Betty noted that they were both tired and then reminded the child that she had to do her work because she was in school. Celine did not protest and resumed working on the presented task. Her tasks included such things as counting objects, color identification, following directions, letter –sound correspondence, and stating her last name when asked. Betty made the tasks something of a "game." She took a turn and then the little girl took a turn. Celine enjoyed this task presentation format.

Meanwhile, Katie worked on a task involving asking questions of people. Because she was non-verbal, she used a switch to activate a recording device that had been programmed with the desired question. Her paraprofessional asked her to choose which question she would like to ask and then recorded it onto the recording device. They practiced using the switch a couple of times and then went into the hall to find a person to ask. At the same time, Tanya, her nurse and another paraprofessional were trying to determine whether Tanya was supposed to be positioned in her prone stander or on the bolster for the next activity. As these different work activities occurred, the paraprofessionals often went over to Betty to confer about their various charges. The paraprofessionals frequently consulted the students' individual data collection books as they worked with the students.

With the first work session finished, the students were cued to move to the calendar routine, a routine that incorporated both the academic and the social. As the students assembled for the routine, Katie immediately tried to pull Celine's hair. Betty matter-of-factly prevented this as she assisted with getting students settled. She kept Katie contained until Katie's paraprofessional got there to resume fully monitoring Katie. The routine was built around the math involved in setting up the calendar. The students selected calendar tasks by using pictures of the different activities within the routine. They worked on identifying numbers, days, and months. The majority of the students clearly had only a very limited understanding of the academics involved in the routine. Their responses were always made with assistance from Betty or from one of the paraprofessionals. In addition to incorporating calendar skills within this activity, the students worked on a variety of social skills and other communication skills. One example of this was the request, "Find your name." When Betty called on a student, that student's paraprofessional presented two name cards. The selected student then pointed to his or her own name. Student responses were rarely independent and any request often resulted in the paraprofessional having to provide some sort of physical assistance ranging from a gentle prompt to an elbow to full physical assistance to get out of a chair and move to a calendar task.

Other examples of embedded communication skills included selecting a friend to take the next turn and saying "hi" to a friend. The student was presented with pictures of two other students in the class and then picked a desired friend for the next task component. After picking from two pictures, the student was supposed to go to stand next to the student that was selected. A variation of this request was the student picking a friend to say "hi" to. After the friend was picked, the student was assisted in saying hi to that individual. The student typically used a switch that was preprogrammed with the greeting to do this. The group members counted along as the selected student completed the presented task. More specifically, it was possible to hear more staff than students counting as the different tasks were completed.

After completing calendar, the students moved onto snack. One of the students was cued to signal "snack" to the rest of the students in the classroom. As they ate, they also worked on learning to ask for more and indicating that they were finished. Katie's snack was possibly the most involved because she used equipment that prevented her from throwing her snack. Her bowl was suctioned to the table. (In fact, Katie was likely to throw any item that was left within her reach whether she was agitated or not.) Following the snack, the students participated in cleaning up, and then toileting opportunities. After toileting was completed the students were assembled for group game. During this routine, students played games, read stories, or listened to learning compact discs. This was a filler activity. As they participated in the group game, the paraprofessionals began taking their lunch breaks so the classroom was understaffed for approximately the next sixty to ninety minutes.

As with the calendar activity, the students' communication needs were addressed throughout the routine. Once again, they chose the game to be played or the story to be read. They chose who would take the next turn or they said "hi" to friends. Specific turns tended to be lengthy because the students had to come in and out of their seating arrangements. As one student took a turn, other students were easily distracted or became bored and irritated with waiting. Once off task, they tended to begin engaging in behaviors. David M. often became aggressive. David S. often became whiny and then refused to make any attempt to participate in the activity. Other behaviors could occur for no easily recognizable reason. Betty could generally handle these glitches in the activity by reminding the offending student that he or she was at school. This was generally effective in stopping the inappropriate behavior. However, such student actions often made activities appear chaotic.

When group game was completed, the students went to lunch. The lunch routine was similar to the snack routine. During this time, staff members were a little freer in their interactions with the students and each other. While the majority of classroom discussion was always focused on classroom and student issues, there was also some non-school related conversation during this period. Betty often briefly removed herself from 1:1 supervision of a student to organize upcoming activities for the afternoon. One of the paraprofessionals monitored Betty's students as this was done. It was the only planning time that Betty received or that she allowed herself to take.

Afternoons in the classroom consisted of a second snack period, and scheduled special or group therapy sessions. As the day began to wind down, the students assisted their paraprofessionals with getting their folders and lunch materials packed. The paraprofessionals completed the daily student checklists—brief reports that told parents how the school day went. The students got a bit of less programmed free time as the classroom staff closed the school day.

Jeri

Jeri also taught students that had been diagnosed as significantly cognitively disabled. The class consisted of Ned, Adam, Keely, and Normand. Three of the four students exhibited aggressive behaviors regularly. Normand was the most difficult of the four students and had a particularly lengthy period of behavioral episodes that spanned several days during the observation period. (His behavior ultimately resulted in the cessation of further observation. It was felt that my presence as an observer was maintaining his negative behavior.) Three of the four students had 1:1 paraprofessional assistants. Normand did not have such an assistant. All of the students required some degree of physical management. Such management typically took the form of implementing behavioral interventions—preventing students from being aggressive, from grounding, or from destroying classroom property. The students also required a significant to moderate degree of physical assistance to complete tasks.

The classroom space was both typical and yet not typical. Typical classroom features included standard areas of activity as well as standard furnishings and tools. Postings addressing a current unit of study, the solar system, were liberally displayed throughout the classroom. Jeri's desk was positioned in the far corner of the room. Behind her desk was a large metal bookcase that was full of pre-school toys that she has removed from the classroom. Her plan was to donate these toys to the district preschool programs. There was a group activity area and a meeting area. Classroom rules and a schedule were present in the meeting area. All classroom postings were written using line drawings generated from the Boardmaker program or a companion program, Writing with Symbols. The meeting board was set up with a series of programmed sentences. These included "We have _____ (for the special of the day)", "The month is ____", "Today is____", "The number (of the date) is ____", and "The weather is _____." Students were typically asked to assist in setting up the various charts and the schedule for the day.

A portable refrigerator, a microwave, and a portable oven, tools that were used as a regular part of the curriculum, were also present among the classroom furnishings. One corner of the classroom held a variety of physical therapy equipment. Such equipment included specialized seating devices, a cloth obstacle course tunnel and a pair of bicycles, both fitted with training wheels, that helped the students maintain balance as they used them. The therapy area was further defined by the presence of a large blue mat, used to take breaks from work.

As the students entered the classroom for the day, their interest in the activities of the classroom quickly became evident. Adam showed great attention to everybody's activities rather than his own routine. He had to constantly be prompted to focus on his work rather than the activities around him. Jeri commented, "Always socializing." Keely was interested in items that Jeri had just placed on the table and became intent on getting these items. Staff noted that her primary descriptor was "very quick." Because of his aggression, Ned was a source of concern to the staff in the classroom, particularly the woman currently working as a substitute with him.

After putting their coats and backpacks away, the students began toileting routines. These routines involved going to the nearby bathroom, using the toilet, and completing morning grooming tasks. As Keely returned from the bathroom, her paraprofessional held her hand. They walked to Keely's work area, where the paraprofessional began orienting a substitute to Keely's individual work. She would soon be gone for a two-week period for surgery. As she moved through the orientation, Keely sat with her head on the paraprofessional's shoulder. She frequently leaned over to hug and kiss the paraprofessional; they have been together since Keely was in preschool. The paraprofessional returned the affection in a similar manner.

Adam and Normand returned from errands that they had been doing with Jeri. Adam immediately came over to initiate contact with me. Normand followed right behind. One of the staff reminded Jeri that they were supposed to be in a special curricular activity. Jeri moved to the schedule and selected the schedule card that displayed "music." Jeri walked to the class with Adam and Normand. Ned and Keely arrived shortly afterward with their paraprofessionals. Keely was very mobile and bouncy; her paraprofessional managed this behavior by holding onto the waistband of her jeans. Adam raised his hand at every question the music teacher asked. He was always part of the larger group as they raised their hands for the teacher's attention. Normand frequently had to be prompted to participate in presented routines. Throughout the class, the music teacher made an effort to include Jeri's students in the presented activities.

With music completed, everyone returned to the classroom for snack. The paraprofessionals assisted the students with everything from communication skills to the actual eating of the snack. Keely's paraprofessional held the snack cake while Keely took individual bites. The paraprofessional noted that it was unwise to put a whole snack in front of Keely at once. Another paraprofessional frequently reminded Adam that he must use his words to ask for things rather than just reach across to grab what he wanted. Sometimes he simply remained sitting motionless in his seat until the paraprofessional nearest to him provided the desired assistance.

Following snack, the students proceeded to the morning group activity. Jeri focused the attention of the group to their schedule for the day. First, she reviewed the activities for the day. Following the schedule review, she asked the students. "Who wants to help do the days?" This question allowed the students to practice the days of the weeks. She selected Keely and Adam to do the days. Keely pointed to the days of the week while Adam recited the days' names, providing her with a voice. Jeri physically assisted Keely with the pointing. As she did this, she also held Keely to prevent her from ripping the materials from the display boards and from grounding (e.g. throwing herself) to the floor. Keely made numerous attempts to ground to the floor and became increasingly amused, as Jeri increased her efforts to prevent the grounding. This type of behavior occurred frequently. She described Keely's behaviors as 'avoidance of work" behaviors. Finally, Keely was directed back to her seat and Jeri presented two day cards to Adam. He was currently working on recognizing the days' names. Jeri asked him to select the day of the week. When Adam incorrectly selected the day, Jeri smiled and said, "See, I told you I was trying to trick you." Adam smiled in response. She used the same board with Normand but tried to use a field of three choices. When he chose incorrectly, she moved back to a field of two choices. When they moved on to counting the days in school, Normand provided verbal assistance while Jeri provided hand-over-hand assistance to Ned, as had been the case with Keely and Adam. Following the counting, they move to graphing the weather.

The music class stood in contrast to a later art class. Upon arrival, the art teacher directed the paraprofessionals to seat Keely and Ned at one table, while he had Jeri seat Adam and Normand at a second table. Adam and Normand were to continue building their Popsicle stick bridges, a fourth grade project. The art teacher pointed out that Adam and Normand were working on this fourth grade project despite the fact that they were fifth graders. The fifth graders were currently involved in creating anatomically correct self-portraits. He made limited eye contact with the students throughout the period and frequently spoke to them through Jeri or the paraprofessionals, very much unlike the music teacher who had directly engaged Jeri's students.

Normand exhibited some obstinate behavior during this activity. He insisted that he needed help when he did not. He also insisted that he would rather be doing nothing rather than working on his bridge. His behavior began to absorb both the art teacher's as well as Jeri's entire attention. Consequently, Keely and Ned received very little attention from the art teacher throughout the entire period. They were left with their paraprofessionals to color on large sheets of white construction paper. Their coloring was more the making of unrelated marks with various crayons than anything else. Later, Jeri said that art was not one of their better routines. She noted that the art teacher was typically not interested in interacting with the students. She added that he rarely had anything planned for them, though he was a bit more open with Adam and Ned than with Keely and Ned.

On occasion, Jeri's students had the opportunity to choose which routine they would like to engage in. This was particularly true of their music routines and band seemed to be a popular routine. Both Adam and Normand participated in playing in the band. Jeri's students generally observed as the band teacher got the session started. Ned was settled next to the door in case he needed to make a quick exit. Tolerating loud sound was frequently difficult for him. Jeri noted that the band teacher gave up one of his preparation periods in order to give Adam and Normand additional music lessons.

The students had indoor recess in their classroom. After recess, they went to lunch in the school cafeteria.

Another regularly occurring routine was cooking. Cooking was particularly difficult to carry out because the classroom did not have adequate cooking facilities. Jeri noted that their cooking activities are oriented both toward life skills and social science standards. At the moment, the class was engaged in traveling around the world via foods associated with specific countries. They were using the different foods as an access point into studying components of geography. So far the students had made pizza from Italy, tea and scones from Great Britain, and a typical Russian breakfast. As with the group meeting routine, Jeri set cooking up in terms of the students making a series of choices. They chose which item to cook, correct measuring implements or other tools, what they wanted to eat or drink and so on. Throughout the routine, Jeri attempted to incorporate academic information, either related to the cooking or to the geography that they were required to be doing. Keely was especially difficult to manage during this routine. Each of her turns was taken with one paraprofessional holding her free hand and a second paraprofessional providing the hand over hand assistance necessary for her to take her turn. As with other task materials, she frequently threw or mishandled the cooking items. She made frequent attempts to exit the routine and often had to be physically returned to the activity.

The final major routine that the students engaged in during school days was individual work routines. Setting up for these routines involved getting each student's individual work bin with work materials and their individual data books. Each student was directed to an individual work area with either Jeri or a paraprofessional.

During one independent work period, Jeri attempted to work with both Adam and Normand. Their first task was a safety word concentration game. Adam attempted to play the game appropriately while Normand spent the majority of time shuffling through a sheaf of papers that he refused to relinquish when the work period began. As they worked, another paraprofessional came over to observe briefly. Adam stopped working to hug her. He was often out of his seat trying to hug adults that were in the classroom. The paraprofessionals noted that he was behaving this way because there were currently so many new people in the classroom. As they continued working on this task, Adam picked the same two cards that he started with. Normand repeatedly attempted to turn over additional cards as he tried to locate matches. His questionable matches were allowed to stand.

Next, Jeri presented a money identification task. The students were asked to identify both coins and dollar bills. As they worked, Adam became bothered by the fact that Jeri had her pen tucked behind her ear. He made numerous attempts to remove it. Normand announced that he was quitting work. Jeri asked him, "Do you need a break?" He responded, "Yeah" and headed to the leisure area.

Jeri set a timer but Normand refused to return to return to work when it rang. She went over to speak to him quietly and he returned to the table to work on a time telling activity. Normand participated in this activity appropriately. However, these work routines later were the catalyst for Normand's multiple episodes of non-compliant behavior. His smaller episodes of non-compliance quickly turned into significant occurrences of aggression and property destruction. On several occasions, Jeri had to send the other students out of the classroom as she worked to manage Normand. Little assistance was provided by administration.

As Adam and Normand worked with Jeri, Keely and Ned worked at their desks with their paraprofessionals. Both engaged in a series of short tasks presented in an applied behavioral analysis format. This involved the presentation of a basic stimulus, followed by the student's response, followed by a reinforcer for a correct response. Both students worked on tasks such as following directions, and receptive identification of colors or coins. Jeri had noted that she was not impressed by the applied behavioral analysis format as a teaching methodology because it had not grown with her students. She also emphasized that the techniques isolated the students from each other.

Concluding Remarks

The teachers have told their stories. Their actions have been documented through multiple observations. Throughout the interviews and observations, issues of interaction with general education, curriculum, and assessment are clearly evident. The classroom activities fall along a clearly evident continuum—from the strictly academic to the access skill level. The activities in the classrooms often show the challenges that can be involved in teaching students with special needs. Chapter Six further examines the meaning assigned to the information provided by the teachers.

Chapter Six
What Do These Experiences Mean—
Interpreting the Data

"[The IEP] is just a piece of the puzzle." (C. Kannon, data collection interview, 2005)

Discussion of Interviews

The Students

The teachers' descriptions of their students suggested several ways of categorizing students receiving special education services. Students are classified according to their skills level. Several of the teachers spoke of their students in terms of their reading ability but reading level as a primary means of categorization is particularly associated with Kristie and to a lesser extent, with Charlotte. The use of the DRA assessment, a simple-to-administer and practical reading level assessment, or other more standardized reading test scores often categorized a student in school. Students were also categorized according to grade level. Grade level becomes more prominent as the descriptor as a student becomes more cognitively involved. This descriptor was particularly important to Charlotte, Marie, and Carlene. Their students were often conceptualized in terms of how far away they were from their prescribed grade level. Betty and Jeri talked of student skills in terms of functioning ability. Their students were often severely limited in their functioning ability. They also often noted that their students were functioning far below their chronological grade levels. Students were further categorized in terms of their educational placement. Whether that class-room placement was appropriate or not was important to these teachers.

Students were categorized in terms of their behaviors and the issue of be-haviors was important for all teachers. Teachers sorted their students on the ba-sis of whether or not they displayed "behaviors" that resulted in disruption to scheduled activities. Behaviors might take multiple forms of expression but were always described in terms of their severity and the degree of disruption that they brought to the general education classroom. A common thread of discus-sion for all of the teachers was strategies to use to manage students' behaviors.

Finally, all teachers talked of their students in terms of the various diagno-ses that they carry. A large part of this is due to the fact that a student's label or diagnosis is often the most important criteria in qualifying for special education services. The diagnosis that a student carries can determine the type of class-room that a student attends as well as the type of instructional strategies used with the student. That diagnosis can come before the student. That is, a student becomes seen as his or her diagnosis rather than the child he or she actually is. The teachers' terminology for conceptualizing their students allowed for the development of the taxonomy presented in Table 6.1.

Table 6.1 Taxonomy of Ways That Teacher Participants Verbalize/Conceptualize Their Students

Category	Terminology	Descriptors
1. Skill level	Reading level	Differential Reading Assessment (DRA)
	Grade level	High, low, below Chronological age
	Functioning ability	High, low, limited
	Educational placement	Appropriate, inappropriate Inclusion
	Cognitive ability	Severe, moderate, high
2. Behavior	Needs	Emotional, social Severe, moderate, high
	Management strategies	Interventions
	Scale	Degree of disruption explosiveness "breakable", "unbreakable" "behavior problem of the school"
3. Disability	Diagnosis	Language-based learning disability Developmental delay, Intellectual delay, Mental retardation Physical disability Autism ADHD (Attention Deficit Hyperac-tivity Disorder)

Note: This taxonomy was developed as part of this study.

Table 6.1 demonstrates to some degree the extent of the student variability that these teachers are typically faced with. The teachers' descriptions indicate the extensive variability that exists among the students who now attend school. This variability encompasses dimensions that go well beyond academic activities. Betty and Jeri, and to a lesser extent, Marie, illustrate this point effectively. The majority of Betty's students function at the access skill level and need supervision at all times. Two of Jeri's students are at this same level. Marie's more challenging students are just approaching the entry point level. Academics are not necessarily the first teaching consideration on the agenda for these students.

Further, participation in academics may become a major issue for certain students. That academics are not necessarily the first teaching consideration is a potentially difficult issue and one that creates important anxiety and pressure in practice for both special education teachers and general education teachers given that academics constitute the primary activity that occurs in schools.

The teachers' descriptions add a new and different type of student to ideas that may be held regarding student diversity. There is a distinct culture evident in special education. As a result, special education adds a stronger dimension of ability to the notions of cultural differences that educators may have and that are often cited as the primary content of discussions of student diversity. The teachers' words and actions further hint at a greater level of flexibility that must characterize special education teacher practice. Special education teachers are charged with meeting the needs of the students that are placed on their caseloads. There is often little choice in what students these teachers will see. In some cases, especially when students exhibit behavioral issues, the special education teacher is often the "last resort." Charlotte and Carlene both provided examples of situations where they note that their classroom was the student's last opportunity for remaining in public school.

Within the context of taxonomic and domain analysis, the teacher conceptualizations of their students allow us to identify specific attributes associated with their categorizations. These attributes allow the teachers to make judgments about applying and/or developing strategies to assist in meeting student needs. These attributes can be arranged in a model that shows the dimensions of the relationship among them. In each case, there is a key question that can be asked. A student is the sum of his or her diagnosis, skill level, and behaviors. A student with special needs is first his or her diagnosis. That diagnosis provides a label; that label is imperative in determining a student's eligibility for special education service. The key question here is does the student belong in the general education classroom? A student with special needs is next seen in terms of his or her ability. This can be conceived of in terms of grade level or functioning level. The concept of grade level is typically associated with students who have a greater academic ability while the concept of functioning level is seen in reference to students who are more cognitively impaired. For students with greater cognitive impairment, teachers often cite functioning ability—often initially thought of in terms of a student's ability to be independent and to address academics, at the beginning of their student descriptions. Functioning ability can further be broken down into levels of need—students can have high, moderate, or low levels of functioning ability. The key question for this categorization is— what can the student do? Finally, a student with special needs can be seen in terms of his or her behavioral needs. As with ability, behavioral needs can be conceived of in terms of their intensity—low, moderate, or high. The intensity of behavioral needs is further defined as a function of the supports that a student requires. So, the key question becomes, what supports are in fact needed or possible within the general education classroom? Taken together, these broad categories—diagnosis, ability, and behavior—become the determinants for a student's classroom placement. And the subject of classroom placement can be the greatest potential source of stress as special education and general education work to come together in the interests of students. Figure 6.1 summarizes the manner in which the attributes of the teachers' student conceptualizations are related.

Figure 6.1 Relationship Between Student Attributes

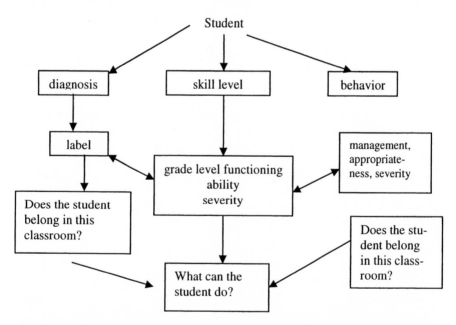

The teachers' verbalizations and conceptualizations of their students and the manner in which their categorizations of the students are organized and related lead to an expanded definition of a typical student. Their conceptualizations further show that special education teachers also think about the appropriateness of certain students for their own classrooms.

Items of particular importance emerged from the teachers' discussions of their students and classrooms. These items often had a dimension of anxiety associated with them. Those points of anxiety included concern over interactions with general education teachers, issues of behavior management, lack of curricular materials, scheduling, and outsider perceptions. *We begin to see that special education teacher practice is characterized by a number of concerns that create anxiety and thus tension in special education and in the interaction between special education and general education.* As will be shown, these concerns further impact other areas of the business of schooling.

Curriculum and Standards

As was the case with the teachers' descriptions of their students, their descriptions of curriculum indicated that the teachers thought of curriculum in a number of ways. Their words provided insight into how they defined and then presented curriculum and the elements of their practice. Further, their words led to an initial categorization scheme for the part that special education teachers play in general education classrooms.

The teachers provided a variety of terms that described curriculum. Kristie referred to curriculum as the framework that you use and as a guide you plug into, a guide that would lead you to where the children needed to be at the end of the school year. Charlotte noted that curriculum was what the state thinks is appropriate for students to learn. She saw the curriculum as the major points that children needed to learn. She added the concept of packaged programs to the definition of curriculum. Her discussion included comments about a variety of different programs that she used with her students. Marie opened her discussion of curriculum by noting that she saw the curriculum as state-mandated. Curriculum, for her, was also something that the state alternate assessment portfolio needed or wanted. Her description of curriculum was perhaps the most technical of the definitions offered by the teachers in that she uses the state terminology— frameworks, strands, and then standards. Carlene noted that curriculum consisted of the subjects that one teaches, subjects that may be directed by the school or by personal choice.

Lastly, both Betty and Jeri added the element of the IEP to the discussion of curriculum. The IEP dictated the manner in which they thought of curriculum. This is so because the IEP determines the skills that students need to work on. While all students receiving special education services have an IEP, the notion of "skills that students need to work on" is more prominent for Betty and Jeri because their students are often typically not thought of in terms of needing or "being appropriate for" academic instruction. For both, curriculum is individualized by students' IEPs and typically begins with a consideration of the social, physical, and communication aspects embedded in activities. Finally, Jeri summed up curriculum as being those skills that students have to work on in

order to become functional and independent adults. Here, she makes use of typical special education terminology—special educators are trained to think in
terms of teaching students to be "functional and independent."

As the teachers discussed curriculum, other dimensions of their positions as
special education teachers emerged. Each teacher engaged in specific tasks related to the presentation of curriculum. Their major task was the delivery of curriculum. In this, they operate just as general education teachers do. At the same
time, all of these special education teachers also differentiated, modified, and in
many cases further adapted curriculum so that it was accessible to the students
that they taught. Carlene placed special emphasis on the fact that she preferred
to select "bits and pieces" of topics from a variety of sources. The primary criterion in this activity was whether or not her students would be able to do the
work. Betty and Jeri both spoke of adapting the curriculum to a level where their
students with significant cognitive disabilities would find some meaning.

The variety of tasks that these teachers engaged in allows for the initial
identification of the different roles that they must fulfill in both their classrooms
and their school settings. Initially, these roles include teaching and supporting
students, creating curriculum, and advocating for their students. Of course, the
primary function for all of these teachers is to teach. In addition to actual teaching, all of these teachers support their students. This notion of support is best
conceived as providing assistance and/or motivation for their students to succeed. The concept of "coach" becomes prominent here. Each successful step that
a student achieves in an activity is a subject for praise and more importantly for
further encouragement.

However, support also refers to the fact that these teachers often find themselves in a secondary supporting situation in general education classrooms. This
was especially true of Kristie and Charlotte. Further, both teachers indicated that
they must conform to what their general education teachers wanted. This indicates that the general education teachers have some degree of power that they
exercise with regard to student acceptance and placement. This conformity typically took the form of a position of subservience in those classrooms where both
of them had limited autonomy. Both described their position and their students
in terms of whether or not they really had a place in the general education classroom. This feeling of being wanted in their classrooms was eloquently yet differently expressed by both. Kristie spoke of the treatment her students received
from general education teachers—some teachers worked to plan their school
days so that Kristie's students were integrated into the classroom. Other teachers
took a hands-off approach—thinking in terms of students as their general education students and the students with special needs as Kristie's students. Charlotte
spoke similarly but added the notion that being wanted in the classroom enabled
the development of nurturing skills.

While each of the teachers functioned as a creator of curriculum; the degree
of curriculum creation that they engaged in was dependent on the functioning
level of the students. Kristie and Charlotte did not necessarily have to create

entire curriculums. Their students were more easily able to work with existing curriculum and materials. However, as students moved along the continuum of services and ability, the degree of curriculum creation necessary became more prominent and more of a task. This was certainly true of Marie and Carlene. Their students were capable of working with a moderate number of skills with some degree of complexity though, they typically could not manage the curriculum pace of a typical general education classroom. They created curriculum accordingly. With Betty and Jeri, the creation of curriculum was significantly more difficult to envision. These two teachers might be faced with the most daunting curriculum task of all. Betty and Jeri were confronted with the multiple tasks of adapting academic curriculum and creating programs for students that have very limited academic abilities. They faced the difficult tasks of balancing the teaching of physical skills that were lacking, and creating a general education context into which to fit those skills. Thus the degree of curriculum creativity that characterizes the different teaching settings changes with the degree of special needs involvement that a student experiences.

These discussions of curriculum again revealed several concerns characterizing individual teacher practice. These concerns included establishing communication with their general education peers, managing the extensive scope of the general education curriculum and the pace of that curriculum, difficulties with the roles that they must play and the need to be an "aggressor" in advocating for their students. Further, all teachers expressed the importance of feeling wanted in their general education classrooms.

The teachers' conceptions of curriculum and the associated categories of knowledge they possessed allowed for the development of the taxonomy of terms presented in Table 6.2.

Table 6.2 Taxonomy of Curriculum Definitions and Tasks

Topic	Terminology	Descriptors
Curriculum	framework you use	structure
	guide you plug into	framework
	guide to teaching	standards
	where the children need to be	blueprint
	the important things	state-mandated
	what the state see as appropriate subject areas	teacher determined self-created
	expectations	
	strands	
	standards	
	what a student needs to work on	individualized
	Individual Education Plan	
	functional	
	life skills	

	individual work sessions	
	purchased programs	Touchmath, Edmark Reading, Explode the Code Phonics, Telian Lively Letters, Hands on Reading Etc.
Tasks	teach	
	support	
	matching students to classrooms	
	aligning the classroom	
	scaling instruction down to the student's level	
	creating curriculum	
	differentiating assignments/curriculum	
	adapting curriculum	
	modifying curriculum	
	finding ways to meet IEP/teaching goals	
Roles	teacher	
	support in special education classroom	
	support personnel in general education classroom	
	advocate	
Concerns	communicating with general education teachers	
	having a handle on curriculum	
	having a lack of curriculum clarity	
	feeling wanted in the general education classroom	
	position in the general education classroom	
	pacing of curriculum	
	managing the extensive scope of the general education curriculum	
	curriculum scope and sequence	

Note: This taxonomy was developed as part of this study.

Table 6.2 demonstrates that there is some degree of variability in how these teachers describe curriculum. Their words indicate that the concept of curriculum is large and subject to interpretation. Additionally, the teachers' words indicate that they have considerable flexibility in meeting the overall goal of educating their students. Each of the teachers provided examples of this flexibility in action. Kristie noted that she could take students out of the general education classroom at her discretion. Charlotte spoke of trying to mirror what goes on in general education classrooms to the best of her ability. Marie independently created a current events curriculum. Carlene stressed that she could select any curriculum that she felt was beneficial to her students. Betty spoke of trying to match her students to the contexts in which they might be educated. Finally, Jeri spoke of trying to match the school's curriculum to her students' needs—one of her most important tasks was to create themes based on the school's curriculum but consisting of activities that incorporated skills that her students needed or had.

These different versions of flexibility with regard to curriculum suggest that special education teachers have some degree of teacher power themselves. At the same time, the degree of that power is very much dictated by what occurs in their teaching settings. Different general education teachers were more or less tolerant regarding their views of what students with special needs were capable of. Not every teacher here had the option of determining the inclusion or the exclusion of specific students.

Turning to the topic of standards, perhaps the most significant point to note is that each of the teachers thinks of curriculum and standards as being relatively synonymous. Curriculum and standards were one and the same. Further, the teachers generally thought of standards and the standards movement as a positive development. The standards movement has caused these teachers to broaden the way that they think of their teaching. Standards helped them to become more organized. Standards have reminded them to consider all aspects of the curriculum, aspects that they might not have previously thought of. Their words further emphasized that there is a division between the types of standards under consideration. The teachers were positive toward content standards but often less so concerning performance standards. Their experiences with the concept of performance standards led to a discussion of state assessment for students with special needs.

Alternate Assessments

It is interesting to note Charlotte's positive spin on the alternate assessment. This is something that personal experience at training sessions has shown is more the exception rather than the rule. At such training sessions, many teachers expressed anxiety and anger at having to participate and at having to present academic instruction to students for whom such instruction might be interpreted as meaningless. Teachers were concerned about an inability to teach life skills—the skills that students needed to become functional. Charlotte's conception of the alternate assessment is also significant for the fact that her experience has typically been with learning disabled students—those students for whom educational teams typically recommend taking the state test, despite fear and often knowledge that the students will be unable to pass, especially as instructional content increases in difficulty as they progress through their schooling careers. These are the students that special educators often think of as being the most at risk regarding participating in state assessments. Test performance will not indicate the true level of knowledge that these students often possess.

Marie's experience with her IEPs is possibly of the greatest significance in this discussion of portfolio assessment. Of the four teachers working with more cognitively involved students, she is the only one who speaks actively of linking her IEPs to the standards she must also document for her portfolios. The alternate assessment process has become instrumental in what has to happen in her classroom.

Marie's thoughts concerning the notion of a "life skills curriculum" are of interest in this discussion. "Life skills" is a term frequently used in connection with students with special needs—especially those with more significant special needs; such students need to learn those skills that will assist them through life. The term is typically used in conjunction with such skills as personal care skills—eating, personal hygiene, and dressing. Prevocational skills and money skills are also often considered to be "life skills." At the same time, the term is one that is inadequately defined or too simply defined. Personal care and prevocational skills do not necessarily provide a balanced curriculum for students with special needs, especially those with significant needs. Her thought that a "life skills curriculum" might be applicable to some but not all students with special needs suggests that curriculum that is oriented toward special education also has the power to sort students. Who determines which student will receive such a curriculum? One might further ask what skill that a student learns is not in some way "life skill?"

Of the five teachers involved in portfolio preparation, Carlene is the most critical of the process. She clearly articulated the prominent negative aspects of the portfolio process. The portfolio does little to show the competency of students who are functioning in the mild-moderate range of intellectual ability. In fact, very few students, regardless of their level of need, are able to pass the portfolio assessment.

The alternate assessment portfolio is also notable for the fact that it emphasizes that language barriers separate special education and general education. The teachers speak of "access skills", "entry points", and "doing standards as written." And as this terminology is considered, other discipline specific terms come to mind. These terms include "life skills" and "functional independence." There is often little discussion of these terms between disciplines.

Betty brings the notion of access skills to the discussion of teacher practice. On the surface, her experience provides an additional example of the differing language between special education and general education. Yet, when we look beyond the surface, it becomes possible to see that special education might bring the knowledge necessary to create an integrated educational system. Entry points provide a necessary additional level of skill identification to the system created as part of the state assessment. Entry points and access skills further provide the deeper means to look at the context of schooling, to fully define the notion of "life skills."

Several teachers made mention of the negative impact on education that portfolios have brought to students with special needs in the state. The teachers' thoughts express the deep concerns held by many special education teachers regarding the need to complete portfolios. These concerns—that participating in the academic assessment is less than meaningful for students with significant special needs, that no matter how hard the students work they cannot pass the test, and as a result cannot graduate from high school, and the fact that placing a student on the portfolio assessment potentially removes him or her from the path of graduation from high school provide examples of major sources of pressure in special education and in the interaction between general education and special education. These are students that were not necessarily accounted for when the mandate to participate in district and state assessments was put into place. The lapse in consideration created by this situation provides possible evidence for the fact that there are two separate systems in schooling today. There is a separate system occupied by the world of general education and a secondary separate system occupied by the world of special education. The difficulties faced by these students further emphasize the division between a special education curriculum and a differentiated general education curriculum. Many teachers believe that there are students that should have a "life skills curriculum" and that there are students who are able to be a part of the general education curriculum. These students have to be assigned to or tracked into the appropriate curriculum. There is little notion of the concept of "participation in the general education curriculum", a key concept of special education teacher training and now, federal law.

The Individual Education Plan (IEP)

Any discussion of the IEP is never far from a discussion of the content of the general education curriculum. Students with special needs often present interesting cases, coming with well-known histories. This is not necessarily the case for students in general education. Further, any discussion of the IEP often leads to a discussion of the appropriateness of the general education curriculum for the student with special needs. The general education curriculum often comes before the student. Students in special education continue to be seen in terms of what they cannot do rather than in terms of what they can do or in terms of what they ought to be doing. Further, the general education curriculum may be deemed inappropriate because the student with special needs cannot perform prerequisite skills.

As they begin developing IEP goals, several of the teachers ask what have become the essential questions in standards-based education—what do students know and what do they need to know? Interestingly, that this phrase is the same important mandate for general education is not as frequently recognized. The recognition of this mandate emphasizes that the task of both disciplines is essentially the same.

That the teachers think about IEP goals being "just a piece of the puzzle" is significant. It speaks to the need to make sure that both special education and general education need to learn to balance the concepts of curriculum and IEP objectives. It is only through such balance that we can begin to understand the notion of accessing and participating in the general education curriculum. Unfortunately, such conversations do not occur frequently.

The development of social science, science, and mainstreaming goals and objectives in IEPs is also of particular interest. IEPs typically do not include objectives for all the subject areas that constitute the general education curriculum. Neglecting to include all subject areas in a typical IEP can make it difficult to mesh the IEP with the activities that occur in a general education classroom. Further, such subject area neglect can facilitate a lessening of inclusion opportunities. A secondary reason for not including such objectives in a student's IEP may also be related to service minutes. An IEP typically specifies the amount of time that a student will be working with the special education teacher for reading, writing, or math. Such times tend to be relatively standardized—one typically sees 30, 45, or 60 minutes teaching periods. These times rarely match the district's specified subject area time. As a result, reading and math instruction typically take precedence over other curriculum areas.

Carlene's acknowledgement of the importance of life skills for students with special needs is one of the major components of special education instruction and remains an important part of curriculum assignment. For some students, the discussion of curriculum continues to center around a choice between a general education curriculum or a life skills curriculum. She is accurate in noting the importance of the fact that not listing a skill in the IEP does not mean the skill will not be addressed. Skills not noted in IEPs are addressed throughout any school day or setting. In fact, this has been the way that the state suggested that daily living skills (e.g. tooth brushing, eating, or bathroom skills), formerly part of many students' IEPs, be handled as standards-based instruction became embedded into the structure of special education planning. Carlene's words remind us that focusing on a purely academic or life skills perspective for skill instruction often neglects the skills that constitute the context of the settings that students must participate in.

Interaction with General Education

Much of the teachers' thoughts on their interaction with various peers centered on opportunities for including their students into general education classes. They tell interesting stories of inclusion into and also separation from the life of their schools. Inclusion (or more precisely, the degree of inclusion) occurs on a teacher-by-teacher basis. All of the teachers noted that there are teachers who are open and teachers who are less open. This was typically expressed in terms of "being invited" into the general education classroom. Yet the teachers' understandings of what "being invited into the classroom" means clearly have different levels. For Kristie, being invited into the classroom had to do with being a "seamless part of the classroom." Her students had all the same materials and opportunities, albeit modified, as the general education students in that classroom. It became difficult to distinguish between any student and the student with special needs. Yet, at the same time, Carlene seemed content that her students get invited to the social events (e.g. birthdays, holiday parties, special work rewards) that occur throughout the school year. Teachers also made note of the fact that going to general education classes is often dependent on student behavior and "appropriateness" for the classroom. Students had to earn the opportunity to go to the general education classroom. Betty must go out, "pound the pavement" and "sell" her students. Ultimately, being a special education teacher could be more about whether the general education teacher is interested and willing to work toward inclusion than about the balanced education of a student with special needs.

Communication with the teachers with whom they worked was an issue for most of the teachers. All expressed the need to have a better understanding of the events that are occurring in the general education classrooms. Scheduling issues can play a major role in whether or not special education teachers have regular contact with general education teachers. Several teachers cited teacher schedules as being problematic. There is often no time to get together with general education teachers. The special education teachers are often running to catch up on collecting the necessary information for planning instruction from their general education peers.

Kristie's comment about not wanting to step on peoples' toes is of special interest in the discussion of interaction with general education peers. In many cases, the special education teacher tried to rationalize reasons for the general education teachers' behavior concerning inclusion. General education teachers do not always accord the same level of tolerance to special education teachers. Kristie's words regarding the possible intimidation of general education teachers regarding students with special needs are significant here. Her words provide both a possible reason for teacher intolerance and also imply that some teachers may not be willing to invest in the professional development necessary toward working with all students. Her words again support and possibly emphasize the idea that general education teachers have some degree of power over who gets into their classrooms.

Charlotte's experience in the area of interaction with general education teachers may be the most notable. She talks of the general education teacher being both focused on students with special needs disrupting the class either through behavior or slowing down the pace of the curriculum. This suggests that in the current world of education, curriculum often really does leave students behind in general education. This is certainly true for students with special needs, but experience has shown that it can also be true for students in general education. The struggling student continues to struggle as school sweeps past them.

Carlene brings the idea of the "inclusion classroom" as a typical placement for students with special needs to the discussion. Her words indicate that it is less that all classrooms have inclusion characteristics and more that the teachers in these classrooms are typically seen as more willing to work with students with special needs. Further, that experience has shown that administration often watches these classrooms more closely in order to ascertain when the teacher might want to take a school year off from classes that are geared more heavily toward special needs students. This provides another example of general education teacher power. She further notes that she is available to provide assistance if the general education teacher is interested in such assistance. Again, such a statement implies and supports the notion that the general education teacher holds a degree of power that can direct the inclusion experience for students with special needs. Carlene's expertise is a function of the general education teacher's desire to seek it out and make use of it. Such ideas are supported by my own teaching experience.

Betty's statement concerning her feelings regarding other teachers working with her may be one of the most poignant statements in the data. She implies that the general education teachers are doing her a favor. Jeri's experience echoes this situation. She too implies that general education is doing her a favor by offering to include or by including her students.

Using teacher perceptions of students with special needs and the appropriateness of general education curriculum as a basis of understanding, one can clearly see that general education curriculum and classrooms have some role as a student sorting mechanism. This assertion is made despite the concerns that educators typically express regarding the concept of academic tracking and the efforts to avoid such practices.

Professional Development

Turning to the closely related topic of professional development, the teachers report great variability in the type of professional development offered. Several of the teachers spoke of the importance of making use of in-house resources for professional development. There is considerable truth in the statement that schools often do not adequately make use of the knowledge that they possess especially as this comes to including different levels of students in general education classrooms. Some districts make use of their in-house resources; others do not. Both Kristie and Charlotte stress the importance of such tactics. Charlotte's experience is particularly interesting because it attempts to get the general education teachers involved in training focused on special education. Marie echoes such thoughts when she speaks of the importance of sharing the Curriculum Resource Guide.

The teachers' characterization of professional development is typical. There is often a significant divide between the training offered to general education teachers and special education teachers. General education is always focused on improving the general curriculum while special education often gets lost in the minutiae of special education. The focus of special education training is often on diagnosis and definition rather than curriculum integration. Charlotte's comments about autism spectrum professional development suggest two thoughts to me as a long-time special education teacher. First, such training focuses more on the discussion of the characteristics of autism rather than focusing on teaching academic content to such students. Secondly, such training is frequently exclusive—the focus is autism, not meeting student needs in accessing the general education curriculum. The implication is that students with autism (or any other specific disability) need completely specialized techniques, and are thus not necessarily appropriate for inclusion in general education classrooms, when in fact this is often not the case.

The exclusion from grade level meetings that several of the teachers talk about is additionally significant. Not being able to attend the meetings where everyday curriculum is discussed leaves the special education teacher at a disadvantage. They are never completely certain of what is happening in the general education classroom. This lack of knowledge contributes to both a sense of separation from the life of the school and a sense of not being truly organized regarding the presentation of curriculum. This sense of separation and disorganization often creates difficulties for the special education teacher around the mandate to access the general education curriculum. Further, the sense of separation between general education and special education increases as professional development opportunities are considered.

That several of the teachers express concern with appropriate training is critical. They point out that there is a disconnect between professional development for special education and general education. Several of the teachers note that much of the professional development offered does not include students with special needs. Many general education professional development topics don't apply to them. The special education teaches are not always required to attend such trainings. My own district frequently does not schedule special education topics for its regular curriculum days. These days are usually spent catching up on the uncompleted paperwork. But, at the same time, the teachers also state that they are comfortable with having the time to work on those items that get lost in the time crunch. Marie's story of having to adapt Greg's desk is the best example of this. Such time is often the only time that they get to complete such tasks. Yet, having time to adapt a student's desk is not appropriate professional development training.

The teachers' thoughts provide insight into the larger issue of district goals for professional development. Public school teachers are required to develop professional goals for each year. Yet, linking those goals to the district is often quite difficult due to a lack of available training options. District professional development often neglects special education needs when planning the topics to be presented to teachers throughout a school year. This is a major point of concern and yet another source of potential separation from the general education system at large for these special education teachers.

Discussion of the Observations

The actions documented in the classroom observations are consistent with statements that the teachers made during their interviews. The teachers' conceptions about teaching are evident in their actions. The observations illustrated several important points made throughout the interviews. The teachers experienced varying degrees of integration into their school communities. They held their students to high expectations of learning, regardless of their level of disability. The observations of the teachers in their classrooms expanded both the number of roles as well as the scope of the roles that a special education teacher might play in the classroom. Finally, these observations provide some understanding into the students' perceptions of themselves in their classrooms as well as their attempts to impact their educational environments. It was these student actions that stood out most prominently during the time that I spent in the teachers' classrooms.

The first, and possibly the most obvious item, to attract interest during the observations is the sense of integration or lack of integration into general education classrooms that these teachers experience. This sense of integration applies to both classrooms and the school as a whole. All teachers experienced different degrees of integration but some instances expressed the issues more effectively than others.

Kristie specifically stressed the importance of being a "seamless part" of the classroom. Her ability to realize this goal is illustrated in her actions (e.g. what she is allowed to do) in the different classrooms she works in. It is a function of the willingness of the classroom teacher to include the students with special needs and to fully utilize Kristie's expertise. The events that occurred during Kristie's math period and her third grade reading period stand in contrast to what occurred during the fourth grade reading block. In her fourth grade reading block, she is clearly in a secondary and subservient position. In her other classrooms, she is much more a harmonious part of the activities. She is a limited partner in the instruction that occurs in the fourth grade math class and a full partner in the third grade classroom. In this third grade classroom, she and her students are fully integrated into the activities in the third grade reading class from the very beginning of the class. Her larger role to play in the third grade classroom than in the fourth grade classroom is likely a function of the third grade general education teacher being new to the classroom but it may also have to do with the fact that the third grade teacher and Kristie, as she stated it, were both "on the same page." Kristie felt that this teacher would "know where she was coming from" as a result of their shared special education background.

Related to the degree of integration into the general education classroom was the sense of being invited into the classroom. In general, the greater the sense of invitation, the better developed were the inclusion opportunities. Charlotte's experiences nicely stress the importance of being invited into the classroom. While needing to be invited into the classroom was less of a concern in her new teaching position, there was clearly a difference between her first grade and her second grade experiences. In her first grade inclusion classroom, she is a part of the classroom, although clearly in a secondary role in that classroom. The general education teacher does work to include her in the daily events of the classroom. Her students do not stand out from the rest of the class in major ways, with the possible exception of Aaron. Aaron clearly makes his presence known in the classroom. At this point, his actions are not so disruptive as to completely interfere with the task of teaching but it is possible to see his behavior becoming more and more of an interference as he grows older. His actions will become problematic as he gets into higher grades where there is such a major emphasis on the academics involved in the state testing. Being a part of the classroom is not the case in her second grade classroom. Here, she is expected to simply remove her two students from that classroom. There is no sense of those students having an integral part in their general education classroom, even though this classroom is also supposed to be an inclusion class.

But it is the experiences of the teachers of the students with significant cognitive disabilities that may be the most telling in this area of integration. Jeri relates stories of how different general education teachers react to the presence of her students in their classes. Some teachers, such as the music teacher, do not allow union contracts, potential discomfort with such students, or the students' lack of ability to complete the planned grade-level lesson to interfere with including them in her classes. Still others are willing to sacrifice preparation periods to offer additional instruction to enhance inclusion opportunities. But there were also those other teachers, such as the art teacher, who interacted with her students on a minimal or even indirect level. And some teachers "just laughed" at Jeri's attempts to foster inclusion. At the same time, Betty's experience with having to "sell" her students to general education teachers is huge. General education is potentially in charge of who might be included and who might not be included. This need for invitation into the general education classroom can result in the students being isolated from the general activities of the school.

However, isolation from the activities of the school was not always the case for these students with special needs. Those students who were more academically capable or who were younger often experienced less isolation from the activities of the general education classroom than those who were older or less academically capable. But the students with greater needs also had important opportunities for social interaction. This was especially true for Marie. Two incidents stand out in her situation. The first incident was the class' entrepreneurial efforts to raise money for class field trips. They ran a coffee business that many of the teachers in the school took advantage of. The general education teachers frequently stopped in to buy coffee and snacks. When they did this, they often checked in to see what the students were currently working on. The second incident of interest in her situation was the traditional student and staff volleyball game that is played as part of the Christmas holiday season. The entire school takes time off on the day that the school finishes for the holiday break to play several games of volleyball. The event was significant because it was one of the few instances where Marie's students were not isolated from the other students in the school. All of them, except for Greg, actively played in the volley ball game. He was unable to participate actively in the game because of his physical issues. The students were clearly accepted as members of the school community at this event.

The teachers held their students to high expectations for their work. All saw their students as capable learners and held them accountable for their learning. This could be seen in the teachers' emphasis on the students participating in their various routines—whether such routines were strictly academic—as was the case with Kristie and Charlotte and to a lesser extent Betty and Jeri, or more functional—as was often the case with the students that Betty and Jeri taught. Betty expected her students to participate in both the calendar routine and to utilize their daily schedules. Jeri created adapted themes for fifth grade science. Carlene worked diligently on spelling multi-syllabic words with her students.

However, Marie provided the best example of high teacher expectations as she allowed her students to drive the curriculum. Two instances stood out over the observation period. The first of these consisted of a discussion of a famous baseball player's salary based on a newly signed deal with the New York Mets. The question of the lesson was what could you buy with an hourly salary of $1,000. She expected active participation and was rewarded by that participation. The boys in the classroom were enthusiastically engaged in noting the types of things that they might buy. Among the items suggested were big screen televisions, Porsches, and a Lamborghini. A second instance was related to the tsunami that had recently devastated Indonesia. Marie had made this event the focus of her computer class. The students worked on-line to research various facts related to the disaster. However, while the students were generally interested in learning more about the tsunami, this was a difficult activity for them. They had to negotiate using the computers, getting on-line, and then reading the information that they found. Marie and the paraprofessionals supported them throughout. All the students in the class provided some fact related to the tsunami.

The observations clearly demonstrate the difficulties in providing standards-based education to students with disabilities. Betty's calendar and group game routines stand out best in this regard. The calendar routine provided both math and communication opportunities. Betty uses this routine to incorporate standards-based number sense into the school day. In addition to working on the days of the week, the students also work on counting the days in the month and days in school, counting to 100 by tens, and counting to 100. The routine becomes more significant as the numbers increase in size. These skills are extremely difficult for the students in Betty's class. It can be difficult to see the purpose of trying to work on increasing number sense with such students. Almost every response must be prompted. It was always possible to hear more staff counting than students counting. The other significant factor in this routine is the amount of physical handling that has to occur with many of the students. The students are in and out of their wheelchairs or other form of adaptive seating throughout the calendar activity. The routine is thus a significant physical work-out as well as an academic context. But the staff offered no complaint.

The teachers all expressed concerns about keeping pace with the general education curriculum. Keeping up with the general education curriculum was often very difficult for their students. Many of the students are working on skills that are significantly lower than their assigned grades. They typically cannot keep up with the classroom pace because it takes a greater amount of time for them to learn new skills. The necessary practice time that these students require is also frequently lacking in general education classrooms. Further, the general education curriculum often proceeds at a standard, lesson-a-day pace. Kristie's and Charlotte's students could not maintain this pace despite the heroic efforts of their teachers. The difficulties associated with this fact were likely evidenced by the general education teachers' reactions to having students with special needs in their classes. Some teachers were concerned that such students would only have a negative impact on their practice. The next day's lesson was always waiting. They would be unable to meet the district-identified goals for curriculum coverage. Additionally, the students' difficulties with keeping up with the pace of the general education classroom often resulted in behavior issues. Such behavioral concerns can result in the removal of a student with special needs from the general education classroom, increasing their isolation.

Betty and Jeri had to search out routines that were appropriate for them to participate in. General education teachers in their settings were constrained at the additional drain these very involved students would place on their often over-burdened schedules. Both teachers struggled to create standards-based in-struction. In both situations, the students typically struggled with the academics involved in such instruction. The time that had been spent on the creation of Betty's calendar routine and Jeri's morning meeting was evident. The difficulty that the students had with the concepts presented was also evident. This situation was also true for Marie and Carlene, though to a much lesser extent.

Each teacher plays a variety of roles in her teaching situation beyond the standard roles related to teaching (e.g. planning and delivering instruction). In-teractions to calm the students are frequent across all teachers. Special education teachers are managers. Students' inappropriate actions are brought first to the adults as a first course of action. The teachers often act as buffers between the students. Marie provided an example of an entrepreneurial role as well as an important example of being a part of the life of the school. Her peers in the school and from other schools in the district made it a point to participate in these activities. Several teachers stopped by to purchase coffee; other teachers and students in the district ordered holiday ornaments made by her students dur-ing their yearly holiday shop activities. All the teachers functioned as "cheerleaders". They constantly worked at keeping the students focused on their task, providing assistance as needed. That assistance always included an element of encouragement as well. All the teachers acted as disciplinarians. Ultimately, Jeri best illustrated this role of disciplinarian as she worked to calm Normand during his extensive behavioral episodes.

Carlene, as most of the other teachers also had to do, frequently had to share information with her paraprofessional or the therapy staff on the run. There was little time built into the schedule to confer with others who also work with the children. Having to share student information on the run also characterized the practice of each of the other teachers. It is particularly prominent in Betty and Jeri's situations. As Carlene spoke of Cary in the situation described in the observation, she noted that she believes that he is just trying to get words out but he doesn't have enough language. Carlene had put herself in the role of interpreter here. This was a role that all the teachers frequently play. They often acted to provide information as to what motivates their students, especially during behavioral issues. Further, they often attempted to assess their students' attitudes regarding their placement in special education.

But most importantly, the observations clearly demonstrate that the students were all able to impact their educational experiences, regardless of their level of disability and the difficulties presented by standards-based instruction. They were able to make connections between their experiences and the outside world. They were able to control activities that were presented. They were able to participate and demonstrate academic progress at their level within the context of the general education curriculum.

The students were often very effective at getting information from those working with them. One incident with Charlotte stands out prominently. She was working with Colin at the time, completing a Making Words activity. The students normally complete the activity using the sound cards that are associated with the Wilson Reading Program. During this lesson, Charlotte was using sound cards belonging to the Lively Letters Program, a letter sound correspondence program that bears some basic resemblance to the sound-learning component of the Wilson Reading Program. The major difference between the two techniques was that the Wilson program uses a series of key words associated with individual letters while Lively Letters teaches a mnemonic story associated with the letter and its corresponding sound. Colin was less familiar with the set of cards being used in this instance. As he read the words, he frequently looked at Charlotte. It appeared that he was looking to her for some silent affirmation that he was correct with his sound blending. This student reaction happens frequently with all the teachers.

The students made clear and definite choices, often using their behaviors to influence those choices. This was nicely illustrated in the routine that Betty referred to in the interviews as "group game." Group game was subject to many of the same difficulties that are noted for the calendar routine. However, the routine was further complicated by the fact that staff were in and out to take lunch breaks. This increased the degree of physical management that must occur during the routine. It's that much harder to physically manage such involved students when all the adults are not present. Further, students responded differentially to presented tasks during the game period. There was a distinct difference in the students' behavior when they were listening to and acting out stories compared to when they were playing games. They enjoyed the stories in which they could mimic story movements or responses. They actively and appropriately participated in these situations. The students did not seem to enjoy the games to the same degree. Inappropriate behaviors often occurred during the game situations, providing an increased level of chaos to the classroom on a regular basis. The students would indicate that they wanted the stories to continue but seldom showed such interest in continuing the game activities.

The students were often quite adept at getting adults to help them, even when they had some understanding of the skills needed to participate. They were also quite successful at influencing the environments that they work in. One snack period in Jeri's classroom was especially noteworthy. The primary topic of conversation was the latest sick call-out by Adam's paraprofessional. She called out frequently. This led to a discussion of Jeri's upcoming absence. With Adam's paraprofessional also absent, there would be no one in the classroom who knows the students really well. Jeri commented, "Be prepared for a fun day." She gestures to Normand and notes, "And this guy will just eat it up." This statement referred to the fact that Normand would most likely exhibit inappropriate behaviors because there will be unfamiliar staff present.

These students were often able to make their disruptive behavior work for them. They understood how to control classroom situations. Student behaviors figured prominently in the presented activities throughout the observations in Jeri's classroom. As Keely misbehaves, Normand also begins to misbehave. Jeri attempted to keep him focused by reminding him that he needed to help cook in order to have the treat and that she is glad when he is doing good work. He behaved momentarily and then quickly misbehaved again. He appeared to be playing a game as well as to understand the difficulties that he was causing. His ability to disrupt the cooking gave the impression that he was in control of the activity.

The majority of the behavioral difficulties originated and was perpetuated by Normand. His attempts to control the activities of the classroom were frequently evident. They could and did occur during all of the activities in the classroom. His behavioral episodes began with the snack episode described earlier and gradually escalated over the next couple of days to a series of major aggressive episodes that finally resulted in the other students being re-located and the classroom organization being destroyed.

During the worst of these behavioral episodes, Normand succeeded in upending tables and chairs, emptying individual work bins, and destroying the leisure area and several of the books that were kept there. His behaviors began early in the school day and continued through the better part of the day.

Throughout the episode, Jeri was in the position of having to contain Normand's behaviors. This essentially meant that she had to place herself in a series of situations that would prevent harm to the other students in the classroom and that would hopefully prevent further destruction to the classroom materials as well as to try to calm Normand, though she herself was at physical risk. As she did this, the paraprofessionals initially attempted to ignore Normand's behaviors. When this became ineffective, they removed the students and their work to the adjoining classroom. There was initially little assistance provided to Jeri or her paraprofessionals by other school personnel. I was left with the impression that they were expected to manage Normand no matter how difficult he became.

At the same time, the students understand actions that please their teachers. They will tell observers that it is important to do good work and that their teachers are happy when they do their best work and behave nicely. They understand that their teachers are in control and that behaviors cannot always lead to the desired results. They understand, even when their teachers are less perceptive, that they sometimes just have to wait the situation out and take whatever consequences are assessed for their lack of ability. Such responses occur even though these are students who can communicate little more than their needs and wants. These students are able to understand the business of school though they may not show these understandings in the conventional manner associated with schools. This is a realization that not every general educator is able to fully accept, either explicitly or implicitly.

Concluding Remarks

The study has presented the teachers' words regarding their experiences and their practices. The teachers' words indicate multiple sources of concern, anxiety, and pressure in their daily practice. Their stories indicate that special education is subject to a noticeable degree of potential chaos. This chaos is created by the interaction between the multiple sources of concern, anxiety, and pressure identified by the teachers. Both systems, special education and general education, are characterized by significant tension. In addition, special education as a system is frequently separate from the general education settings in which it was intended to function.

The teachers' classroom actions have been documented. The idea of chaos that began to emerge during the discussions was evidenced in the classroom actions of all the teachers. Both data sources allowed for the identification of significant issues and concerns contributing to the shaping of special education teacher practice. All of the teachers were faced with a number of difficulties associated with their students and their teaching that they needed to work through. In many cases, these difficulties were obstacles to effectively completing their teaching tasks. These issues and concerns that the teachers identified in word or through action drive the analysis that is presented next in Chapter Seven.

Chapter Seven
Special Education Teacher Practice Revealed

"I don't think that people really know what goes on inside of this classroom."
(M. Konners, data collection interview, 2005.)

Chapter Four presented data summarized from the teachers' multiple interviews. The teachers expressed their thoughts regarding their students, their classrooms, curriculum, standards, the IEP, alternate assessment, professional development, and their interactions with the world of general education. Chapter Five provided individual vignettes of teaching, assembled from representative routines that occurred in individual classrooms. These vignettes provided illustrative segments of a school day in a special education classroom. Such vignettes might be interpreted from the perspective of a day in the life of each these teachers. Chapter Six presented a discussion of those interviews and observations. These chapters have demonstrated that the teachers share similar thoughts and experiences regarding their positions as special education teachers in public school settings. The complexity and apparent chaotic nature of special education teacher practice are evident in the words and actions of the teachers participating in this study as well as my own practice as a special education teacher. Special education practice incorporates dimensions that extend and in many cases go beyond academic activities. These dimensions were described as part of a taxonomic and componential analysis presented in the preceding chapters. This chapter builds on those analyses, providing further understanding of special education teacher practice.

The Students and Classrooms: Codes and Themes

The teachers' descriptive responses to the interview questions presented in Chapter Four yielded a series of codes describing additional concepts associated with their students and classrooms. These codes represent items of importance to special education teachers and further expanded the content of the typical general education categories previously noted in the earlier chapters.

Special education teachers encounter several teaching variables in addition to the traditional variables of schooling. While planning and delivering curriculum remain the starting point for all teachers, these teachers must also balance the interaction of such variables as administrative support, standards and state assessment, the students' perceptions of receiving special education and any behavior that might be associated with those perceptions, great variability in student ability as well as student behavior, and significant differences in educational philosophy. All of these tasks are carried out with students that often have major difficulty with completing conventional academic tasks. Teachers used different terms to describe similar situations. Several data codes were present across all teachers while other codes were mentioned minimally. As a result, it became possible to collapse this initial list of data codes into a shortened list of essential codes. Several codes that were mentioned minimally were dropped from further analysis at this time. A few codes were retained and elaborated on later in the analysis. These essential codes focusing on the students and their classrooms are summarized in Table 7.1.

Table 7.1 Essential Data Codes: Teacher Descriptions of Students and Classrooms

Code	Frequency of teachers	Code	Frequency of teachers
challenges	6	administrative support	3
connections—gen. ed.	6		
teacher power	6	language of education	3
student attitudes	5	teacher roles	3
adaptability	5	curriculum/standards	2
expectations/success	4	access	2

Teachers spoke of the frustrations and concerns that they encountered in their teaching situations. The essential code became "challenges in teaching in special education." The challenges of teaching in special education encompassed issues with teacher power, expectations for student performance, administrative support, student variability, and curriculum and standards. Student variability was best represented in the discussions of student diagnoses. They also spoke of student attitudes and success, participation, school inclusion philosophy, and connections to their assigned general education classrooms. The essential code here became connections to general education. General education teacher attitudes and the notion of an informal degree of power emerged from the teachers' discussions related to their connections to their general education classrooms. These codes provided broad threads of discussion as the analysis proceeded.

All teachers spoke in some ways of the challenges of teaching in special education. Their challenges included the level of acceptance that they felt as they worked with their assigned students, and the different roles that they occupied. Charlotte, Carlene, and Betty specifically noted administrative support as essential to the tasks that they needed to accomplish while the other teachers spoke of the topic incidentally. Charlotte's thoughts centered on challenges created by what she felt was a lack of administrative support. This lack of support hampered her ability to provide instruction to her students. On the other hand, Kristie was very positive about the administrative support she received. Her district was actively involved in trying to create increased inclusion. Carlene was very positive about the administrative support that she received. Betty was also positive concerning the administrative support that she received. Interestingly though, this support was essentially associated with the purchase of equipment or teaching materials. This was also the case with Marie's experience. Jeri's administrative issues centered on not being able to rewrite her IEPs.

All the teachers indicated that their students demonstrated a broad range of ability levels. In addition to this, there was frequently no pattern to the manner in which the disabilities manifest themselves. For the students diagnosed as learning disabled, some students decoded but did not comprehend. Others comprehended but did not decode. Both skill sets are major pieces of the instruction that occurs in elementary schools. Students could often acquire concrete skills but could not apply those skills. The teachers must be flexible enough to continue their practice under these conditions. Further, the amount of practice that can be necessary to acquire any skill can be enormous. Such extensive variability in practice characterizes the experience of all the teachers, but is particularly prominent for the students with greater levels of disability, such as those taught by Marie, Carlene, Betty, and Jeri. They must be able to meet the different manifestations that student disabilities can take.

The teachers often engaged in trying to put themselves in their students' situations, of trying to understand how their students felt. Of interest in Kristie's student descriptions is her emphasis on hoping that her most challenging child would not notice that other children were more academically capable than he was. Her students' feelings are of importance to her. Her quick empathy toward her students' feelings ably illustrates the role of student advocate. This is a role that characterizes each of the teachers, either explicitly as in Kristie's case, or implicitly as in the case of the other teachers. Of even greater significance in her descriptions is Kristie's emphasis that "progress is progress." This is an example of student advocacy at its most powerful. General education is often a world in which students are expected to make grade level leaps in progress. Such expectations suggest a conventional interpretation of schooling. Students generally learn at a predictable rate. Students making slow or limited progress are often looked on less satisfactorily than typical children. Special educators must see beyond this interpretation. They must be able to communicate what the students can do in order to offset the myriad of issues created by what the students cannot do.

The teachers' student descriptions further emphasize the importance of both perseverance and the complexity of working as a special educator. Kristie's description of her student with behaviors, "the behavior problem of the school," provides one of the clearest examples of this. This student was capable of doing the presented work but regularly chose not to. She was expected to continue to work with this student despite the behaviors he engages in. Each day, she must be ready to get him engaged in his academics. At the same time, working with such students provides one illustration of the complexity of the field. Her comment that "this student was unbreakable," despite all her efforts, is particularly telling. Special educators are supposed to be able to "cure" inappropriate behaviors, despite the fact that years of teaching experience and work with students with behavioral issues tells me that we can manage inappropriate behavior but not cure or completely eliminate it. Kristie kept trying different strategies but was unable to get this student appropriately engaged. Further, working with such behaviorally involved students is not always an equitable expectation. Students who do not behave conventionally can easily be ejected from the activities or supervision of general education classrooms. Special educators often become responsible for such students. They seldom have choice regarding which students they will work with.

Kristie is not alone in having to show perseverance in oftentimes-unique situations. All of the teachers were able to offer stories of a similar nature. In some cases, the issues were behavioral in nature. This characterized Charlotte's experiences. In most cases, the issues were a combination of lowered cognitive ability complicated by disruptive behavior. Marie and Carlene provide the best examples here. They often worked with students that supposedly "just couldn't survive in the mainstreamed classroom." No one in their districts ever completely defined the meaning of that phrase. Finally, Betty and Jeri shared stories of the difficulties they encountered in developing and providing general education curriculum to students working at the level of the access skill.

Charlotte's student descriptions illustrate teacher practice components of variability, complexity, and flexibility, as well as the perseverance just discussed. She uses a standard definition of learning disability in describing her students. They are typically identified by the level at which they fall behind grade level. As with Kristie, Charlotte talks of the difficulties of working with students with behavioral difficulties. Charlotte's student description is notable for the emphasis she places on managing behaviors. She deepens the notion of the complexity of being a special educator when she adds the idea of not being able to follow classroom routines and expectations to the definition of behavioral difficulties and when she notes her desire for increased behavioral strategy training. She implies that the skill to be able to follow classroom routines and expectations is something that students are expected to inherently know or at least learn quickly and then retain. Yet, the inability to retain skills is often one of the significant determinants of special needs. Charlotte's emphasis on the need for strategies to manage behavior provides a first hint that teachers of different disciplines, general education and special education, having different knowledge bases. These different knowledge bases do not always interact well together. Special education teachers must have content knowledge as well as "special knowledge" necessary to assist their students. In Charlotte's situation, she implies that she was supposed to have increased knowledge of behavior management strategies.

Her discussion of her students with the greatest needs brings attention to the term "access". Charlotte uses the term in relation to her students who were just below grade level. In some ways, this is a typical definition of the term "access." Charlotte uses it to mean working on the standard general education curriculum. Yet, the term is more often seen in reference to students with greater cognitive needs, where it generally refers to providing general education instruction to all students regardless of cognitive level, through modification and adaptation. What is interesting and surprising in her use of the term "access" is that she uses the same meaning as those working with students with more significant cognitive needs. This provides a potential connection between meeting the needs of students with different levels of disability. All special education teachers need to have some understanding of this term. Interestingly, however, the only other teacher who mentions the term "access" is Kristie. I would have expected the other teachers to use the term more so than Charlotte or Kristie. Thus, the term "access to general education" may be used more in the literature than in actual teacher practice. Further, the term may be thought of as more appropriate to students with learning disabilities rather than students with other diagnoses of special needs.

Carlene brings the topic of school inclusion philosophy to the discussions. Her description of her student with ADHD brings to mind the question of criteria for inclusion, something that is frequently mentioned in inclusion workshops. Determining criteria for inclusion is perhaps the biggest complexity of all in current discussions of education. It would be interesting to know how the determination was made that certain students could not be in the general education classroom. From Carlene's discussion, it appears that decisions of placement are made on the basis of the child meeting the criteria for the classroom rather than the classroom working to support the child's presence there. Carlene's mention that some of her students cannot function in a large group further suggests that the group comes before the individual.

Despite the fact that educational theory speaks of individual learning rates and the unpredictability of such rates, differentiating instruction and meeting the educational needs of all students, general education settings can still be places where student conformity is the ultimate goal. Success is often measured by the fact that students do what they are supposed to do in fourth grade in the way that fourth grader students typically complete a given skill, regardless of whether or not the student can perform in that way. From my own practice, the student who cannot hold a pencil properly is still going to do his work in cursive handwriting because that is what fourth grade students do. Such an attitude is often a source of stress for special educators. Carlene's description of her autistic student becomes particularly important here. This boy has made significant gains during his time in Carlene's classroom. Yet, not everybody would immediately recognize and appreciate the degree of the gains that students such as this do make.

Once again, Kristie and Carlene remind me of a similar situation in my own practice. I received a student who was considered by earlier teachers as incapable of learning academic skills and unable to be in a general education classroom. "He had an IQ of 58." As he enters third grade, this student has begun to read, can identify numbers at a second grade level, can add and subtract multi-digit numbers using the Touchmath technique from memory and has begun to understand the concept of regrouping among several other academic skills. I would say that this student is clearly capable of learning academic skills. However, his continued difficulties with not being able to work independently typically lessen the importance of the skills that he has acquired. General education teachers may be more concerned that such students cannot follow the dismissal routine in the first few days of school than with making a place for them in their classrooms.

Carlene's description of her students is also notable for its discussion of criteria for moving on. She links moving on and out of the isolated classroom directly to having less behaviors and a diagnosis that does not imply the need for instruction delivered in a separate setting. Receiving special education services is not necessarily a desirable thing. Her discussion illustrates the important emphasis that education places on diagnosis and categorization. The diagnosis and the category often exist separate of the students. It is also interesting that Carlene links inclusion to higher functioning students. The students who are more able to follow the general rules and procedures of the general education classroom are the ones that are typically seen in those settings. It is acceptable to remove other less desirable students from general education classrooms. Such a perception is consistent with available research data (Lipsky & Gartner, 1997; Soodak, et al. 1998). Further, it is my assertion that this perception seems to be true of much of general education, despite research to the contrary that indicates that all students can benefit from inclusive settings (Browder & Spooner, 2006; Downing, 2002; Lipsky & Gartner, 1997).

Marie, as with the first three teachers, notes a wide range in ability levels in her students. She initially describes her students in terms of both disability and skills. She notes the difficulty of trying to determine exactly where some of her students are regarding what they can do. This can be a complex task, made more so, because the students' skills are not always stable. That is, skills can be present on one day and gone the next, only to reappear at another time. That skills can skip out and reappear is further indicative of the perseverance that must also characterize what Marie does on a regular basis.

Of particular interest in Marie's student descriptions is her questioning of whether two of her students are appropriately placed in her classroom. This is significant and is illustrative of the fact that special education teachers also think of their students as fitting a certain model of what students in a given classroom should generally look like, as seems to be the case with what can be observed in general education classrooms. Marie's experience further illustrates that her entire curriculum can change as different groups of students come to her. She has moved from a curriculum encompassing primarily pre-academic skills to one that incorporates third and fourth grade mathematics skills and fifth grade science and social studies skills. Thus, special education teachers must also often reinvent themselves based on their students.

As she describes her two lower-functioning students, Marie indicates that she must think of finding ways for them to interact with the materials of the curriculum. This attention to methods of interaction may be more prominent with Greg than with Asia. Marie talks of using sturdy materials and coming up with a way for him to easily turn pages. As with Charlotte, Marie is speaking of access to the general education curriculum. She clearly indicates that this is the goal of her teaching but she does not make use of the term "access" at this point. The necessity of finding methods of interaction with the curriculum also emerges in the student descriptions provided by both Betty and Jeri, below. But again, the actual term "access to the general education curriculum" is not directly used.

Jeri's description of her students also emphasizes a standard manner of describing students, especially those with more significant cognitive disabilities. Students are typically first described in terms of their functioning level and their disabilities. Her discussion of wanting to change her students' IEPs is of interest in that it clearly brings school context into the story. Jeri indicates that she would like to change her IEPs but seems to be implying that she cannot do this because they were just recently written. The school's interest is to keep the system functioning but this may at the expense of the students. It would be difficult to administratively rewrite these documents.

Jeri's difficulty with her IEPs is another indication of the tensions that exist over being a special education teacher. That tension is clearly illustrated in the workings of the power structure present in her school. It appears that Jeri is constrained in rewriting her IEPs by typical practice in the school in which she teaches. Rewriting her four IEPs would require additional time from all those involved in the IEP process and staff time is frequently stretched beyond its limits in special education. Districts sometimes try to avoid additional meetings if possible. So Jeri must demonstrate considerable flexibility as she works within the classroom structure that she has inherited and moves toward re-aligning that classroom with her understanding of what she is supposed to be doing.

Betty's description of her students indicates that she has the greatest range of functioning ability in her students. She has had students who work on beginning academic skills as well as students working on functional skills, skills that would be described as access skills. She is the first of the teachers to mention the use of the term "hands-on" and to suggest the necessity of adapting curriculum as well as making instruction meaningful for her students as part of the initial descriptions of her students.

The concept of instruction being meaningful is particularly important. The teachers all speak of making their instruction meaningful, yet there are no clear guidelines about what this really means. Trying to define it is an activity that can cause significant stress for educators both in special education and general education. There is little agreement on what constitutes success for these students. Students with special needs are frequently held to performance criteria derived from the world of general education. These criteria are often unattainable for many students with special needs. The best example of this is the notion that these students can successfully take the state assessments. Further, regardless of the effort put forth by the students and their teachers, these students are unlikely to pass those assessments as present educational policy exists. Such a definition of success in school is both implausible and improbable for these students.

That all the teachers talk so much of diagnosis is of interest. Diagnosis appears to precede anything else that happens with the students, especially as they demonstrate greater disability levels. It is important to note that a diagnosis is necessary in order to receive services. However, the emphasis on diagnosis noted here seems less related to eligibility of service than to sorting of students. Special education teachers also categorize their students, just as other educational professionals do. The emphasis on diagnosis and categorization has an additional, and perhaps more important significance. *There is a separate language that characterizes special education practice.* It is a language that intensifies the potential degree of chaos that exists with special education. For example, outsiders do no often understand the complexities of the various diagnoses and categorizations or teaching methodology that exists in special education. These are not frequent topics in general education professional development. Then, there is also the fact that the same separate special education language can often be contextually defined. The same term can have different definitions based on district policy. Further, districts, and sometimes teachers, often use items such as program descriptors to their advantages. Notably, there are infrequent attempts to create links between the languages of special education and general education.

All the teachers, with the exception of Kristie, offer student descriptions that may be considered more as student profiles. The students stand out as individuals in their particular classroom. Kristie's student descriptions indicate that her students are less separate from the make-up of a general education classroom. For some special education teachers, student categories are based on academic abilities. All teachers categorize their students in terms of levels of abilities. Often times, Kristie and Charlotte's students typically are working on academic skills that are just below or only moderately below their grade level curriculum. At the same time, as Marie indicates, the students can also be working on extremely low academic skills, as was the case with Asia who could only count to three but was in the fifth grade. For Marie, this student is probably her lowest performing student, yet for Betty or Jeri, this student might be considered one of their higher students. Student academic ability clearly has an impact on the practice of these teachers.

For other special education teachers, the categories are based on the degree of assistance or support needed. This is true, especially as you consider the students that Betty works with. Betty provides information that shows the true range of students that receive their education in a public school setting. That range includes far more than just students working with traditionally conceived academic curriculum. The teachers think of their students in terms of their interaction with the curriculum and where they are in terms of where they should be. As the students increase in the level of need, there appears to be less separation from an individual curriculum that they need to learn. Students are seen as individuals with needs rather than as students interacting with a pre-determined curriculum. However, it is that concept of the pre-determined curriculum that often results in certain students being removed from general education classrooms. The academic skills of a task outweigh the social skills that can be embedded in that task's completion. General education often does not consider other skill areas within an academic lesson as valid, as a goal of instruction that can be equally important. The disruption to a given academic lesson is all that is seen.

The teachers spend considerable time thinking of their connections to general education classrooms. Important beliefs about teaching become evident in these discussions. Further, these discussions emphasize additional aspects of the tensions involved in being a special education teacher. Kristie uses the term 'integrate' rather than 'inclusion' as she describes her activities. The need for integration is important to her. It is important to her that her children not "look different" from the other children in the classroom. Kristie suggests that her students may need help but that they are not really any different from other learners in the classroom setting. She seeks a sort of invisibility for her students and for herself. Her students provide just another facet of the learning diversity that characterizes present day classrooms. She speaks very highly of being a "seamless part of the classroom". This is not always a position that a special education teacher enjoys. Kristie values her own integration as well as the integration of her students.

Yet, for Jeri, the connection to the general education classroom takes a much different form. The socialization aspect of the connection to general education is clearly important as an educational goal for her. She seems especially pleased that visitors now think of her classroom as more of a classroom. Here, she is comparing her classroom and its organization to other classrooms in her setting. It is important that her room looks like it fits in with the rest of the school. As a result of this belief, she takes such items as common classroom postings and adapts them to her needs.

Jeri's students will not have isolated individualized work areas. Her emphasis on not being secluded is also important. Special education classrooms can have a tendency to create their own level of isolation. This isolation can occur as the classroom is set up to accommodate student differences…for example, creating individual work areas, using rigid classroom areas such as the meal area, the therapy area or the relaxation area, and labeling supplies and the schedule with line drawings. Such actions can emphasize the differences in student need rather than be seen as a method of accommodation in order to participate in or access the general education curriculum. This can be especially true of using pictures to label the schedule and classroom routines. For example, I was once told that using pictures to label the classroom and adapt routines was inappropriate to the general education classroom because the students who were struggling with reading but who were not officially identified as having special needs would use the pictures rather than attempt to read the schedule or the lunch menu. Isolation from general education can also happen as teachers individually structure their classrooms as a result of their available materials and district policies. Additionally, classroom materials are sometimes lacking and are often significantly different from those used in general education. These materials can also be very difficult to obtain. District policies can be more supportive of isolation rather than integration.

Several of the teachers go on to imply that there is an unofficial teacher power as well. It appears that the classroom teacher has an "unofficial" power in welcoming or not welcoming the students with special needs into the classroom. And as previously noted, the special education teachers here must conform to the routines of the teachers with whom they work. In commenting that she doesn't want to "step on people's toes", Kristie occupies a subservient role in the classroom. Her practice must operate around the position her students hold in the general education classroom. Charlotte's practice also provides evidence of this subservience to the general education teacher. She typically did not lead any instruction in the first grade inclusion classroom during the observation period.

Throughout her description, Kristie's role in providing voice to her students' feelings is evident. She speaks often of what she believes the students feel as a result of their special needs. At the same time, there is some smaller hint that student voice is less recognized in elementary schools than in middle or high school settings. Even though students may say that they do not wish to go to a pull-out setting, they are seldom given the opportunity to not go. Other teachers also perform similar actions for their students. Many of them offered stories where they attempted to interpret their students' feelings. In fact, this skill is often a basic element of special education teacher training, especially as it relates to behavior management techniques. Understanding behavior management techniques begins with the attempt to infer the meaning of difficult behavior. An inference is an interpretation based on the setting and on prior knowledge. What is it that one thinks a behavior or an action means?

That Kristie emphasizes that it was her choice to pull her second graders out potentially indicates that she has also has some power as a special education teacher. However, such a decision could also have been motivated by the fact that the classroom in which this child was placed was unable/unwilling to meet the child's needs. In essence, Kristie may be unable to buck the system. In actual practice, she may not have had the opportunity to remain in the classroom. She certainly implies this when she notes, "that being new to the school, I didn't want to step on any toes." Further, Kristie was very concerned that she would be seen as overly "pushy."

Both general education classrooms and special education classrooms have an "in and out" nature to them. There is the in and out aspect related to special curriculum subjects. Special education, however, brings with it an increased degree of that in and out, creating significant disruption to the students' education. Students may leave a general education classroom for a variety of different services. Teachers may want to plan these student absences so that they do not conflict with various curricular subjects. This can, and often does cause scheduling difficulties for arranging services for students with special needs. The key difference between Charlotte's first self-contained classroom and a general education classroom is twofold.

There is a different nature to the "in and out" of a special education classroom. IEPs typically allow for short periods of intervention. The time periods that Charlotte may see students is always less than the scheduled time a general education classroom may be working on reading or math. Further, Charlotte may have to take students from various classrooms, again causing scheduling difficulties. The second difference between Charlotte's classroom and the general education classroom is that she has three different grade levels to keep abreast of. The potential difficulty here is that she has more than one curriculum to master in addition to working with her students with their various special needs. Sometimes the schedule allows for convenient grouping—where generally the special educator has a single grade, with potentially one curriculum, and sometimes it does not. There are often times when the special education teacher is trying to cover several levels of grade specific material with the students at the same time. It is important to note that while this poses a possible problem for the special education teacher, it does not lessen the difficulties that a general education teacher may face with the need to differentiate instruction for the range of students that may be in a typical general education classroom. However, it is also true that the functioning range of the students in the special education setting is likely to be significantly greater than what would be seen in the general education setting.

Of the three situations—time periods, schedules, and curriculum issues—having less than the prescribed time to work on subjects such as reading or math is the more significant. Less time with students who take longer to learn is not productive. Further, such lessened teaching times creates situations of isolation such as those described by Kristie when she speaks of her students' return to their general education classrooms in the middle of lessons. The returning students frequently wind up in the back of the room, outside of the lesson currently in progress.

Betty's selection of the term "program" to describe her classroom is potentially significant. The use of "program" is something that all of the teachers, with the exception of Kristie, make use of. It is a term that poses some difficulty in that it serves to separate the special education classroom from the general education environment of the school. The students in these classrooms attend "programs" housed in a given elementary school rather than the elementary school. The term suggests that special educators frequently fall prey to thinking of themselves as separate from the world of general education. Thinking of oneself as separate from the general education setting in which one is situated significantly contributes to the sense of tension in interacting with general education that has become evident in the data. Feeling separate can certainly impact the ability to interact and integrate productively with the larger general education setting.

Charlotte, Marie, Carlene, Betty, and Jeri all describe separate classrooms that have generally separate activity areas. For Charlotte and Marie, there are student desk areas. Carlene's students do the majority of their work in small group formats, at small tables. Betty and Jeri have routine/group areas and what they describe as individual work areas for each student. The individual work areas for Betty and Jeri are of interest in that they emphasize the idea that the students will learn more effectively if they are put in "a distraction free environment." The idea of the "distraction free environment" is something of a common conception for educating students with special needs. However, the observations clearly demonstrate that the special education environments in this study offer multiple kinds of distractions. Experience also shows that there is no such thing as a distraction free environment. In addition, the students are frequently able to act upon those distractions to their advantage. Further, the removal to that "distraction-free environment" precludes natural opportunities to learn those social skills that are frequently mentioned first when developing educational plans for inclusive opportunities. Inclusion sometimes tends to be seen only in its social context and not in any academic context. This is especially true for students such as those in Betty and Jeri's classrooms.

The teachers' descriptions of their students and classrooms and the various threads of the analytical discussion led to the identification of several major elements of special education teacher practice. The data presented in this section illustrate that special education teacher practice is characterized by variability, complexity, flexibility, perseverance, and some sense of separateness from the larger world.

Of particular importance in the data codes was the special education terminology used by the teachers. Specific terminology was often associated with students, materials, and teaching arrangements. This specific "language of special education" began to emerge most clearly with Betty's descriptions, though each teacher had multiple instances of specialized terminology. Diagnoses, adaptive equipment, and assistive technology are most prominent in Betty's descriptions of her teaching situation.

Curriculum, Standards, and Assessment: Codes and Themes

As with the discussions of students and classrooms, the teachers' discussions of curriculum showed both variety and depth. Curriculum is the framework, structure and blueprint for what they teach their students. Curriculum is a matter of the different educational programs and materials that the school uses or that can be purchased. Curriculum is a creative task of individualization and developing goals for the IEP. Curriculum is determining how selected material is taught. Curriculum is created through teacher selection, differentiation, accommodations, modifications, and adaptations. Curriculum is the task of meeting the individualized goals set in the IEP.

The teachers' words yielded a series of codes that can be used to further develop thoughts on answering this study's questions addressing special education teachers' experience and practice as they encounter the general education curriculum and standards as well as the concept of access to that curriculum and standards-based education. Again, as in the section addressing students and classrooms, several data codes were present across all teachers while other codes were mentioned minimally. The teachers sometimes used different terms to describe similar concepts or situations. Their individual codes were contracted into a reduced list of essential codes. These essential curriculum related codes are presented in Table 7.2.

Table 7.2 Essential Data Codes: Teacher Descriptions of Curriculum and Standards

Code	Frequency of Teachers	Code	Frequency of Teachers
concerns	6	state assessment	5
definitions	6	adaptations	4
student skills	6	modifications	4
links to general education	6	purchased programs	4
standards	6	accommodations	2
teacher roles	6	access	2
training	6	accountability	2

Again, the topic of concerns/frustrations or challenges was prominent in the discussions. Here the concerns were related to delivering curriculum and standards-based instruction. Teachers were sometimes unsure of the purpose of such instruction for their students, but, at the same time, they generally felt that the mandate to include their students in such instruction helped them to see beyond their usual practice. Several of the teachers emphasized that standards-based education was responsible for making them consider curriculum areas that they might not have previously thought of. Student skills figured prominently in all of the discussions related to curriculum. Other prominent codes in the discussion included adapting and modifying curriculum, and finally access, even though most of the teachers did not actually make use of the term, as previously noted.

The teachers' definitions of curriculum showed both similarities and differences. The similarities in definitions indicated that teachers saw curriculum as a framework or a guide to what children needed to know. Kristie noted that curriculum was also a blueprint for what she needed to be teaching. Charlotte described curriculum as a framework for what children needed to know. Marie and Carlene also thought of curriculum in these terms but both added additional dimensions to the topic. Marie clearly stressed the fact that there was a significant element of a state mandate incorporated into curriculum. This was exemplified in her emphasis on both the state frameworks and the Curriculum Resource Guide, a document that breaks each educational standard down into its components parts and provides ideas concerning making those standards available to all students in school. Marie saw this guide as her most important curriculum tool. Charlotte mentioned the Curriculum Guide as well. However, for her the Curriculum Guide was more associated with completing alternate assessments rather than a piece of the curriculum. Carlene emphasized an additional dimension to curriculum by noting that it can be school dictated, but at the same time, sometimes dictated on your own. She also spoke of student ability to complete a task as being important in selecting curriculum activities.

The teachers often spoke of the necessity of creating curriculum. For some, this was a small-scale task. For others, the creation of curriculum was major. There was first the Individual Education Plan and then the mandate to incorporate standards-based instruction into that document. Carlene was the first of the teachers to note the teachers sometimes dictate that curriculum, and all, but Charlotte, provided examples of acting on this dimension. Kristie pointed out that she frequently takes the important topics in the curriculum and then adapts them to the books and the writing that her students are currently working on. That Charlotte did not mention this aspect of curriculum is likely a function of the fact that she is new to her teaching position (as well as being the newest teacher participating in the study). Marie provided her often student-driven current events curriculum, a curriculum that evolved out of a specific moment in her teaching.

Each of the teachers spoke of both adapting and modifying curriculum either explicitly or implicitly. Both Kristie and Charlotte, and to a much lesser degree, Carlene spoke of access. As noted in the descriptions of the students and the classroom, that not all teachers used the term access or even seemed to be aware of its existence is of special interest. Kristie and Charlotte were the only teachers in the group to make consistent use of the term "access" in the context of general education curriculum, though Carlene did mention it in passing. The teachers displayed different understandings and uses of the term.

Marie is the first to make mention of the concept of practicing various curricular skills. Thinking of the need to practice skills, a concept greatly emphasized in a recent course of differentiating instruction for special needs students, leads me to wonder about the true feasibility of practice such as Marie describes. Such practice works for the students that Kristie and Charlotte work with. Practice can also be effective for the students that Marie and Carlene work with, though it loses some effectiveness. Practice as noted here works less well for the students with Betty and Jeri. Their students require enormous amounts of practice to learn the simplest of skills. One possible reason for difficulties associated with the effectiveness of practice may be the sizeable amount of material that constitutes school curriculum. It is frequently difficult to provide sufficient practice given the rate at which the general education curriculum moves.

Within the area of providing general education curriculum to students, Marie is the first teacher to describe incorporating the alternate version of the state assessment into her everyday practice. (The alternate version of the state assessment is a portfolio assessment version of the standard test. Many students in substantially separate placements become involved in completing it.) She assigns one of her paraprofessionals to work on its organization daily. This focus has two points of importance. The first point of importance is that alternate assessment requires a significant amount of time to complete. The second point is that alternate assessment becomes increasingly difficult to complete depending on the grade level at which one teaches. Teachers working with older students, those entering fifth and sixth grade must focus on both different and additional curricular areas. That is, in addition to constructing portfolios for math and reading, these teachers may be required to also complete portfolio work in science and technology and history and social science.

Providing such a range of instruction can be difficult and may be implicated in the removal of students with special needs from general education settings. First, the instruction in the general education classroom becomes increasingly more complex and thus harder for students with special needs. Second, it becomes necessary to group students in to a classroom where the required instruction can be provided. Students may need to be removed in order to address the subject areas needed to complete the portfolio. This poses considerable additional difficulty that is closely related to managing an already overburdened curriculum load. Marie's alternate assessment situation also characterizes Jeri's teaching efforts. She too has students at multiple portfolio levels in her classroom.

Several of the teachers discussed the importance of having curriculum materials. Many of the teachers made mention of the variety of purchased programs that they had access to. Such programs consisted of curricular materials that were geared to students with special needs or that were useful in providing standards-based education. These programs included such materials as the Edmark Reading Program or The Hands-On Reading Curriculum that Betty spoke of. More prominently, several of the teachers spoke of not always being included in the ordering of curricular materials, which while a potential oversight, often impacts their ability to provide and modify general education curriculum. In my own personal experience, new curriculum materials are not always provided for special education teachers. Teachers' resources may or may not be available. In support of this, I was presented with the situation of teaching reading to a student working on or above grade level who could not be in a general education classroom because of behavioral issues. I was supposed to do this without the third grade reading series, with a schedule that placed me out of the classroom for approximately 50% of the school day, and with my usual caseload of students with significant to moderate cognitive disabilities still in tact. Situations such as these, though not intended to be intentional, emphasize that there is often a lack of equity in the situations experienced by special education teachers.

The new special education teacher frequently acquires whatever the departing special education teacher left behind. Carlene found it necessary to spend considerable time searching out material to use to develop her curriculum. Her comments lend support to an interpretation that the special education classroom can be very much a reflection of the current teacher's decisions or beliefs. Her description of her classroom material situation certainly implies that the special education classroom often became what the teacher brought with her. This shows up clearly in Jeri's situation. She completely reconfigured the purpose of the classroom when she entered it. This is certainly different from the new general education teacher who enters the classroom with the school's curriculum and a basic set of curriculum supplies, at the very least.

Carlene's description of materials and their impact on curriculum remind me of yet another personal example of the curriculum issues that a special education teacher might face. Several years ago, I contacted my district's curriculum director for a copy of the revised district curriculum as well as copies of the standards based units that had been created as part of the current professional development initiative. My request was greeted by several seconds of silence and then, "Well, what do you need that for?" I answered, "So that I could create modifications and adaptations of the unit activities." I never received a copy of the curriculum or the units. I was left with the impression that the need for modifying and adapting curriculum for students with special needs remains a misunderstood topic. This is an impression that has not changed over time. Further, the idea of adapting curriculum is an issue that affects students with all levels of special needs; this is not an issue that affects only students with moderate or significant cognitive or learning disabilities.

The term "access" surfaces again and is of specific interest for two reasons. I would have expected that all of the teachers would have made consistent use of the term, given that this is one of the primary goals of being a special education teacher. "Access to the general education curriculum" is a current axiom of the special education version of standards-based instruction. I specifically expected the use of this term with Betty and Jeri, more so than the other teachers in the group. Instead, Betty stresses the individualized nature of curriculum for students such as hers, while Jeri stresses individualization that lacks perspective. That is, Jeri provided several examples of previous curriculum provided by other teachers that was non-functional. As already noted, "access to general education" is a term often associated with students having significant cognitive disabilities and increasingly more documented in the literature. Related to this and possibly of the greatest interest in the discussion was Carlene's comment that she would rather integrate bits and pieces of curriculum materials and adapt rather than access. This lack of use of "access" potentially emphasizes that in addition to the divide between general education and special education, there is a significant divide within special education. Special education teachers define their own terminology differently.

All six teachers generally thought in terms of equating curriculum and standards as they responded to interview questions. None noted a significant difference between the two topics. Standards provided the content for the curriculum that their districts used. Curriculum content and assessment were essentially separate topics. The notion of performance assessment really did not emerge until the teachers began talking about the negative impact of participating in the state assessment process, as it currently exists.

The Individual Education Plan enters the discussion of curriculum here. Both Betty and Jeri open their curriculum discussions with a consideration of the IEP. Betty's comment regarding her desk as a place to securely hold her IEPs is notable both for its humor and for what it says about the tasks that the special education teachers must cope with. While the IEP is the major document of special education, her comment about it being filed safely indicates that it is by no means all that the special education teacher manages in a typical day in the classroom. Betty knows the contents of her IEPs but also must attend to the overall organization of the school day.

The emphasis that is typically placed on meeting individualized goals of an IEP may be significant in configuring special education classrooms. Students with special needs may be placed outside of a general education classroom because of the perception that they must learn prerequisite skills before being allowed to enter that classroom or because the activities of a general education classroom may be seen as beyond the abilities, and therefore inappropriate for the student with special needs. Further, too much emphasis on individualization may preclude the opportunity to create some essence of a standardized curriculum. There is little sense of the concept of making the curriculum fit the student. Curriculum from the special education perspective would best be seen as a malleable item that can adapt to those that it is designed to serve. One does not always get the sense that this is the case in general education settings.

As the teachers' discussions of curriculum and standards show more clearly, there is a separate well-developed language associated with special education that is quite different from that used in general education. Special education teachers speak in terms of accommodations and modifications, of adapting and modifying schoolwork, of access to the curriculum, of entry points and access skills, of data collection. They do not, as a point of emphasis, speak of differentiated instruction, a current major theme of general education instruction. This well-developed language of instruction in special education is separate from the language of instruction in general education. It can be difficult for special educators and general educators to communicate effectively.

The topic of standards-based assessment, and more specifically, alternate assessment brings new codes to the study. These codes included attitudes toward the state assessment, concerns toward the state assessment, and a separate assessment language. This separate assessment language is further incorporated into that larger language of special education. As previously noted, that language provides a significant point of separation between the special education system and the general education system.

The teachers have clearly developed thoughts regarding the impact that standards-based assessment has had on their teaching. For the most part, their thoughts regarding such assessment are positive. All the teachers cited the fact that standards-based instruction had led them to improve their teaching, primarily by pushing them to see the possibility of teaching topics that they had not previously considered. Charlotte and Marie's thoughts stand out here. Charlotte stressed the importance of the state assessment and the training that she has received in increasing her ability to create learning opportunities for her students. She specifically noted the importance of the "entry point." Marie detailed the importance of the state Resource Guide in helping her to create educational opportunities for her students and in helping her to improve her level of accountability in her classroom. Carlene added the importance of the element of "the essence of the standard"—the core concept embedded within a given standard to the discussion. The state has provided each special education teacher with this resource guide. It breaks each of the state standards down to its basic element and also provides examples of possible ways to present that concept to students with special needs. Yet, this text remains confined to special education departments rather than "marketed" and presented for general use in schools. In my own experience, the additional copies of the document that my district received initially were closed up in the special education office file cabinet and later returned to me to the "alternate assessment person" when that file space was needed. No attempt to disseminate the information to others in the school was made.

At the same time, the teachers also expressed specific concerns with the mandate to participate in the state assessments. The greatest concern noted by the teachers is the fact that the majority of students who participate in an alternate assessment are unable to pass that assessment. They are consequently going to be unable to graduate from high school in the present high-stakes testing environment of the state. Carlene further noted an issue with just how much students with greater cognitive disability understand of such instruction, especially as they move into middle school and beyond. Other concerns were related to the considerable amount of time that it takes to complete an alternate assessment and to issues with the fact that the assessment can be seen as a measure of how well the special education teacher can follow directions for producing a portfolio.

The teachers also spoke of the impact of curriculum and standards and professional development on their practice. There are few attempts in general education settings to link discussions of curriculum and standards to special education. There is no talk of linking the special education standards language to its general education standards language counterparts. That is, general education teachers are rarely aware of the concepts of access skills and entry points. Once again, we see the existence of different languages characterizing and separating disciplines that should co-exist. Unfortunately, the disciplines are instead somewhat mutually exclusive.

A similar statement of mutual exclusiveness between special education and general education can be made regarding professional development. A major element of this discussion was the teachers' emphasis on whether the offered professional development was appropriate. Generally speaking, the teachers felt that district professional development was not appropriate. Professional development offerings seldom fit into the activities that typically occurred in their classrooms. These discussions continued to support a growing conception that general education and special education are frequently separate entities in the same setting.

Interactions with General Education Teachers: Codes and Themes

The teachers' words yielded a series of codes that can be added to the development of answers to this study's questions addressing special education teachers' practice and experience. Again, as in the previous sections, several data codes important to the topic of interactions with general education teachers were present across all teachers while other codes were mentioned minimally. The teachers sometimes used different terms to describe similar concepts or situations. Their individual codes were contracted into a reduced list of essential codes. The codes addressing interaction with general education teachers are summarized in Table 7.3.

All of the teachers spoke of the factors that impacted their interactions with the general education teachers with whom they regularly worked. They eloquently commented on the importance of the notion of invitation into the general education classroom and the openness of the general education teacher

Table 7.3 Essential Data Codes: Teachers' Characterizations of Their Interactions with General Education Teachers

Codes	Frequency of Teachers
factors impacting (invitation/openness)	6
communication	5
inclusion	3
implementation	3
planning	3

toward students with special needs. When the students with special needs and special education teacher felt welcome in the classroom, the students enjoyed greater integration into the life of the classroom. If the students and teachers felt less welcome by the general education teacher, the level of integration was less. This was well illustrated by the treatment Kristie's students in their reading class. The students were less welcome; less integration into the activities of the classrooms was apparent. Additionally, the majority of their interactions with the general education teacher were punitive in nature [from LF's observations]. At the same time, her third grade students who were welcomed in the classroom enjoyed a much more positive experience.

The Observations: Codes and Themes

The observations were notable for three concepts important to this study. While additional specific teacher roles (e.g. advocate and cheerleader) began to emerge from the interview data, the observations significantly expanded the number of roles that special education teachers occupied across their practice. These roles ranged from communicator to entrepreneur to cheerleader to manager to interpreter. Each teacher occupied different role sets. Where they occupied similar roles, those roles were structured by the settings in which the teachers taught. Table 7.4 summarizes the variety of roles that these special education teachers must play as they go about their teaching.

Several of the roles that the teachers occupy stand out. These include the roles of advocate, creator, and manager. Student advocacy is deeply ingrained in all that these special education teachers do in a given school day. All of the teachers participating in the study work to meet the identified needs of their students. Fulfilling this objective often requires communicating with general education teachers, cheering students on for successes of any degree or magnitude, and assisting students in behaving appropriately. The most important aspect of their advocacy role is communicating the importance of including students with special needs into general education classrooms. However, as the study findings indicate, the advocacy role is best developed in Kristie's situation. She speaks directly of advocating for students and also makes note of having to become more aggressive in her efforts to get her students better included into their general education classrooms. At the same time, it is important to note that this role

is perhaps easier for her because she normally teaches students with high incidence disabilities, those students who typically have increased access to general
education settings from the outset.

Table 7.4 Special Education Teacher Roles

Roles	Frequency of Teachers	Roles	Frequency of Teachers
manager	6	creator	4
intermediary	6	director	3
enforcer	6	consultant	3
cheerleader	6	entrepreneur	1
coach	6	aggressor	1
advocate	5		

The need for such advocacy is perhaps of greater necessity for other teachers participating in the study. This might be especially true for teachers of students with greater handicaps. It becomes more difficult to see the efficacy of
including such students in general education classes. Meeting the challenge of
increasing inclusion is often more of a battle. The advocate role is additionally
important for its potent impact on school philosophy. For example, Kristie saw it
as her responsibility to aggressively pursue inclusion for her students. Her desire
was to make sure that other teacher, especially her fourth grade reading teacher,
got on board with the school philosophy of inclusion.

Other prominent roles for these teachers included curriculum creator and director. In many instances, these teachers found themselves simultaneously in
roles of creator and director. They were faced with creating and delivering curriculum and also with the additional task of directing several assistants as their
teaching plans were put into action. This duality frequently complicated the
work that these teachers did. The role of manager was important to all six teachers but perhaps best developed in Betty's case. Betty had to manage her complicated staffing schedule in addition to her teaching activities.

Conclusions

The students and their actions are clearly evident in the activities that occur
in a special education setting. What their teachers chose to do in the classroom
shape and define their experiences. Those experiences are influenced by the
challenges noted throughout the interviews. The multiple concerns, pressures,
and frustrations noted by the teachers point to significant tension in the practice
of special education. There can be an initial impression that a special education
setting is disorganized and lacking in coherent routines; an impression that leads
to the notion of chaos. However, this impression of chaos is far from the reality
of the situation. The most important task of the special education teacher is the
management of the chaos that can ensue in a special education classroom or

setting and additionally as special education attempts to interact with general education.

The analysis presented here led to the development of themes important to the practice of being a special education teacher and essential to the study's central question—how does being a special education teacher manifest itself in the broader world of elementary general education? The study data produced three major themes—the elements of special education teacher practice, a significant sense of tension between general education and special education, and a distinct separation between the special education and general education systems. Additionally, the interactions that occur between special education and general education are often dominated by a notion of general education teacher power.

As a whole, the teachers' descriptions of their practice reveal the great student variability with which they must contend. This variability may begin with meeting academic needs—the typical business of schooling, but it extends far beyond just academic needs. This is perhaps best illustrated by the task of incorporating standards-based instruction into the instruction provided for Betty's students and to lesser extent Jeri's students. Both teachers have students working at an access level of skills. It is difficult to see the connection between academics and physical and social needs with these students and it is certainly valid to ask what the point of standards-based instruction might be for these students? On the other hand, student variability is also an issue for Kristie and Charlotte. In their situations, the ability to engage in academics is more recognizable, yet, the students still struggle significantly with making the ideal kind of school progress—that of grade-level progress. Carlene and Marie confront such student variability from yet another angle. In both situations, and especially, in Marie's, their classrooms may have to serve students of similar disability but at greatly different cognitive levels. So Marie finds herself doing fifth grade science with the majority of her class and having to find ways for her significantly cognitively handicapped students to participate in that instruction.

The teachers' descriptions of curriculum enhance their descriptions of their students and their classrooms. Curriculum becomes just as variable as the different students that come into public education. These different curricular needs add another dimension to the practice of special education teachers. These teachers spend a considerable portion of their time creating the materials that they use to teach. Special education teachers are also faced with the larger problem of meeting their students' complex arrangement of needs in less time than general education teachers are typically provided with. The practice of these teachers is structured by a variety of scheduling concerns. These concerns frequently dictate the effectiveness of the services that are provided to students with special needs. Additionally, the pace of classroom instruction can seriously impact meeting needs especially for those students with greater academic capability.

The data show that special education teachers have specific teacher roles that they must play in schools and general education classrooms. Their traditional roles include support teacher, student advocate, coach, and classroom teacher. Each one of these roles is further broken down into finer gradations of activity and sometimes the roles overlap. In the role of support person, the special educator first assists the student with the work that the classroom teacher assigns. This is what is typically seen when the special education teacher is working in a more inclusive setting. Kristie could often be seen in this role. Charlotte's practice also demonstrated many examples of providing student support. The overlapping nature of being the classroom teacher as well as the support teacher characterized the practices of Carlene, Marie, Jeri, and Betty. The ideal classroom role in the inclusive setting was the co-teacher. This was defined as being an active equal, "seamless", part of the classroom instruction. Being a "seamless part of the classroom" is a position that Kristie clearly aspires to. Sadly, she was the only teacher who was able to achieve any real degree of such opportunity to be fully included in the classroom.

The roles that special education teachers occupy are significantly increased when the observation data are examined. Further, these roles are often subservient to the organizational structure of the general education classroom. The special educator's power is limited when compared to that held by general education teachers. Their practice is often structured by meeting the needs of the general education teachers with whom they work or perhaps to whom they are assigned. Both Kristie and Charlotte provide examples of this. Kristie's level of integration is different in each classroom in which she provides services. Charlotte occupies a significantly subservient role in her classroom at this point in time.

Based on the information provided by Kristie, Charlotte, Marie, Carlene, Betty, and Jeri, it can be noted that there is a distinct sense of separation between the systems of special education and general education in public schools. Special education teachers often exist in a world that is subservient to the larger world of general education—there is typically one school but two systems. Further, various tensions permeated the data analysis. These tensions characterized every area of teacher practice discussed in the study. Specific concerns were identified by each of the teachers participating in the study.

Kristie's primary issues were related to issues with her interactions with her general education peers. Many of the other teachers spoke of behavior problems as major issues. (Kristie did make mention of behavior as well. However, such issues were not primary for her.) Charlotte made numerous mention of problems related to behavior management. Special education frequently becomes the setting for those students who have difficulties behaving. Added to this were her concerns with a lack of administrative support. Marie's experience with Greg illustrated the behavioral concern. His refusal to work as well as his physical needs made her question the appropriateness of his placement in her classroom. She also experienced behavioral issues with several of the students in her classroom. However, she appeared to accept such behavior as more of a given. Carlene also spoke of issues of behavior. However, her comments were related to the idea of student behavior as a major criterion for placement decisions in her district rather than to needs and methods of behavior management.

Of all the teachers participating in the study, Jeri had the most difficult behavioral issues to deal with. One student in her classroom was very difficult to manage and on one occasion destroyed the classroom during a lengthy and intense episode of non-compliance. Jeri and the class were left to manage this student and try to keep the classroom running for the majority of this time. It was only after two continuous days of such behavior that the administration intervened.

Yet, despite the fact that Betty's practice was also rife with behavioral concerns, this was not her chief issue. The larger issue for Betty was coping with her complicated staffing schedule. Managing that schedule made life in the classroom very disorganized and at times chaotic. At the same time, Betty was not alone in citing scheduling concerns. For both Kristie and Charlotte, schedule issues interfered with time to communicate with general education teachers and with professional development opportunities. Charlotte could frequently not attend grade level meetings because either she or her staff were doing general education duties. Kristie had to choose between her two assigned grade levels when considering grade level meetings. Jeri also experienced issues with scheduling, but more so with staffing in general. She frequently found herself in the position of trying to schedule extra special classes for her students as documented in the students Individual Education Plans. However, she often encountered difficulties in achieving this as a result of teacher contracts and teacher acceptance. But the major issue for her was the lack of a classroom paraprofessional. While she had several additional adults in the classroom, they were there in the capacity of providing 1:1 assistance to her students. This typically made it impossible for them to provide her assistance with creating learning materials for the students. Also of issue for Jeri was the fact that sometimes the paraprofessionals invoked their role as 1:1 assistants as an excuse for refusing to assist in the reinvention of the classroom, something that they did not completely understand.

Carlene's significant issues came about from having to build a resource of classroom materials. She had noted that when she went to her classroom, there were virtually no materials available. Other teachers echoed her concerns with the lack of materials. For the most part, this lack of materials took the form of not having copies of teacher manuals or the practice materials for district curriculum. She also expressed particular concern with the role that the state assessment played in what she had to accomplish.

All of the teachers talked about issues with curriculum. The teachers generally noted concern with issues of curriculum development, modification, and pacing. Curriculum development became a much greater issue as the student's functioning levels were considered. Betty and Jeri frequently had a very difficult time creating a meaningful curriculum that balanced the students' physical and social needs with accessing the general education curriculum. The notion of accessing the general education curriculum was also frequently left undefined and so these teachers created activities that they perceived as being consistent with the general education curriculum. All of the teachers had issues with interacting with general education around curriculum and its delivery. Keeping pace with the general education curriculum was a significant concern for the majority of the teachers.

The tensions identified by the teachers existed within each component of the normative model of education used to structure the study. Further, the tensions identified by the teachers exist both within the special education system and outside that system as it worked to integrate itself into the larger general education system in which it exists. These tensions are summarized in Table 7.5.

Table 7.5 Tensions Within Special Education and General Education

Normative Model	Tensions	Major Issues
I. Curriculum	content	materials administer vs. create
	skills	can do, cannot do ought to do
	accessing standards	validity of access expectations to perform at grade level
	adapting/modifying differentiation language of standards	appropriateness
	purposes of education	definitions life skills access to general education curriculum
	needs vs. pre-determined curriculum	
	curriculum creativity	degree of creativity knowing what to include individual creation
II. Teacher Actions	communication opportunity teacher power	lack of time to be included

III. Instruction and Learning	content	adapting/modifying
	placement	
	behavior	
	creating curriculum	
	lack of materials	
	special education students vs. general education students	your students/my students
IV. Evaluation and Assessment	state assessment	
	passing courses and graduating	
V. IEP	goals and objectives	
	integration/inclusion	
	purpose of education	role of context

Summary

These teachers all struggled with extensive student variability, curriculum issues, and instructional questions within their classrooms. As the interviews have shown, the teachers here confronted their own questions of teaching students with disabilities that were unlike those they normally taught. The teachers all labored to create and also to deliver curriculum for their students. They worked diligently to provide appropriate instruction for their students even in those situations where it was clearly evident that it would take years for the skills attempted to be acquired. They questioned their efficacy—were they missing important aspects of the general education curriculum as they worked with their students? The interaction of these areas of tension in the classroom could be perceived as chaotic—especially to the outside observer The tensions that began in special education settings were only amplified as special education teachers interacted with the general education settings in which they taught.

Special education's attempts to integrate itself into the general education system tended to increase the level of perceived tension as well as to intensify the separation between the two systems. All the teachers recounted stories of trying to balance standards-based instruction and assessment, keeping pace with the general education curriculum, and most poignantly of requiring invitation into general education classrooms. They contended with difficult student behaviors on a daily basis, behaviors that typically resulted in quick removal from the general education classroom. They often questioned their understanding and knowledge of curriculum. They were very concerned about not forgetting important curricular topics. They struggled with communicating instructional information and philosophy. District resources and the perception of separate educational mandates significantly impacted the level of tension that existed between the two systems.

In summary, this study has used the voices of special education teachers to describe teaching practice. These special educators provided information regarding the nature of their teaching practice as well as identified a series of tensions that created a sense of chaos in that practice. They further emphasized the fact that special education and general education exist as two separate cultures in many public schools. The final chapter of this book focuses on the answers to the study questions, suggests a "managed chaos" model of practice for the special education teachers and offers recommendations for managing the chaos and the separation that currently exists in educational settings.

Chapter Eight
Special Education Teacher Practice—Managed Chaos

"I recall watching Ed Sullivan when I was little. A semi-regular performer on the show was this man who spun plates on long thin poles. He would spin more and more plates and run back and forth among them trying to keep them from crashing to the floor and shattering. That's what teaching in special education can be like...you run from plate to plate trying to keep the thing in proper motion...(L. Ferrelli, author, 2007).

This study had its roots in a personal examination of the fit between core concepts of educational theory and practice and special education. Its purpose has grown and in the end, become two-fold. The first purpose was to tell a personal story of being a special education teacher and finding some answer as to how those core concepts of educational theory and practice fit into my own special education experience. As I engaged in this task, I realized that I was telling not just a personal story, but also a story for an under-represented group of teachers. And so, the second and larger purpose of the study was to examine the experience of other special education teachers. What story did their experiences tell? Did those experiences match those that I have had? How?

Study Questions Answered

As all teachers do, special education teachers go about the business of educating the students that they serve in several ways. The pilot study focused on how teacher practice developed over time. It set the stage for developing a deeper understanding of the experiences of general education teachers and was used to build the framework for this study of special education teachers. Special education teachers clearly had a role to play in general education settings. That there was a connection between general education and special education was articulated in the pilot study teachers' discussions of the students that they regularly encountered. Both pilot study teachers exerted significant effort to educate the students, with or without disabilities that they were presented with. And, it was those students with disabilities that often presented the greatest challenges to teacher practice. As I analyzed the data from the pilot study, I continued to think in terms of achieving a greater understanding of special education teacher practice. The special education teachers who took part in this study came to special education through personal experience and through a desire to work with students that were often left on the periphery of the general education settings in which they participated. Their words show that they think deeply about their place in the current world of elementary education.

This study has allowed me to illuminate the practice of special education teachers through their words and their actions. The work was initially conceived to answer questions related to participation in an alternate assessment process for students with special needs and special education teachers' belief systems related to that topic. It became a larger study of special education teacher practice.

What do special education teachers think and do as they educate the students they work with? First and foremost, these teachers think of their students and what they need in order to become learned and functional members of society. They clearly believe that students with special needs are able to learn whatever material they set out to teach. For the most part, the teachers believe that they have a valid role in the general education system, though their words often indicate a significant separation from that system. It is important to note that they do not all espouse total inclusion. The hope of inclusion for their students is always considered a worthy goal. Yet, they are comfortable with the still standard student placement continuum and the idea that not every student may be able to be included in a general education classroom. These teachers see themselves as advocates for their students though they do not all specifically use that term to describe what they do for students as they work to include them in general education. These teachers act as communicators, as liaisons between their world of special education and the larger world of general education. They provide the materials, strategies, and information concerning how to work with students with special needs. They work diligently to educate other professionals concerning the needs of students with disabilities. Ultimately, they provide voice for those students who cannot speak for themselves. Thus, advocacy is an important component of special education teacher practice.

These teachers understand that there is a specific power structure in the current educational system and that they are often in the position of having to work within and around that power structure. This is best illustrated in their words concerning their interactions with the general education teachers with whom they regularly work. Ultimately though, these teachers believe that the system can be and perhaps should be improved. Better integration for all students with special needs is possible through combined effort aimed at integration with the world of general education.

The concept of teacher belief systems became operationalized in terms of teacher practice. More specifically, the important questions became: 1) what were the elements of special education teachers' daily practice, 2) what do the experiences and resulting practice for these teachers look like and what factors were similar or different in special education teachers' experiences, and finally, 3) how did current reform initiatives in standards-based education and accountability impact practice?

1) What are the elements of special education teachers' daily practice? Special education practice is built upon the ideas of *support and flexibility*. The teachers in this study had one overarching purpose—supporting their students as they negotiated their school days. Providing that student support was built on flexibility. The participating teachers were required to fit into the special education and inclusion systems in place in their schools. Fitting into these school-based systems was two-fold. The teachers were well aware of the existing power structures in their schools and in general education. All of them related stories that reflected an understanding of where and how their students fit into the general working of the school. This typically took the form of showing understanding of scheduling and student placement issues. At the same time, the teachers were also aware of the fact that fitting into a general education classroom was sometimes centered on the desires of the general education teachers with whom they worked. General education teachers were open or not so open to the presence of students with special needs in their classrooms. Feeling invited into the general education classroom and being a part of the activities of that classroom determined whether the students with special needs and their teachers felt accepted into that classroom.

As indicated by the study data, feeling accepted into the general education classroom was highly valued by the teachers and often impacted the learning that occurred for their students. The importance of such acceptance was best illustrated by Kristie's words concerning being a "seamless part" of the activities occurring in the classroom and by Charlotte's recognition that her day went more smoothly when the general education teacher readily accepted the presence of her students with special needs in the classroom.

The role that acceptance into the general education classroom played in the education of the students with special needs was also well illustrated throughout the teacher observations. This was especially true of Kristie's students. The students in her classes were treated differently as a result of the classroom teacher's interest in inclusive practices. As previously noted, the students in the third grade classroom were best integrated into classroom activities. The only item

differentiating their literature circle from the rest of the class's literature circles
was the fact that they were working on an easy-reader chapter book. In the
fourth grade math class, her students gradually got more involved in participating in the class geometry lesson. However, in the fourth grade reading class,
most of the interactions between the classroom teacher and these students were
disciplinary in nature. Kristie remained somewhat on the sidelines of any activities in that classroom.

Charlotte's first grade situation also provided evidence for the importance
of acceptance, in this case, the response to a difficult student. Aaron spent much
of his time trying to get a reaction from either the classroom teacher or from
Charlotte. Neither teacher typically responded to his inappropriate behavior.
They did, however, always make a point of responding to any appropriate classroom behavior. Aaron was accepted regardless of his behavior. Thus special
education teacher practice was significantly impacted by acceptance from the
larger general education system.

Student *variability* characterizes the practice of special education teachers.
The teachers in this study work with a vast range of student ability. Kristie and
Charlotte work with students who are characterized as "below grade level"; students working below grade level typically can work with standard curriculum
materials. At the same time, Betty and Jeri work with students who are learning
to walk and to communicate with individuals around them. Yet, both pairs of
teachers are working within the same current mandate to access the general education curriculum and to show progress within that curriculum.

These teachers have all mastered whatever situation they find themselves in
and must adapt to the students that are placed in their care. The students that
they regularly work with can vary greatly in ability and in behavioral need. Students with behavioral issues often cause the greatest difficulty for the special
education teacher. These teachers are frequently looked to for curing students'
behavioral issues. All of the teachers participating in the study have students
with behavioral issues. Kristie worked with *the* "behavior problem of the
school". This was the student that refused to complete the majority of his
schoolwork despite the fact that he was capable of doing so. Charlotte had
Aaron who was often in control of any academic activity presented. Betty had
several students in her classroom that displayed aggressive behaviors, as did
Jeri. While the idea of *adaptation* also characterizes general education teachers,
the primary difference between the two is that general education teachers have
some ability to choose the students that they work with while special education
teachers do not.

Many of the teachers shared stories that illustrated that fact that general
education teachers have a certain degree of informal power in determining the
make-up of their classes. There are procedures in place in the general education
system that allow general education teachers to initiate new placements for students exhibiting academic issues or problematic behavior. These students can be

referred and are sometimes picked up for special education service. While such placement circumstances are usually behavioral in nature—a student's actions may be so problematic that he or she disrupts an entire class, removal from classes can and still does occur as a result of low cognitive ability. Such ability to choose the students with whom you work is less common in the world of special education but not unheard of. For example, recall that Marie was concerned about Greg's presence in her classroom. As it turned out, Greg was sent to a new placement, one that was considered "more appropriate" for him, as the observations were concluded.

Special education teacher practice is further characterized by *perseverance*. The teachers in this study often work with the same group of students over several years. In following their students from grade to grade, they note the slow progress that many groups of students with special needs make. These teachers become adept at presenting and representing instruction until they find that one method that works for that one particular student. This is the essence of adaptation, modification, and accommodation. Perseverance is also exemplified in the teachers' dealings with the students with behavioral issues. These teachers typically stay with the students throughout the difficult episodes and constantly work to assist them with learning to control their inappropriate behaviors. As the data have shown, it is often those student behaviors and their management that are primary elements in the perception of a chaotic nature of special education practice.

Like general education teachers, special education teachers work closely with curriculum. Such curriculum work poses interesting issues for the special education teacher. Perhaps the most basic issue in such work is that special education teachers can rarely pick up the designated curriculum or teacher's guide and teach the scheduled lesson. Thus, special education teacher practice is characterized by curriculum *creativity*. Some degree of accommodation or modification is always necessary for students with special needs. The degree of accommodation can range from simple modification of existing activities to intensive adaptation of those activities to completely different curriculums. Marie's experience with her current events curriculum provides the best example of this. She created an entire curriculum model for her students. A variation on this understanding of curriculum creativity is the fact that special education teachers often find themselves in a position of having to reinvent themselves within the context of the students that enter their classrooms. Both Marie and Carlene experienced this as their classroom populations changed across time.

In addition, the special education teacher frequently has to determine what components of the school curriculum can be presented to his or her students. Teachers working with students who have greater cognitive ability often find managing general education curriculum an easier task than teachers working with students who have greater impairments. Several of the teachers in the study offer stories of their concern with whether or not they selected correctly from among the vast array of curriculum choices. Teaching methodology literature in special education often speaks to the notion of "cutting the clutter"—reducing curriculum to its essential elements but offers little in the way of procedural guidance for completing such a task. Further, such activities often occur with little district or individual school guidance. There is a limited mind-set regarding adapting and modifying curriculum in the daily workings of general education. The typical response remains—the student with special needs cannot do the work, why should he or she be subjected to the pain of trying?

A final important element to special education teacher practice is *advocacy*. The teachers in this study all functioned as student advocates. They provide material, strategies, and information concerning how best to educate students with special needs. They may provide voice for students who are seldom heard. All of the teachers participating in this study actively thought of their students' feelings concerning having special needs. Kristie and Charlotte both expressed significant concern about how their students reacted to their special needs. Marie wondered whether Greg understood that her classroom was the best place for him. Carlene spoke of the importance of feeling safe during the education process. When her students felt safe with their environment, behavioral issues were less likely to occur. Further, all six teachers made efforts to interpret the meaning of their students' needs and as well as their behaviors as they negotiated including those students in general education classrooms.

But the most important aspect of the element of advocacy in special education teacher practice lies in the fact that all of these teachers work to "sell" their students to the larger world of general education. These teachers actively seek out general education teachers who are experienced with working or who are willing to learn to work with students with special needs. This can provide a significant teaching challenge to the world of general education, especially if the students with special needs are significantly cognitively involved as is shown by Betty and Jeri's experiences.

In summary, special education teaching situations—whether in general education classrooms or in special education classrooms are composed of significant variability, support, flexibility, the degree of acceptance, adaptation, creativity, perseverance, and advocacy. Each of these characteristics is constantly in play. Students and activities typically exhibit greatly divergent levels; levels that often display greater range than is found in the general education classroom. Some students may be working on addition and subtraction while other students are just developing beginning counting ability. Some students may be working on answering literal comprehension questions while other students are learning the letter-sound correspondence essential to literacy at the same time. Special education teachers further do not always find themselves in equitable situations in public schools. The task of accessing the general education curriculum is similar for all teachers but the accomplishment of that task can be seriously hampered by not having access to the same materials that general education teachers.

2) *What do the experiences and the resulting practice for these teachers look like? What factors are similar or different in special education teachers' experiences?* The experiences and practices of these teachers are influenced and shaped by their students and the settings in which they teach. The findings presented in this study demonstrate how variability, desire for acceptance, perseverance, adaptability, creativity, and advocacy led to greatly different teaching situations. Context is clearly important in the individual practices of these special education teachers. The primary difference among the teachers in this study is the type of student with whom they generally work. A typical range of student with special needs is represented in the variety of classrooms that the teachers work in. That range of student and classroom covers the special education service continuum. There are students in inclusion-based classrooms, students in self-contained classrooms geared toward academic resource, and students functioning in the severe range of cognitive development, students working on developing access skills. My own experience as a special education teacher falls between the students in a low-academic ability self-contained model and students who are in the severe cognitive range of student ability. Different teaching contexts result in different teaching experiences.

The teachers in this study demonstrate different needs regarding presenting and creating curriculum. Kristie and Charlotte are able to use the district's general education curriculum and supplement with lower level materials that are matched to the students' ability levels and the required skills. Marie and Carlene have some of this ability but the frequency with which they are able to do this begins to decrease. Carlene expresses the issues related to creating curriculum best when she comments that she prefers creating her own curriculum. The most important criterion in such creation of curriculum is her assessment of whether she believes that her students will be able to learn a presented skill. Marie also expresses her issues with presenting curriculum clearly when she notes that she cannot just pick up a curriculum guide and say, "Okay, we'll do this lesson today in math." Betty and Jeri have the toughest task with regard to general education curriculum. They are faced with the problem of not only selecting topic areas from the general education curriculum, but also with significantly adapting those activities so that their students can participate in the activities. Both teachers have distinct examples of making this work for them. Communication and assistive technology is embedded into all of Betty's group oriented activities as was demonstrated throughout her observations. The students are familiar with the use of photographs, line drawings, and voice output devices to interact with their peers as they work in groups such as morning meeting or calendar. In Jeri's case, she has created her "Trip Around the World" theme to develop a link between the geography curriculum that she is supposed to access and to life skills. The students develop food preparation skills as they prepare foods associated with the different countries. Food preparation and the skills that are associated with it are skills that the students will need as they become independent adults.

The teachers' experiences demonstrate the variability of service arrangement cited as in issue in the literature (Lipsky & Gartner, 1997; McLaughlin et al., 1998; Raber et al., 1998; Thompson et a., 2000). Kristie and Charlotte work in settings where there are currently no students functioning in the severe range of cognitive disability. Marie and Carlene each have one or two students in the most significant range of cognitive disability. Betty and Jeri have classrooms devoted to students with the most significant disabilities. The level of inclusion for all students is different for each teacher. Kristie and Charlotte are considered to be inclusion teachers. The other teachers experience inclusion on a more limited basis. And, as noted elsewhere, what is similar and significant in each case is that all the teachers express the importance of being invited into the general education classroom and that the quality of the inclusion experience for students with special needs in general education classrooms is often very much a function of the manner in which the district organizes their special education services.

Kristie's district holds the most promise for the continued development of inclusive philosophy. A major focus of its professional development is student-centered planning for students with special needs, a current cornerstone for developing viable inclusive models (Ford et al., 1989; Giangreco, Cloninger, & Iverson, 1998). This notion of person-centered planning from a primarily academic perspective is further documented in special education teacher methodology literature (Browder & Spooner, 2006; Downing, 2002; Janney & Snell, 2004). Each district talks about inclusion but so far has achieved varying levels for that inclusion. The notion of sorting the students according to their ability level is evident as you listen to the teachers speak of both current and past students. Interestingly, this talk is consistent with an idea that inclusion is appropriate for some students but not all. This idea still has viability, whether appropriate or not, in training programs for special education teachers. Students and teaching specialties are differentiated and as a result sorted. Further, the teachers in the study appear to feel comfortable with this tendency to sort students. The primary difference between Kristie's district and the other districts in the study is likely a function of the fact that at the moment, Kristie's district has no students considered to be severely cognitively handicapped in the true sense of the definition. That is to say, while the teachers all talk of certain students being "severely" handicapped, they use this phrase as a general descriptor of ability rather than using the phrase in a more official diagnostic capacity.

The variability in the district philosophy of service provision impacted the range of classrooms that I examined. Inclusion was most prominent in Kristie's setting. Charlotte experienced both inclusion and pull-out activities. As the students' needs became more involved, the degree of inclusion tended to decrease. Marie and Carlene were both in self-contained settings. They often had to seek out appropriate opportunities for interaction with the general education classes in their schools. Betty and Jeri had to "sell" their students in order to find inclusion opportunities. Yet, the districts in which these teachers taught offered philosophy statements considered to be inclusive. The range of inclusive experience presented here lends support to the notion that inclusion in actual practice is heavily influenced by a student's academic capability.

An observer unfamiliar with the world of special education might look in upon the different classroom situations and see disorganization, a lack of structure, and a sense of little connection with what is commonly considered to be the business of schooling—reading, writing, and arithmetic—especially as self-contained settings are considered. There appears to be limited consistency in a classroom where every student might be working on a different academic level, exhibiting behavior problems related to task completion or social competency. In addition, students who may be working on developing mobility, communication, or self-help skills can complicate the academic-oriented activities in such classrooms.

The impression of lack of organization is far from the reality of the situation in the classroom that serves students with special needs or for the inclusion specialist. As any classroom teacher does, the teachers in the study have specific strategies for organizing their classrooms. The concept of routines is prominent in each of the teachers' practices. Most of these teachers have established these routines for themselves. The classroom is their space. Their routines include schedules, transitions, and academic periods. They account for how the day and the activities are carried out.

The situation is slightly different for Kristie and Charlotte. Both must make themselves fit into the routines that are organized by the general education teachers with whom they work. This can go smoothly or not. Fitting into such pre-existing routines is potentially more difficult than having the opportunity to create individual personal routines. The degree of fit into those routines can impact the level of integration that the special education teacher is able to achieve for his or her students. Kristie expresses this best when she speaks of her students looking just like every other student in the general education classroom. In some classrooms, her students could not be singled out of the general mix of students; further, she often functioned as a co-teacher rather than as an assistant to the teacher.

But perhaps the most significant difference between the experiences of these special education teachers is related to student behaviors. Recall that each of the teachers related stories about different students with behaviors. They managed these behaviors with differing degrees of administrative support. All made note of the fact that student behavior seriously impacted student placement. The notion of placement was most prominent in the cases of Marie and Carlene. Both expressed the power of student behavior as determining whether or not a student might be able to "make it" in a general education classroom.

Academic ability played a role in this idea of "making it" in the general education classroom but its impact was much less significant for these teachers.

   *3) How do current reform initiatives in standards-based education and
accountability affect special education teacher practice?* As we know, there is
an extensive and well-developed literature on school reform (Cuban, 1993;
Kennedy, 2005; Kliebard, 1995; Lipsky & Gartner, 1997). Naturally, that reform
expands to the practice of special education. Given that the question of standards-based reform and assessment was the initial impetus for this study of special education practice, some note of the teachers' response to it remains warranted.

   In general, the teachers' interactions with standards is generally expressed
positively, despite major issues of coming to terms with how some of their students were going to demonstrate standard-based knowledge. All of the teachers
noted that the incorporation of standards into their teaching has improved that
teaching. Several broad thoughts are important here. Charlotte makes mention of
the fact that working on standards at a lower level than grade level is a valid use
of the standards. Carlene beautifully expresses the thought that standards have
made her more aware of teaching topics that she might not have previously
thought of. Betty supports this thought when she talks of her interaction with
standards. Marie brings the importance of accountability to the discussion. Standards have made her more accountable for the topics that she teaches. In the
past, she may have done units "for fun." Now, she expends great effort to gather
evidence to show just what her students have done with an assignment. The importance of this statement is not to be taken lightly. Collecting data and evidence
other than work samples to show progress, while a familiar component of special education methodology, is not necessarily as familiar to the world of general
education.

   Yet, important concerns with standards-based education and accountability
are expressed when the teachers discuss their interaction with these reform initiatives; the teachers have strong feelings regarding assessing their students with
special needs. It is clear that when the teachers are talking about standards, they
are talking about content standards. In general, the teachers see the mandate to
provide standards-based instruction as a method to have increased access to
general education curriculum. The concerns with standard-based education
come when the topic of accountability is introduced. Carlene speaks for several
of the teachers in the study as well as for many special education teachers in the
field when she expresses her thoughts about the negative impact that state assessment participation carries with it. Major issues remain with the fact that
many students with special needs simply cannot pass the test. The scoring system is not sensitive enough to allow for these students to pass. Further, the assessment is the key to whether or not a student graduates from high school.
These issues of not passing the test and the associated consequences become
more prominent when the teacher works with students who have greater aca-

demic ability. The issues are also there, but to a lesser degree, for teachers working with students who are significantly cognitively disabled.

Carlene also provides voice to questions of the purpose of state assessment participation as well as the validity of components of the teacher training for the alternate assessment. She is not alone when she points out that she can essentially determine her students' scores on an alternate assessment before she submits them. The alternate assessments do little to provide information that will assist the teacher in improving instruction beyond the previously noted expansion of curriculum content. Her comments regarding the validity of "accessing the standards" are important. Alternate assessment training examples provided by the state demonstrate students participating in a variety of standards. Carlene questions what these students really understand from such participation. Her questions suggest that even special education teachers may not fully understand the variability that students with special needs can display. There is a lack of understanding regarding teaching certain groups of students. This lack of understanding contributes to the potentially chaotic nature of special education in elementary schools. Further, the questions elicited as a result of participation in the state assessments only emphasize the separation between special education and its counterpart, general education. General education leaves one with the impression that curriculum and assessment are direct and easily scheduled and completed; while special education students remind us that this is not typically the case. What works for the student in general education is less likely to work as well for the student in special education.

The teachers' thoughts regarding the relationship between curriculum, standards, and professional development are particularly significant. All of the teachers make note of the fact that they would appreciate continued training in curriculum and standards. This is probably best expressed in the fact that all of the teachers state that they would like the opportunity to take part in grade level meetings. However, they are also comfortable with being separated from that professional development or with a lack of appropriate professional development training. These oversights in planning leave these teachers with time to complete tasks that they might otherwise not have time for. Carlene also emphasizes the importance of providing refresher training on making the best use of standards-based instruction. There is considerable truth in the fact that doing things in a familiar way can offset the full integration of standards-based instruction into everyday teaching.

As a group, these now "answered" questions formed the components of the overarching study question of the study—how does being a special education teacher manifest itself in the broader world of elementary education; stated more practically, how do special education teachers function in the general education settings in which they find themselves?

A Tale of Two Cultures

The data presented has allowed for the identification of several important themes in special education. These themes include *the elements of special education teacher practice, tension, chaos,* and ultimately *separation*. The multiple teacher concerns and frustrations that are documented within this study are elements that create the tension that characterizes special education teacher practice.

Multiple data codes identifying teacher concerns and frustrations are identified in the data. They led to the determination of tension as an important theme. These codes are summarized and ranked in importance in Table 8.1. The strongest tension related features noted by the teachers participating in the study included the challenges of being a special education teacher, the existence of a certain degree of informal teacher power, concerns over the ability of students with special needs to meet the performance requirements of standards-based education and state accountability systems, and the importance of feeing invited into the general education classroom.

Table 8.1 Summary of Essential Data Codes Indicating Tension in Special Education and General Education

Topic	Code	Rank
students/classrooms	challenges	high
students/classrooms	teacher power	high
students/classrooms	student attitudes	high
curriculum/standards	concerns	high
curriculum/standards	definitions	high
curriculum/standards	standards	high
curriculum/standards	teacher roles	high
curriculum/standards	state assessment	high
interaction with general education	factors/invitation	high
students/classrooms	admin. support	moderate
interaction with general education	inclusion	moderate
interaction with general education	implementation	moderate
interaction with general education	planning	moderate
students/classrooms	curriculum/standards	low
students/classrooms	access	low
curriculum/standards	access	low
curriculum/standards	accountability	low

- Codes indicated in the data of five or six teachers were ranked as high. Codes indicated in the data of three or four teachers were ranked as moderate.
- Codes indicated in the data of one or two teachers were ranked as low.

It is this theme of *tension* that potentially has the greatest prominence as a study finding. The tensions reported by the teachers participating in the study are often realized in a context of *chaos*. Understanding and addressing the intertwined tensions and chaos evident in the teachers' descriptions of their practice lead to the realization that special education and general education exist as two separate worlds. This is despite the fact that the creation of two separate worlds was never the intent of special education law. That law was intended to allow access to public education, to facilitate inclusion for a population of students that had previously been denied the opportunity to adequately and actively participate in the general education system.

The recognition of these tensions in special education and general education lead to the broad study finding of separation. Again, multiple data codes led to this determination of separation as an important theme. These codes are summarized and ranked in importance in Table 8.2.

The strongest separation related features noted by the teachers included teacher adaptability with regard to the range of students that they might be required to work with, as well as more curriculum task specific related issues such as the need for adaptation and modification. Both caused some degree of separation from the general education world. The degree of variability possible and the concept of adaptation are not necessarily well understood in general education practice. The curriculum task specific features were ranked as moderately important to the special education teachers. The separation related to these areas is important to note given that in many ways, current educational programming still follows a somewhat lockstep curriculum embodied within the lists of skills that are considered important for children to know and be able to do and perhaps more importantly how they show what they know. There can be little time to incorporate specialized programming and instruction into the frenetic world of the general education classroom. There is a high degree of conformity regarding the identification of tensions and issues of separation among the teachers participating in this study. These conformities exist irrespective of the levels of ability that characterize the students that they teach.

Table 8.2 Summary of Essential Data Codes Indicating Separation in Special Education and General Education

Topic	Code	Rank
students/classrooms	adaptability	high
curriculum/standards	student skills	high
curriculum standards	links to general education	high
curriculum/standards	training	high
interaction with general education	communication	high
students/classrooms	expectations/success	moderate
students/classrooms	language of education	moderate
students/classrooms	teacher roles	moderate

curriculum/standards	adaptation	moderate
curriculum/standards	modifications	moderate
curriculum/standards	purchased programs	moderate
curriculum/standards	accommodations	low

- Codes indicated in the data of five or six teachers were ranked as high. Codes indicated in the data of three or four teachers were ranked as moderate.
- Codes indicated in the data of one or two teachers were ranked as low.

The world of public education documented in this study is subdivided into two separate cultures—a culture of special education and a culture of general education. There are numerous definitions for the term "culture." Culture can be seen as essentially everything that has been learned or produced by a group of people, as ways of interacting with people, as patterns of play and work, and as the social institutions of society (Spradley & McCurdy, 1972). The teachers participating in this study identified a variety of elements important to the cultures of special education and general education. This section summarizes the significant aspects of the distinct cultural components of those two worlds. Elements of several cultural components—physical, social, linguistic, and ideological-political—are discussed.

Within the realm of the physical setting, the important elements of distinction between special education and general education include teaching setting, equipment, teaching tools, and finally technology. The special education teacher is apt to teach in a variety of settings within an elementary school. She may go into the general education classroom for periods of time, as was the case with both Kristie and Charlotte. She may also be assigned to her own classroom, as was the case with Marie, Carlene, Betty, and Jeri. For these last four teachers, their classrooms were similar to general education classrooms in that they were the primary arbiters of how the classrooms were set up and what occurred in those classrooms.

The more significant classroom situations illustrating the theme of *separation* would be those of Kristie and Charlotte. In both situations, the special education teachers were in secondary positions in their general education classrooms. Kristie followed the routines put in place by the general education teacher in her classrooms. She had various degrees of classroom interaction in the classrooms in which she was observed. In one classroom, she was an active co-teacher. She taught lessons and also served as a general resource to the new third grade teacher. Kristie often provided advice on following school procedure for this teacher who had recently transferred from another school in the district. In a second classroom, Kristie played an active role in the class but her activities tended to be secondary to what the general education teacher had organized. Kristie was aware of the fact that she was a visitor, albeit a useful and valued visitor, to this classroom. This is best evidenced by a situation in which she referred to classroom jobs in the first person but then quickly switched to the less descriptive third person. "My paper passer" quickly became "the paper passer." In the third classroom, Kristie had only a limited role to play—in most instances during the observations, she did little more than move about the classroom offering minor assistance to all students while the general education teacher conducted a whole class read-aloud.

The objects, tools, and organization of the classroom space for special education classrooms and general education is frequently different as well. When factors such as these are considered, Marie, Carlene, Betty, and Jeri are often working in more distinct situations. This is especially true of Betty and Jeri. The physical set up of their classrooms are significantly different from the typical general education classroom. There is less a sense of a whole classroom in their situations than of a series of individual schedules needing to be followed. This separates the student both from his special education classroom and also from any general education classroom that he or she may have interaction with. Betty's classroom stands out in particular. Amidst the expected classroom furnishings was a vast array of specialized physical positioning equipment, items that were both difficult to manipulate and that would potentially be perceived as interfering with the flow of activity in a general education classroom.

Another significant aspect of tools separating special education and general education in the study was the use of picture and object devices. Both Betty and Jeri's classrooms were characterized the use of line drawings and objects to create schedules and to communicate. Picture and object use is often essential to the instruction of students with significant cognitive needs. Such schedules formed an important part of the students' literacy instruction. But what is interesting regarding the use of such schedules is that some general education teachers can be resistant to their use. In an example from my own experience as a special education teacher, pictures were seen as interfering with the skill development of the general education students. The teacher did not want picture support for the classroom schedule or the lunch and job charts because it would allow the less motivated students to avoid reading the words used on the charts. I interpret this as an unwillingness to see beyond the conventional way of doing things. Such unwillingness sells students short in the long run.

Within the realm of the social setting, the important elements of distinction between special education and general education include the activities that students participate in. Teachers, both in special education and general education, and school administrators often talk in terms of social inclusion. This term typically refers to allowing students with greater disabilities to attend recess and lunch with their general education peers. What is less often said is that these time periods are typically the more unstructured times in the day. These times are often not useful educational periods because teachers and paraprofessionals are often on duties or breaks. Such practice lessens the educational opportunities provided to students with special needs. Further, focusing only on those routines typically thought of as social separates students with special needs from the richness of the academic activities that regularly occur in the general education classroom. Every activity has some social aspect to it. For example, math class is not simply math class. It is also following the routine, getting proper material, following directions, and listening to the teacher or teachers, all elements of an eventual workplace.

In addition, the pace at which curriculum must be covered often precludes addressing the social aspects of instruction in general education classes. The teachers' words and my own experience as a special education teacher support this assertion. The teachers acknowledge that general education classrooms frequently do not have the ability to slow down to work on the less academic aspects of curricular activities. They must do a lesson or more a day; there is no time to wait for slow students to become comfortable with, much less learn, the material presented. These issues intensify once a student enters third grade, the first year that state assessments are administered in the state in which the majority of the teachers participating in the study taught. In essence, the rapid pace of curriculum delivery seldom matches the manner in which students learn. To the observer, the curriculum moves along at its pre-determined pace and it is hoped that the students can keep up, despite teachers who will tell you that the best feature of the move to standards-based instruction was the notion that teachers are no longer able to just "plow" (progress) through that curriculum (P. Monty, Pilot Study, 2002). As previously noted, it has been the extended experience of these teachers as well as my own experience, that students with disabilities need more time than to learn the material than the current curriculum pace allows. Learning is not something that can be timed into neat categories and specific blocks of time. It is not something that can necessarily occur with a single presentation of material.

Within the linguistic dimension of culture, the important elements of distinction between special education and general education include the student descriptive device, curriculum, and language of instruction. A special education teacher often describes her students in terms of diagnostic device and then in terms of skills. While this may be explained by the fact that diagnosis is a key criterion in determining a student's eligibility for special education services, it is also a key component in separating students from one another. Diagnosis often provides the criteria for determining curriculum and for inclusion opportunities. *Special education students become their diagnoses.* A general education teacher thinks in terms of the curriculum and then the student. It is not hard to hear the belief, "that topic is not appropriate for those students", expressed.

Curriculum thus acts as a kind of sorting tool for students with special needs. Students with high incidence disabilities, those who are often more academically competent or capable, are usually considered to be more appropriate candidates for inclusion in the general education classroom. The presence of such students in general education classrooms as well as the belief that general education curricula is more appropriate for such students, as noted in the literature review, are also well documented in practice. It is important to note that special education teachers are also accepting of curriculum as a sorting tool. They sometimes expressed the idea that their students would just not be appropriate for the general education classroom.

However, the most significant aspect of separation between the worlds of general education and special education are the different "languages" associated with the disciplines. Examples of these different languages are presented in Table 8.3.

The chart below represents some of the points of comparison between special education and general education. Students with special needs are often seen in terms of their diagnosis and their functioning level rather than as representative of their grade level. Students eligible for special education services are often represented by their IEPs rather than by the grade level curriculum. This IEP can be primarily academically based as in the cases of Kristie, Charlotte, Marie, and Carlene or more socio-communicative based, as in the cases of Betty and Jeri. Special education teachers are trained to think in terms of data-collection. Such data collection typically addresses developing task analyses for skill instruction; frequency counts of isolated behaviors, and time samples. General education teachers focus on creating work samples, on what is more commonly referred to authentic assessment.

Table 8.3: Summary of Significant Separate Educational Terminology

Topic	Special Education Term	General Education Term
student	diagnosis	grade-level
content	IEP	curriculum
	individual	district
	curriculum creator	curriculum presenter
	goals/objectives	lesson plans
	accommodations	
standards	entry points	skills
	access skills	standards as written
instruction	adaptation	differentiation
	modification	
	"progress is progress"	grade-level progress
assessment	portfolio	state-assessment
	data-collection	grades
	work samples	assignments

However, of the items noted in the chart, the most significant terms are those that are instruction related. As previously mentioned, special education teachers talk of accommodations, modifications, and adaptations while general education teachers talk of differentiation. A similar separation occurs when discussing standards. Special education teachers, especially those working with students who are significantly involved, are apt to speak in terms of student addressing entry points and access skills while general education teachers speak of students in terms of needing improvement, proficiency, or advancement. From my position of straddling both worlds of special education and general education, I see that there is a connection between the two sets of terminology. Concepts such as entry points and access skills must be seen as valid levels in the categories that educators create to organize their students. Such concepts become truly valid only when they can result in an opportunity for these students to pass the state assessment for graduation purposes. Further, these ideas of entry points and access skills expand the educational context for all students in public education.

Several of the teachers speak of a lack of curricular materials. For some, this meant not having any materials when first starting in a classroom. Others noted the fact that the school doesn't always order general education curriculum material for them. Still others spoke of often having to scramble to borrow necessary materials from general education teachers. At the same time, the teachers also noted that their special education departments were often more than ready to supply materials. The important point concerning such materials though, is that these materials were often unrelated to general education instruction. Adaptive equipment could be readily ordered, yet, the materials that should form the basis of adapted instruction were frequently far harder to get.

Last, the ideological-political dimension of culture provides its own elements of distinction—resources, teacher status, and finally student expectations. These elements point to the inequity that often exists between special education and general education. Separate is not equal in these instances. An important finding emerging from the work presented here is the role that general education teacher power plays in the work of special education teachers.

General education teacher power is often associated with the education presented to students with special needs. Findings in this study clearly indicate that the special education teachers often occupy subservient roles to the general education teachers. The special education teachers clearly operated according to the desires of the general education teacher to whom they were assigned. General education teachers typically have a greater sense of choice when faced with educating students with disabilities. General education teachers often have a choice about whether they will accept "inclusion class." There are mechanisms of student removal from the general education classroom that the teachers are able to make use of. But the more significant facet of this notion of general education teacher power is that general education teachers often can choose whether or not they will work with students with disabilities. This choice can run the range between actually working to have troublesome students removed from the general education setting to the more subtle "my students vs. your students" attitude demonstrated by some general education teachers who have students with special needs in their classrooms. All of the teachers participating in this study emphasize, often eloquently, stories of the importance of being invited into general education classrooms or of the importance of role of openness on the part of general education teachers.

And finally, separate but not equal also refers to the manner in which students are educated. There is an element of low student expectations often associated with students with special needs. The students that are more academically capable are the students that are typically considered as appropriate for inclusion. Other students with special needs are ranked according to their ability to demonstrate pre-requisite skills for the general education academic environment. There is the impression that curriculum is something that the students must be able to do rather than a tool for organizing what they need to learn. Grade levels result in a lock-step system that is frequently insensitive to students with special needs. Again, special educators can fall prey to this line of thinking. All teachers have noted the problems that can arise when students cannot perform certain skills.

These elements of distinction between special education and general education enhance the notion of separation between the two worlds. This becomes a second important finding of the study. Bridging the differences between the disciplines of special education and general education and bringing the two systems together must become the task of both special and general educators.

The Model

As previously stated, one plan for this study was the development of individual theories of teachers' practices and settings. In some respects, this goal was achieved. I say this in a broad sense. All practices were student-driven in terms of the IEP. This is the mandate of the IEP. Yet, each teacher's practice demonstrated differences as a result of district practices and teacher actions. This is consistent with research emphasizing the importance of context in educational practice and reform. Each practice can be characterized in specific ways. Kristie and Charlotte demonstrated somewhat standard practices. This is to say they were primarily driven by the general education curriculum. For Kristie, "Curriculum is just not off the cuff . . . I take the important things from the curriculum and I adapt them to the books and the writing that my students are doing." Charlotte differed from Kristie in that she had some portfolio experience. That experience offers the potential for increasing inclusion for students with special needs as seen in her words regarding the use of "entry points." Both desired to be a "seamless part of the general education classroom." Marie provides the best example of state mandated reform taking hold in practice. She went from touching on science and social studies because it was fun to developing data based projects for her students to complete. Her practice is also perhaps the most individualized in that she allows or is able to let her students frequently create their own curriculum. At the same time, Carlene has a much more modi-

fied version of creating curriculum. She creates curriculum in a somewhat similar fashion to Marie in that she picks and chooses topics of instruction based on
whether or not her students might be able to learn them. She thanks her district
leaders for allowing her this freedom. However, her students do not determine
curriculum in the same manner that Marie's students often do.

While all students receiving special education services have an IEP, the notion of "skills that students need to work on" is more prominent for Betty and
Jeri because their students are often typically not thought of in terms of needing
or "being appropriate for" academic instruction by a larger world. Betty's situation is somewhat conventional in that her practice is highly influenced by having
to match her students to the curriculum frameworks rather than create a responsive curriculum for her students. Her practice experience is also disturbing in
that she speaks of having to "pound the pavement" as she approaches general
education providers in her school to achieve inclusion for her children. And
Jeri's practice experience is perhaps the most constrained, despite her efforts to
institute what she considered to be best practice for students with significant
special needs. In her case, when she speaks of her concerns with her students'
IEPs, she implies that her district is motivated by saving resources.

In a more specific sense, the different characterizations of teaching presented by each of the teachers are all influenced by the themes noted in this
study. That is, they are driven and shaped by the challenges and concerns leading to a sense of both tension and separation. My analysis of the data collected
for this study suggests a model for providing some answer to the overarching
question of the study, for understanding how being a special educator manifests
itself in the broader world of general education. That model incorporates a notion of what I have termed, "managed chaos." This term arose from an early data
analysis discussion during which the perception of "chaos" was noted.

Chaos is something of a generic term that is defined in terms of disorganization, confusion, or a lack of order. "Managed chaos" is an additional generic
term that addresses bringing order to a noted lack of organization. It is a term
that can be applied to complex situations in business, industry, health care, and
even family care. An Internet search for "chaos" using the Google search engine
revealed approximately 2 million hits. Narrowing that search to education and
then to special education reduced the number of hits, though such hits still num-
bered over 1.5 million for each. Further, chaos is a concept that is appropriate to
the public school setting. Experience has shown that if one wants to observe
such educational chaos in general education, visit a school as state testing approaches. Normal activity gets lost and chaotic in test preparation. I selected the
term "managed chaos" to characterize my study's findings because the term
accurately articulated both the complexity of the task of being a special educator
in an elementary school and the importance of balancing the component elements of that task. This model is illustrated in Figure 8.1.

The model of "Managed Chaos" begins with the components of the normative model that was created to structure the study. These components include instruction and learning, teaching actions, the general education curriculum, and assessment and evaluation. These components are mediated by the IEP document; that is, they are incorporated into a student with special needs' educational plan. This mediation is represented in the diagram by the special education system touching on the larger general education system. The components of the normative model can result in significant chaos when the complexity of teaching students with a variety of special needs is added to the educational system. Further chaos results as general education teacher power impacts both instruction and the special education teacher. Such power can often act to constrain special education teacher practice and can impact the quality of the education that is offered to students with special needs.

Figure 8.1 A Model of Managed Chaos

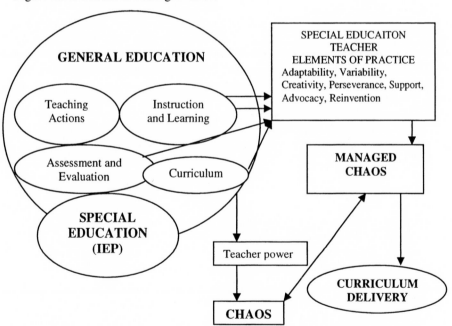

The special education teacher is responsible for incorporating the components of the normative model into teaching practice, represented by the multiple arrows that connect general education to the special education teacher. The special education teacher balances the elements of the normative model through the elements of special education teacher practice identified in this study. These elements include adaptability, variability, support, flexibility, creativity, perseverance, and teacher reinvention. That teacher practice can be constrained by an informal element of general education teacher power. My work has shown that general education teachers have some ability in impacting who gets into their classrooms as well as the quality of the education that is offered to students with special needs, intensifying the impression of disorganization. Special education teacher practice acts to mediate and balance the chaos that can ensue, leading to the concept of "managed chaos." It is this concept of "managed chaos" that results in effective curriculum delivery for students with special needs.

At the same time, it is important to note that the educational chaos is never completely managed. The constant tensions that exist in the educational system as the systems of special education and the general education attempt to integrate often result in the resurgence of chaos. The special education teacher must also manage these resurgences of chaos as well as the daily activities of teaching. This study has shown that, in fact, the practice of special education on a student-by-student basis is neither disorganized, nor chaotic, nor unconnected to the world of general education.

That same practice of special education is also not a separate entity and should not be seen as such, although educators are often inclined to do so, even in 2007. However, it is my assertion that 'chaos' is often how special education is viewed by both general educators and sometimes by special educators as well. At the same time that the special education teachers in this study noted multiple tensions leading to an illumination of two separate educational worlds, they were also comfortable with the continued notion of the long established continuum of services—that some students might not belong in general education settings. Such a perception serves two purposes. The current conception of the continuum of services and its sorting of students acts as a tension-reducer between special education and general education. It allows for students that have greater difficulties to be removed from the mainstream. It also allows for a continued separate and unequal status for special education teachers. But, while such beliefs reduce tension between the two cultures, they do little to work toward the integration of the cultures.

Returning to the opening of this chapter, it is the special education teacher's responsibility to balance the elements identified as essential to special education teacher practice—to keep those "plates" that contain the elements of special education teacher practice—adaptability, flexibility, support, variability, perseverance, creativity, advocacy, and reinvention—spinning. Thus, the model describing special education teacher practice becomes one of "managing the chaos" that ensues as special education interacts with general education in public school settings.

Review of Data Interpretations

The sample of teachers participating in this study was one of convenience. I worked with teachers who expressed interest and willingness to participate. The inclusion of six teachers in the study provided multiple sources of data as a control for bias in the information collected. I was further fortunate in that fact that I had two teachers from each of general categories of special education—inclusion specialists, teachers in a substantially separate setting, and teachers working with students with significant cognitive disabilities. This allowed for some degree of comparison both across the six teachers and within each of the teaching categories. There was general agreement of experience within the teachers' situations both across the six teachers and within each teaching specialty. That each teacher provided similar information and examples suggested that a descriptive accuracy was present in the data set.

In addition, the teachers' words were checked against a series of multiple observations. These observations confirmed the elements of special education teacher that were identified by the teachers. Student variability, curriculum creation, teacher perseverance, and teacher flexibility and adaptability were readily observable in the daily practice. Confirmations of these components were observable with all teachers, though the manner in which these variables presented themselves was often quite different. Student variability was most apparent when the students with greater cognitive handicaps were observed. Their teachers confronted students with a range of skills that typically do not regularly immediately register within academic settings. At the same time, variability was also apparent with the students with greater academic skills. Skills ranged from reading isolated words to reading entire grade level texts with no comprehension. The importance of curriculum creativity was also readily apparent. The teachers of the more handicapped students were constantly in the position of having to create entry points into the standards-based instruction of their schools. Such materials were easily observable in their classrooms. These teachers were clearly adaptable as well as flexible. Adaptability was apparent in teacher discussions of having to reinvent themselves according to the students that came their way. Teacher flexibility was essential in dealing with the behavioral issues that so many of the students with special needs exhibited.

During the final phases of the data analysis, outside educational providers were asked to review and confirm the interpretations and analyses that I had made of the data. These reviewers were recruited to protect against research bias and assumptions held concerning activities of general education. They were individuals who were currently special education teachers, individuals who worked in combined special education and general education positions, and finally, individuals with primarily a general education back-ground. All reviewers were given access to interview transcripts and data interpretations.

In general, the reviewers were in agreement with the interpretations that were made regarding the roles that special education teachers played in general education settings. They offered comments that suggested that the elements of special education teacher practice were accurately identified. This was especially true of the reviewers who were currently special education teachers. These reviewers were ready to add their own examples illustrating the identified elements of special education teacher practice to those that had already been documented. These individuals were also in agreement with the interpretation of the existence of two separate cultures existing in one setting. Once again, they were ready to offer their own personal illustrative examples of feeling separated from the activities of their general education settings. One reviewer, in particular, noted the political elements within the discussions of special education teacher adaptability. This reviewer cited concerns with whether the teachers participating in the study were aware of and accessed union rights regarding their positions in their settings. These comments were of particular interest given the fact that most of the teachers offered justifications for the behavior of general education teachers in situations involving the inclusion of students with special needs. A few teachers talked of the role of unions during interview sessions but it was also clear that they did not necessarily act on their concerns over certain episodes of treatment from their general education counterparts.

Reviewers working in combined special education/general education positions also noted agreement with the interpretations in the study. They were further able to provide comparative comments regarding the interpretations made as part of the study. For example, one reviewer commented that while she was in agreement with the notion of separation between the special education system and general education system, it was also important not to lose sight of the demands that the world of general education places upon its teachers, a major element of the current context of education and something that I was concerned about doing as I interpreted the data, given my long experience in special education. She acknowledged the importance of making note of this fact within the interpretations of the study data. This reviewer was very much in agreement with the interpretation that the general education teacher wielded some degree of power, a power that was often considerable in nature, and in the ways in which students with special needs were accepted into their classrooms.

All reviewers were in agreement with the broad interpretations of the data provided here. They felt that this study, given the data on which it was built, presented an accurate picture of the nature of being a special education teacher in today's complex world of general education.

Managing the Chaos

"The greatest thing in this world is not so much where we are, but in what direction we are moving." (unknown)

"Managing the chaos" is dependent on understanding the teaching system in which the chaos occurs. Bronfenbrenner (1979) noted that explanations for what we do and think are found in the interactions between the characteristics of people and their environments, past and present. We exist in a variety of settings that are composed of activities, interactions, and roles. Teaching does not occur in a vacuum. Teachers develop their practice as they interact with the components of teaching and with the students they encounter. The teachers and students are actors in an environment. These environments extend beyond the behavior of individuals to encompass functional systems within and between settings that can be modified and extended.

Bronfenbrenner's work has spurred other researchers to further develop the concept of the ecological framework and apply it to educational settings. These researchers have noted the importance of both the multiple variables that constitute an educational system—variables such as those composing the normative model used in this study—as well as the interaction between these variables (Radford, 2006), the necessity of multidisciplinary study for understanding educational systems (Jacobson & Wilensky, 2006), and finally the importance of the organization and its goals in school learning and improvement (Collinson, Cook, & Conley, 2006). The settings and the school cultures that are built around the interactions between the teachers and their environments provide contexts that shape, dictate, and potentially constrain educational practice.

This study has documented the importance associated with the interactions between special education and general education teachers as well as the difficulties that can be associated with those interactions in special education teacher practice. It further illustrates that individual practices differ across student abilities and school settings. These interactions, as well as the tasks and tools of teaching students with special needs, and individual school variability in practice impact what these teachers are able to accomplish. While not the focus of this study, the ecological framework briefly described provides a powerful tool for developing a deeper understanding of special education teacher practice as well as the increased understanding of the role of special education in the broader world of general education. There is a clear need for additional research.

Recommendations

The findings of this study lead to several specific recommendations addressing the "managed chaos" that permeates elementary level special education and its' interaction with general education in schools and are intended for both special education and general education professionals. They will help to reduce tension within both disciplines as schools become more successful at reducing the separateness between special education and general education through increased integration and inclusion. The study will be of special interest to special educators because it presents their experience and thus corrects the issue of their lack of representation in the educational literature. General educators will see opportunities for school reform in the study.

The teachers participating in this study note a variety of tensions that impact their positions as special educators. These tensions include general education teacher perceptions, general education teacher power, separate languages that divide special education and general education, and limited time to communicate with their general education counterparts. The teachers make their desire for increased training clear. They all note a desire for additional standards-based training and curriculum training. This desire for training is inspired by their stories of having limited inclusion in such training in their schools, as well as by their student needs. It is hoped that considering these recommendations and ultimately acting on them will lead to an increased level of integration between special education and general education.

1) Districts need to be more honest, forthright about inclusion. Districts must develop an inclusive philosophy of education that truly includes all students. It is vital to recognize that there are multiple sources of tension between special education and general education, as shown by the findings of this study. Steps must be taken to create a district and a school context and culture of one educational system, a system that does not separate its special educators from its general educators. Such a philosophy must further focus on creating a district specific definition for the term "access to the general education curriculum."

2) Districts need to recognize all students as learners. Educational research overwhelmingly illustrates that all students are learners. Special education was created for the purpose of assisting that group of students who do not learn conventionally or who do not learn at a "normal" regular pace. However, as the study findings suggest, general education curriculum has a sorting function embedded within it. Teachers, both in special education and general education often note there are skills that some students cannot do. One result of such information is a tendency to think first of students in terms of what they cannot do rather than what they can do. Typically there is limited consideration of adapting the curriculum to the student so that the student with special needs can remain with peers.

It is imperative to look at both what students can do and what they ought to be doing; such consideration creates the impression that these students are also learners. It is this context of what students ought to be doing that provides a curriculum that matches and that can grow with the student with special needs. Access to the general education curriculum is a key to the context for what students with special needs ought to be doing. Focusing on the student rather than the curriculum and testing provide a starting point. We must move beyond the conception of separate special education curriculum and general education curriculum based upon a lock-step set of pre-determined skills.

3) Special education teachers have to learn to think in terms of general education curriculum as the appropriate context for their students. The majority of the teachers participating in this study express the need to have a better understanding of the events occurring in the general education classroom. This is best addressed through creating and increasing opportunities for special education teachers to communicate with their general education peers. It is just as appropriate to think of the non-academic components of academic skills as well as the academic skills. In addition to learning math content, students are also learning how to follow routines, how to gather appropriate materials, and how to potentially attend to different instructors and directions. Content area instruction is not just about the academic content. Students with special needs should not have to "earn" or "buy" their way into a general education classroom through the demonstration of a series of prerequisite skills.

4) District wide professional development activities and in-house training opportunities should focus on the integration of special education and general education curriculum. It would be appropriate to focus on the development of district training programs that expand the knowledge of both special education and general education teachers already in practice. Standards and curriculum training should include both special education teachers and general education teachers. Attention should be given to creating links between special education language and general education language in that training. It is unfortunate to note that education trainings are not appropriate to special education students.

5) Districts need to create a single language of special education and general education. The study findings demonstrate the separate languages of special education and general education. The concepts and goals of each discipline are similar but the terminology is different. I would argue that differentiation in instruction is appropriate to any student in public school. Differentiation in general education is an additional name for the special education concepts of modification and adaptation. Special educators differentiate instruction on an ongoing basis. However, they refer to the task in terms of modifying or adapting instruction. The ideas of points of access and entry into the general education curriculum must be seen as valid academic understanding in their own right. It is counter-productive to maintain a separate language for each discipline. Such an action can only continue the separation of the two disciplines.

6) The creation of curriculum should address all students. The teachers in the study all indicate that they would like to have the opportunity to participate in general education curriculum meetings. Districts have to take a role in determining the core components of the curriculum. It is not appropriate to say that certain students should not be exposed to curriculum topics because the material is beyond them. Special education experience often shows that this can and frequently does happen with students with special needs. As previously noted, inclusive methodology speaks of "cutting the clutter" in the curriculum—of reducing the curriculum to its most essential elements of knowledge. Individual districts speak of "exposure" to the general education curriculum. However, that same methodology seldom addresses strategies to achieve an understanding of the curriculum's essential elements. Districts should develop strategies to create and integrate curriculum for all students. The concept of "exposure" to the curriculum must be clarified in a practical manner. Standards-based educational literature and the state Curriculum Resource Guide provide viable starting points to develop such strategies.

7) Districts should work toward a goal of bringing curriculum development tools such as standards-based educational literature and the Curriculum Resource Guide into regular interaction among both special education and general education professionals. General education speaks of aligning curriculum to standards and of creating curriculum maps. Developing a set of district wide curriculum entry points (e.g. a set of skills that are both academic and more realistically achievable for many students with special needs) would be a powerful action. Such action might also help to reduce the tensions created by the rapid pace that the general education curriculum must keep.

8) General education curriculum must examine its current content and pace. If, as teachers who had the opportunity to attend a year-long standards-based education seminar in order to train them to become teacher leaders for their schools, are accurate in the assertion that standards-based units were to lead to all children developing some sense of essential knowledge for important topics, then curriculum pace must be manageable. The pace of the current curriculum cannot continue at a topic a day, with double math and reading sessions as the state testing approaches. Teachers require the opportunity to actually teach a skill so that their students can develop fluency with that skill.

9) Special educators and general educators must share their knowledge. The study findings indicate that the essential mandates of special education and general education are similar. The essential questions for both are –what is it that students need to know and be able to do? It would be valuable for special educators and general educators to sit down and examine points of convergence between them in the context of general education curriculum. Staffing schedules must allow special education teachers to be available to actively participate in grade level-meetings. The teachers in the study all indicate the troubles and frustrations with interacting with their general education peers that their schedules cause. This inability to attend grade-level meetings potentially keeps the special education teacher in a secondary teaching position because they are always in the situation of not knowing what is required of their students. Inability to attend meetings and interact with general education peers precludes the opportunity to share knowledge between the disciplines. The teachers' note, "But we don't share…not until someone comes looking for the information." To that end, and to address the fact that there are vast numbers of teachers, both in special education and general education, already practicing in schools, I would create a model for the creation of in-house staff development programs that would lead to the sharing of teacher knowledge.

It is only through sharing of individual knowledge that a whole district-wide educational technology can be created. These teachers are well versed in the methodology that will aid general education teachers in seeing the points of access and entry into the general education curriculum and in seeing beyond academic content. For example, teaching methodology typically noted as specific to students with significant cognitive needs provides some essential concepts to achieve these ends. Ecological assessment and task analysis are of great importance in seeing beyond the academic in an academic routine. Special education methodology does not need to be kept exclusively within special education. Further, it is such sharing of knowledge that allows for the effective use of in-house resources—the teachers themselves, that creates professional development that may actively be used by the teachers who participate, and that ultimately contributes to building the needed bridges between special education systems and the general education systems.

10) Districts must recognize the existence of the "two cultures" reality that exists between special education and general education. They must take steps to resolve the separations between the two systems. Failure to do so must be interpreted as not only a failure to integrate the system but also as recognition that it remains acceptable to treat certain populations as unequal.

11) Acting upon the recommendations presented to this point might best be achieved through expanding general education teacher programs. Teacher education programs need to recognize the full meaning of student diversity. This study has shown that the extensive variability of the students that now attend public schools goes well beyond the commonly known understandings of student diversity. I would specifically add a component that addressed working with students with a range of special needs to general education teacher preparation programs. This component would likely take the form of *a set of core special education courses embedded in the general education teacher preparation program*. General educators especially need an opportunity to see students with more significant needs in order to appreciate the learning that can take place.

In closing, in their 1998 synthesis of the literature addressing best practices in inclusive schooling, McGregor and Vogelsberg noted that current discussions of best educational practice often emphasized the need to create responsive learning environments. Such environments incorporated student diversity through an array of strategies that planned for the full range of learners that might be encountered in public schools at the design point of instruction and stressed teaching problem solving, and an active use of assessment connected to learning and teaching. We currently consider these same topics though the terminology has changed. Today, we think of the standards-based instruction focusing on problem solving and the application of knowledge, universal curricu-

lum design, and person-centered planning. It is essential to create caring and
supportive learning communities for all students. Achieving best practice as
identified in the research will require significant school restructuring in order to
address the issues identified in this study, to provide the time necessary for professionals to develop curriculum, and to share their knowledge. And so there is a
final recommendation.

     12) ***Policy makers must consider the effects of reform on teacher practice.***
The results of this study lend some credence to a belief that the present emphasis
on high stakes testing has had a negative impact on developing useful inclusive
opportunities for students with special needs. Policy makers need to look at and
understand the qualitative effects of high stakes testing on school. Teachers are
frequently thinking in terms of "not having enough minutes in the day" in order
to integrate students or to truly make use of formative assessment—to reteach
skills so that mastery can take place. Too rapid curriculum pacing impacts the
tension and separation that are evident in the educational system. Students who
struggle and their schools with them are frequently left behind on the basis of
missing single test questions. Students with more significant needs may not be
able to graduate because they cannot pass the test. There is no time for developing mastery of content. There is too much content to master. Test results designed to improve accountability must be used formatively as they were intended rather than punitively. Future educational reform efforts must address
these concerns.

Suggestions for Future Research

     This study illustrates the practice of six special education teachers' practice.
Its findings indicated that there are multiple tensions that exist within special
education and between the interaction of special education and general educa-
tion. Two separate cultures—special education and general education—are evident in the data. There is a sense of polarization in these two cultures. It is "special education" and "general education"; there is little sense of *the* educational
system. This study's findings, together with the recommendations that were
generated as a result of its completion, suggest several areas of future research.

     The topic of this study emerged from a reading of the research literature
identifying variables that impact the overall education that students receive. This
literature provided great insight into my understanding of the process of education and teacher practice but also revealed that there was only a limited match
between the core concepts of educational theory and practice and special education. This is to say that there was limited research regarding the variables of
education and their application to special education teacher practice. As such,
this study is original. Studies focused on the practice of special education teachers were virtually non-existent. The practice of special education teachers has
been a neglected area of research. Additional research focusing on the practice
of special education teachers is warranted. It would be beneficial to develop

teacher lore for special education similar to the teacher lore that exists for general education teachers. My study might serve as a catalyst to such research.

Special education as an individual system and as a system that must integrate into a larger general education system has identifiable tensions. This study identified several such tensions. However, the tensions that have been identified are potentially applicable to only this group of teachers. Research addressing tensions in special education with additional groups of teachers would be valuable. That research should include additional samples of special education teachers in each of the specialties identified in my study as well as samples of special education teachers in specialties not specifically identified here. Further, such research should take the form of both additional qualitative studies as well as larger more quantitative studies. This study sought to identify important categories of special education teacher knowledge. Quantitative research might make use of these categories and expand them to include much larger populations of special education teachers.

The research literature demonstrated that two disciplines—special education and general education are frequently not presented as being part of the same larger venue of public education. This study supported the notion of the existence of separate special education and general education cultures. Further, it was also apparent that the notion of two separate cultures is one that is perpetuated by both special educators and general educators. Special education teachers often express comfort with the continuum of service delivery and with the sorting of students according to functioning level. Some students are considered to not be appropriate for certain settings. As a result, they require placement outside the general education classrooms. On occasion, special education teachers demonstrate reluctance to participate in general education curriculum. It is still possible to hear the complaint that students with special needs don't need a general education curriculum, they need "life skills." Further, special education teachers also see the general education curriculum ahead of the students. Certain students with special needs can't be in the general education classroom because they are lacking in specific academic skills.

But again, this is the reading that results from this group of teachers and this data set. The teachers here did question certain student placements, easily accepted the removal of certain students from their general education classrooms, and were content, in some cases, with very limited contact with the general education classrooms. Further, the teachers sometimes questioned the efficacy of the concept of accessing the general education curriculum for certain students. Is the existence of two separate cultures present in other special education teachers' experiences? Will the occurrence of separate cultures in other special education teachers' experiences resemble the findings documented in this study? What are the characteristics of other special education teachers' experiences? Additional studies of special education teachers cultural systems, in other geographical regions in the United States and perhaps abroad, would be beneficial. Further studies should focus on other special education teachers in the specialties in my study as well as special education teachers in specialties not specifically identified here.

There are multiple variables that interact to create the complexity that exists within an educational system. This study has documented that these variables often interact to create the separate cultures of special education and general education. There is a sense of dysfunction to the existence of two separate cultures in schools. Yet, integration and inclusion often remain desired goals. Such integration is likely to be context specific. Further research regarding alternative plans for integrating the two systems and managing the current dysfunction is essential. The teachers' provided valuable information leading to recommendations that would allow for the integration of special education and general education, if considered at the level of policy.

However, as this area of research is considered, it is important to note that inclusion remains a continued topic of research. Despite the general positive vein of this research, there continue to be questions regarding its success at the levels of both practice and policy. Given that special education teachers are often somewhat comfortable with the current state of special education service delivery, it would be of great benefit to expand the existing research addressing the performance of students with special needs in specific settings. Would the results of such research support the continued existence of the current continuum of services or would its results support continued and/or increased movement toward inclusion?

Additionally, and in light of the present focus on meeting the requirements set out by the No Child Left Behind Act, research addressing special education's focus on making use of the general education curriculum would be of great value. Given that many special education teachers often express the belief that their students simply cannot pass state assessments as they presently exist, is a more separate special education standards-based academic curriculum and testing system a viable answer? What might that curriculum look like? How might that curriculum be developed? Where should that curriculum be delivered—how might such a curriculum change the ways that educators think of inclusion? Would a separate curriculum adequately address the questions and pressures created by the rapid pace kept by the general education curriculum as it too struggles toward "proficiency for all students" by 2014?

Finally, it would be of great interest and benefit to study the children, their families, and their communities. My study demonstrated in small ways, that students with special needs, even those diagnosed as or considered as significantly cognitively handicapped, are very aware of their environments, are able to connect their experiences to the larger outside world, act purposefully to impact that environment, and make progress in the academic arena, the general education curriculum. Further ethnographic study surrounding these areas is both warranted and expected. It is well past time for giving this population, this group of "Others", their full voice.

Final Thoughts

I write the final thoughts closing my study as the new 2007 school year is beginning. Its findings resonated as I sat first in the auditorium listening to opening day speeches, attended the first of my professional development days, and finally, as I spent the first four days attempting to set my teaching schedule. The elements of chaos, those "spinning plates", were once again in motion. The separate worlds of special education and general education were made starkly clear as the speakers presented numerous general education exemplars of "excellent standards-based projects." Special education went unacknowledged save for a mention that the district's difficulty in achieving adequate yearly progress could be traced to such subgroups as those students receiving special education services. The teachers' words, "but we don't share" echoed in my thoughts.

The two separate worlds were further emphasized in the professional development schedule. General education teachers attended training on vertical alignment of the curriculum, while special education teachers were sent to Medicaid billing and instructed to spend the afternoon engaged in clerical activities such as software training and photocopying. It was difficult to see how such activities would be useful in improving student performance. Creating access to the general education curriculum will continue to be difficult so long as thought is not given to integrating special education and general education.

However, the most distressing aspect concerning the opening was the presence of so many of the tensions that were identified by the teachers participating in my study. Scheduling was something of a nightmare; the tension created by the sense of invitation into general education classrooms, as well as the active utilization of the general education teachers' power within their classrooms was palpable. The teachers' words were with me as I listened to concerns about having too many people in the classroom at any given time, making changes to schedules, and what certain students could and could not do. Most significantly, my mind was pre-occupied by the teachers' words regarding assessing the level of invitation into classrooms. If general education teacher complaints began immediately, difficulties with integrating students with special needs were soon to follow. Some complaints began immediately. And, in fact, one teacher began complaining of what the students with special needs could not do before noon of the first day of classes. It will be a struggle keeping those general educators calm.

The participating teachers understood and clearly articulated their sense of separation from the activities of their schools. Providing voice to these special education teachers and indirectly to their students has shown that there is a definite sense of polarization in the elementary school settings. This polarization is not conducive to providing the education that all students are entitled to or to building the necessary bridges between special education and general education. We cannot afford to waste time any additional time on it.

This study has identified students with special needs and their teachers as "Others"—"those who live just beyond the territories" of general education, as "human beings who speak in strange tongues and who practice unusual customs (Bohannon & van der Elst, 1998, p. 3)." It has documented content specific to those "strange tongues" and "unusual customs" of special education. It has helped to demystify those "strange tongues" and "unusual customs." This study has demonstrated that in spite of its languages and customs, the world of special education shares many similarities disguised by these different languages and customs. Such knowledge is instrumental in understanding No Child Left Behind's call to reach proficiency for all students. The special education experience shows that it is difficult to make global statements concerning student proficiency and school performance for all students. This becomes one of the greatest sources of tension and potential separation between special education and general education.

We have the knowledge that we need to reduce the tensions that exist between special education and general education. Using that knowledge, we have the ability to build the necessary bridges between special education and general education—to create a single educational system. It is our responsibility as educators to make adequate use of that knowledge. Putting our vast knowledge of education and the skills that we have developed in teaching to proper use is *true accountability* and *real progress* for the students that we teach, regardless of whether we are special educators or general educators.

Post script

Interestingly, I find myself once again reflecting on the material that comprises this work before the reader , in 2009, at the beginning of another school year. This time, I can make note of some potentially positive notes, though the circumstances surrounding them was one of "dire consequences." The district finds itself in a position of "restructuring based on meeting state testing goals. Opening day speech content consisted of topics such as improving team work in the system, of remembering that AYP status is met as a result of everyone working together to meet the educational needs of students. Professional development discussion offered hope that the system would work toward making use of the knowledge that we have—of actually taking professional development and practically incorporating it into current practice. There was distinct emphasis on creating and using formative assessment practices toward the education of students. Perhaps there will be hope for slowing down the juggernaut that general education so often appears to be.

But, on the other hand, so much of what I wrote in this text earlier remains evident through these first few weeks of school. The description and interpretations of special education teacher practice remain as noted. There remains a distinct separation between general education and special education and issues related to separate languages and knowledge bases as well as misunderstandings of student expectation remain prominent. The desire and need for feeling invited into the general education classroom is readily apparent. Where invited the sense of tension is minimal; where less invited the sense of tension is enormous. This notion of what students can do and ***what they can't do*** and the impact on tolerance, invitation, and potential future tension is palpable. The general education curriculum waits for no one.

As school year routines are being established, that there has been little change between the original closing and this postscript is somewhat disturbing. We so often do not act on what we know…it's time to put that knowledge to use. And yet, while all that has come before remains unsettling, I also remain convinced that we really do have the knowledge to build those bridges between special education and general education—to create that single educational system. We really do have the knowledge to create true accountability and make progress for all the students in the school system. It is this hope that ultimately sustains those of us who become educators.

Appendices

Appendix A: Interview Protocol

Introduction to the Interview Protocol

I am interested in learning how you, as a special education teacher, organize and understand your practice. My curiosity was inspired by my own experience as a special education teacher and by the recent mandates that all students participate in the general education curriculum and in state assessments.

My opening questions were defined after a review of the literature on teacher development and from the teachers' personal experience. Following the literature review, I created a model of teaching. This model encompassed five categories: (1) curriculum, (2) teacher actions, (3) instruction, (4) the Individual Education Plan (IEP), and (5) Evaluation and Assessment. The majority of the questions in each of the categories of the model of teaching presented here were generated during a pilot study exploring teacher beliefs about their teaching. This interview protocol is used as part of the data collection procedures for my dissertation. Examples in the data are used to clarify the terms used to describe your understanding of your teaching.

As part of our interview sessions, you will be asked questions from each of the categories in the model of teaching that I developed. We will begin with questions related to teaching in general. The questions in the first three categories of the model—curriculum, teacher actions, and instruction and assessment—relate to your understanding of teaching in general. Following this, we will talk about the IEP (Individual Education Plan) and your understanding of evaluation and assessment as it relates to educational reform and portfolio assessment. As our discussions are completed and analyzed, additional questions specific to your situation may be generated and discussed.

Curriculum

- Describe your classroom for me. (ex. physical space, materials, decorations etc.)
- Describe what you will do over the first few weeks, the next few weeks, etc.
- Describe how you organize/prioritize curricular elements. (math, reading, science, social studies, functional etc.)
- Describe the ways the students interact with the curriculum. (ex. the work, the routines etc.)
- Describe your contact with other teachers (ex. grade level meetings, teaching contact etc.)
- What does the term "curriculum" mean to you?
- When do you update curriculum?
- In what ways do you update curriculum?
- Describe your experience with district professional development.
- Describe your approaches to professional development. (ex. district vs. personal)

Teacher Actions

- Describe the general organization of your school year (main things that happen—beginning in September and moving toward June).
- Describe a typical day from start to finish.
- Describe how you organize an incoming class.
- What do you do to prepare for the first day of school?

- When do you begin thinking of the first day of school (for a new year)?
- In what ways do you go about grouping the students (home-bases, pods etc.)?
- When you think about your students, how do you categorize them? (strengths/weaknesses, labels etc.)
- What are your joys/frustrations at being a teacher?
- What are some of the specific problems that you have encountered as a special education teacher?
- In what ways did or do you cope with difficulties or problems that you have encountered in your teaching?
- What is your favorite aspect of being a teacher?
- Describe your preferred teaching techniques.
- Describe the ways that you engage the students/keep the students involved.
- What does a good teacher need to know and be able to do? Why do you list these particular attributes?
- Trace your career as a teacher. Talk about how you got to your present position.
- What are the events (that you've experienced) that have shaped your teaching?
- What are the important concepts and materials (books etc.) that have shaped your teaching?
- Who are the important people that have shaped your teaching?
- What is the most important thing to you about being a teacher?
- How would you define yourself as a teacher?
- Teacher literature speaks of reflecting on personal practice. What are the ways in which you think about or reflect on your own teaching?
- What are the ways in which you, as a teacher, stay engaged (life-long learning etc.)
- What are the most important things you've learned about teaching during your career? How did you learn them? How have these things changed over your career?

Instruction and Learning
- Describe what you do to plan a typical lesson. What do you do first, next etc.)
- Describe the types of lessons that you normally do.
- Describe a successful student.
- Can you characterize the school year you have just completed? What were your biggest accomplishments? What were your biggest difficulties/problems?
- Describe how the students interact with you and with each other. (students in special education and general education)
- What is the basis for this description of the students' interactions?
- What are your expectations for the kids?
- What is the basis for this description of your expectations?

IEP
- What do you think about as you begin developing a student's IEP?
- How do you plan objectives for an IEP? (Ask about academic or functional teaching orientation etc. here)
- Describe the different things that you teach?
- Where do the different things that you teach originate?
- What are the ways that you interact with the general education classroom?

- What are the ways that you interact with other special education teachers in your building? In your district?
- What do other school personnel think of the students in special education?
- How do you know what other school personnel think of the students in special education?
- What concept words describe special education? (ex. co-operative grouping, guided reading etc.)

Evaluation and Assessment

- What comes to mind when I say "assessment"?
- What are your preferred techniques for assessing the students?
- What comes to mind when I say "standards"?
- Tell me what standards are.
- Describe you experience with standards up to the present. (attitudes toward, training in etc.)
- How have/have standards changed your teaching/planning?
- Describe your experience with alternate assessment.
- What role do you see the students playing in all the talk about standards?

Appendix B: Terminology Glossary

ABA training with discrete trials

ABA uses the principles of behavioral learning/modification identified by researchers such as B.F. Skinner, to set up an environment in which children with autism learn as much as they can as quickly as possible.

Children with autism typically do not learn much from their environments. They are often capable of learning, but it takes a very structured environment, one where conditions are optimized for acquiring the same skills that typical children learn "naturally." ABA is all about the rules for setting up the environment to enable our kids to learn. The major point of ABA is to teach the prerequisites to make it possible for a child to learn "naturally."

The most common and distinguishing type of intervention based on applied behavior analysis is **discrete trial teaching**. It is what people most often think of when you say "ABA" or "Lovaas method." Briefly: the student is given a stimulus--a question, a set of blocks and a pattern, a request to go ask Mom for a glass of water--along with the correct response, or a strong 'hint' at what the response should be. He is rewarded (an M&M, a piggy-back ride, a happy "good job!") for repeating the right answer; anything else is ignored or corrected very neutrally. As his response becomes more reliable, the 'clues' are withdrawn until he can respond independently. This is usually done one-on-one at a table (thus the term table-top work), with detailed planning of the requests, timing, wording, and the therapist's reaction to the student's responses.

DRA

The Developmental Reading Assessment is an assessment tool used by many elementary school educators help identify student's reading ability and level, document progress, and tailor teaching to drive effective reading instruction. The DRA consists of a series of quick and easy to administer stories that assess the student's accuracy, fluency, and comprehension.

Edmark Reading Program

The Edmark Program provides students with one-on-one teacher-to-student lessons. The program teaches 150 words chosen from the Dolch Word List and first-grade readers, as well as regular plural, tense, gerund endings, capitalization, and punctuation. The program uses a process that teaches a word, introduces its meaning, provides comprehension practice, and uses the word in the story context. All learning modalities are incorporated the instructional sequence. Carefully planned introduction of words and evolution of sentence structure promotes language development. At 10-word intervals, review and test activities are provided, allowing teachers to test student knowledge of the words they are learning. Short instructional steps, repetition, and constant positive reinforcement build student self-confidence. Supplemental teaching materials are available, including additional practice sheets and a spelling component. While the program can be useful for many students, teachers often express some reluctance at its use given that the stories used in instruction are of limited interest.

Essence of the Standard

"Essence of the Standard" is the term used in the state Curriculum Resource Guide (see below) to refer to the essential component(s) of identified academic standards.

Frameworks, Strands, and Standards

"Frameworks", "Strands", and "Standards" are the terms used to describe the academic standards in the state in which the study was conducted. "Framework" refers to the broad curriculum area. "Strand" refers to the more specific areas of that curriculum. For example, math is broken down into number sense, patterns and algebra, measurement, geometry, and data and statistics. "Standard" is the specific learning goal of the academic strand.

Functional Life Skills

"Functional life skills" is a term that is often open to a variety of definitions. It is typically used to describe skills that are self-help and sometimes vocational in nature. Teachers in both special education and general education can often be heard to use the term in instructional planning.

Mayer-Johnson computer programs

Boardmaker and Writing with Symbols are two picture-based computer programs that are commonly found in special education classroom. **Boardmaker** is a program that allows teachers to quickly select and obtain line drawings of any number of items and routines that are likely to occur in educational settings. Such drawings are typically used to create student schedules, academic supports, communication supports, and to adapt instructional activities. **Writing with Symbols** is a program that provides a word processing capability using line drawings consistent with the Boardmaker program.

Resource Guide to the Curriculum Frameworks

The Resource Guide is a publication of the state Department of Education. Designed specifically for students with significant cognitive needs, the document takes each of the standards identified in the state Curriculum Frameworks and breaks it down into its component parts, identifying its "essence". In addition, suggestions are offered for designing standards-based instruction for such students.

Non-verbal Learning Disability

Nonverbal learning disorders (NLD) is a neurological syndrome consisting of specific assets and deficits. The assets include early speech and vocabulary development, remarkable rote memory skills, attention to detail, early reading skills development and excellent spelling skills. In addition, these individuals have the verbal ability to express themselves eloquently. Moreover, persons with NLD have strong auditory retention. However, four major categories of deficits and dysfunction also present themselves. These categories include motoric (lack of coordination, severe balance problems, and difficulties with graphomotor skills), visual-spatial-organizational (lack of image, poor visual recall, faulty spatialperceptions, difficulties with executive functioning and problems with spatial relations), social (lack of ability to comprehend nonverbal communication, difficulties adjusting to transitions and novel situations, and deficits in social judgment and social interaction), and sensory (sensitivity in any of the sensory modes: visual, auditory, tactile, taste or olfactory).

*definition of executive functioning: Neuropsychological functions including, but perhaps not limited to, decision making, planning, initiative, assigning priority, sequencing, motor control, emotional regulation, inhibition, problem solving, planning, impulse control, establishing goals, monitoring results of action, self-correcting.

502.4

502.4 is one of the state prototypes for identifying educational placements for students with special needs. This particular prototype refers to the substantially separate classroom. Other program prototypes include 502.1 (the general education classroom), 502.2 and 502.3 (the resource room), 502.4i, (public separate day class), 502.5 (private separate day class), 502.6 (residential facilities), 502.7 (home/hospital setting), and 502.8 (programs for preschool-age students).

Bibliography

Ayers, W. (1989). The good preschool teacher: Six teachers reflect on their lives. New York, NY: Teachers' College Press.

Barnes, D. (1992). *From communication to curriculum*. Portsmouth, NH: Heineman.

Bechard, S. (2000). Students with disabilities and standards-based reform. Policy brief. Aurora, CO: Mid-Continent Research for Education and Learning. (ERIC Document Reproduction Service No. ED449623)

Bohannan, P. & van der Elst, D. (1998). *Asking and listening: Ethnography as personal adaptation*. Prospect Heights, IL: Waveland Press, Inc.

Bronfenbrenner, U. (1979). *The ecology of human development*. Cambridge, MA: Harvard University Press.

Browder, D. M. & Spooner, F. (2006). *Teaching language arts, math, and Science to students with significant cognitive disabilities*. Baltimore, MD: Paul H. Brookes Publishing Company.

Bruner, J. (1977). *The process of education* Cambridge, MA: The President and fellows of Harvard College.

Center for the Future of Children (1996). *Special education for students with disabilities*, 6. Los Angeles, CA: The David and Lucille Packard Foundation.

Clandinin, J. & Connelly, M. (1986). Rhythms in teaching: The narrative study of teachers' personal practical knowledge of classrooms. *Teaching and Teacher Education, 2*, 377-387.

Clark C. M. & Peterson, P. L. (1986). Teachers' thought processes. In M. C. Wittrock (Ed.), *Handbook of research on teaching*, (3rd ed. pp. 255-296).

Collins, J. (1986). Differential instruction in reading groups. In J. Cook-Gumperz (Ed.), *The social construction of literacy*, (pp. 117-137). NY: Cambridge University Press.

Collinson, V., Cook, T. F., & Conley, S. (2006). Organizational learning in schools and school systems: Improving learning, teaching, and leading. *Theory Into Practice, 45*, 107-116.

Cuban, L. (1993). *How teachers taught: Constancy and change in American classrooms, 1890-1990*. NY: Teacher's College Press.

Downing, J. (2002). *Including students with severe and multiple disabilities in typical classrooms: Practical strategies for teachers*. Baltimore, MD: Paul H. Brookes Publishing Company.

Downing, J. (2006). On peer support, universal design, access to the core curriculum for students with severe disabilities: A personnel preparation perspective. *Research and Practice for Persons with Severe Disabilities, 31*, 327-330.

Elbaz, F. (1981). The teacher's practical knowledge. *Curriculum Inquiry, 11*, 43-71.

Elliot, J. (1997). Invited commentary. *Journal of the Association for Persons with Severe Handicaps, 22*, 104-106.

Elliot, J. L. & Thurlow, M. L. (1997). Opening the door to educational reform: Understanding standards. Minneapolis, MN: National Center on Educational Outcomes. (ERIC Document Reproduction Service No. ED412719)

Evans, C. (1991). Support for teachers studying their own work. *Educational Leadership, 48*, 11-14.

Friend, M. & Bursuck, W. D. (2002). *Including students with special needs: A practical guide for classroom teachers*. Boston, MA: Allyn and Bacon.

Ford, A., Schnorr, R., Meyer, L., Davern, L., Black, J., & Dempsey, P. (1989). *The Syracuse community-referenced curriculum guide for students with moderate and severe disabilities.* Baltimore, MD: Paul H. Brookes Publishing Company.

Gamoran, A., Nystrand, M., Berands, M., & Lepore, P. C. (1995). An organizational analysis of the effects of ability grouping. *American   Educational Research Journal, 32,* 687-715.

Giangreco, M. F., Cloninger, C. J., & Iverson, V. S. (1998). *Choosing outcomes and accommodations for children (COACH): A guide to educational planning for students with disabilities,* 2nd ed. Baltimore, MD: Paul H. Brookes Publishing Company.

Gorden, R. L. (1975). *Interviewing: Strategies, tactics, and techniques.* Homewood, IL: Dorsey Press.

Holly, M. L. (1989). *Writing to grow.* Portsmouth, NH: Heinemann.

Hunsaker, L. & Johnston, M. (1992). Teacher under construction: A collaborative case study of teacher change. *American Educational Research Journal, 29,* 350-372.

Jacobson, M. J. & Wilensky, U. (2006). Complex systems in education: Scientific and educational importance and implications for the learning sciences. *Journal of the Learning Sciences,* 15, 11-34.

Janney, R. E. & Snell, M. E. (2004). *Modifying schoolwork,* 2nd ed. Baltimore, MD: Paul H. Brookes Publishing Company

Janney, R. E., Snell, M. E., Beers, M. K., & Raynes, M. (1995). Integrating students with moderate and severe disabilities: Classroom teachers' beliefs and attitudes about implementing an educational change. *Educational Administration Quarterly, 31,* 86-114.

Johnson, B., Bowman, A., & Hall, J. (1990, February). The journal as a research tool. Paper presented at the Association of TeacherEducators, Las Vegas, NE. (ERIC Document Reproduction Service No. ED322106)

Jorgensen, C. M., Fisher, D. & Roach, V. (1997). Curriculum and its impact on inclusion and the achievement of students with disabilities. Pittsburg, PA: Allegheny-Singer Research Institute. (ERIC Document Reproduction Service No. ED409684)

Kampfer, S. H., Horvath, L. S., Kleinert, H. L., & Kearns, J. F. (2001). Teachers' perceptions of one state's alternate assessment: Implications for practice and preparation. *Exceptional Children, 67,* 361-374.

Kavale, K. A. & Forness, S. R. (2000). History, rhetoric, and reality: Analysis of the inclusion debate. *Remedial and Special Education, 21,* 279-296.

Kearns, J. F., Kleinert, H. L., Clayton, J., Burdge, M., & Williams, R. (1998). Principle supports for inclusive assessment: A Kentucky story. *Teaching Exceptional Children, 31,* 16-23.

Kearns, J. F., Kleinert, H. L., & Kennedy, S. (1999). We need not exclude anyone. *Educational Leadership, 56,* 33-38.

Kelchtermas, G. & Vanderberghe, R. (1993, April). A teacher is a teacher is a .... Teachers' professional development from a biographical perspective. Paper presented at the meeting of the American Educational Research Association, Atlanta, GA. (ERIC Document Reproduction Service No. Ed360292)

Kelsay, K. L. (1989, March). A qualitative study of reflective teaching. Paper presented at the meeting of the American Educational Research Association, San Francisco, CA. (ERIC Document Reproduction Service No. ED352320)

Kennedy, M. (2005). *Inside teaching: How classroom life undermines school reform.* Cambridge, MA: Harvard University Press.

Kennedy, R. L. & Wyrick, A. M. (1995, November). Teaching as reflective practice. Paper presented at the Annual Meeting of the Mid-South Educational Research Association, Biloxi, MS. (ERIC Document Reproduction Service No. ED393850)

Kleinert, H. L. & Kearns, J. F. (2001). *Alternate assessment: Measuring outcomes and supports for students with disabilities.* Baltimore, MD: Paul H. Brookes Publishing Company.

Kleinert, H. L., Kennedy, S., & Kearns, J. F. (1999). The impact of alternate assessments: A statewide teacher survey. *Journal of Special Education, 33*, 93-102.

Kleinert, H. L. Kearns, J. F., & Kennedy, S. (1997). Accountability for all students: Kentucky's alternate portfolio assessment for students with moderate and severe cognitive disabilities. *Journal of the Association for Persons with Severe Handicaps, 22*, 88-101.

Kliebard, H. M. (1995). *The struggle for the American curriculum: 1893-1958.* New York, NY: Routledge.

Lieber, J., Capell, K., Sandall, S. R., Wolfberg, P., Horn, E., & Beckman, P.(1998). Inclusive preschool programs: Teachers' beliefs and practices. *Early Childhood Research Quarterly, 13*, 87-105.

Lipman, P. (1997). Restructuring in context: A case study of teacher participation and the dynamics of race, ideology, and power. *American Educational Research Journal, 34*, 3-37.

Lipsky, D. K. & Gartner, A. (1997). *Inclusion and school reform: Transforming America's classrooms.* Baltimore, MD: Paul H. Brookes Publishing Co.

Malouf, D. B. & Schiller, E. P. (1995). Practice and research in special education. *Exceptional Children, 61*, 414-424.

Massachusetts Department of Education. (2006). Resource guide to Massachusetts curriculum frameworks for students with disabilities. Malden, MA: Massachusetts Department of Education.

McGregor, G. & Vogelsberg, R. T. (1998). *Inclusive schooling practices:Pedagogical and research foundations: A synthesis of the literature that Informs best practices about inclusive schooling.* Baltimore, MD: Paul H. Brookes Publishing Company, Inc.

McLaughlin, M. J., Henderson, K., & Rhim, L. M. (1998). Snapshots of reform: How five local districts are interpreting standards-based reform for students with disabilities. Alexandria, VA: Center for Policy Research on the Impact of General and Special Education Reform. (ERIC Document Reproduction No. ED423653)

Pajares, M. F. (1992). Teacher beliefs and educational research: Cleaning up a messy construct. *Review of Educational Research, 62*, 307-332.

Patton, M. Q. (2002). *Qualitative research and evaluation methods, (3rd. ed.)* Thousand Oaks, CA: Sage Publications.

Peterson, P. E. & West, M. R. (Eds.) (2003). No child left behind? The politics and practice of school accountability. Washington DC: Brookings Institution Press.

Peterson, P. L., McCarthey, S. J. & Elmore, R. F. (1996). Learning from school restructuring. *American Educational Research Journal, 33*, 119-153.

Osgood, R. L. (2005). *The history of inclusion in the United States.* Washington D.C.: Gallaudet University Press.

Raber, S., Roach, V., & Fraser, K. (Eds.) (1998). The push and pull of students with disabilities in standards-based reform: How does it affect local school districts and students. Alexandria, VA: Center for Policy Research on the Impact of General and Special Education Reform. (ERIC Document Reproduction Service No. ED417531)

Radford, M. (2006). Researching classrooms: Complexity and chaos. *British Educational Research*, 32, 177-190.

Richardson, V. (1990). Significant and worthwhile change in teaching practice. *Educational Researcher, 19*, 10-18.

Richardson, V. (1994). Conducting research on practice. *Educational Researcher, 23*, 5-10.

Richardson, V., Anders, P., Tidwell, D., & Lloyd, C. (1991). The relationship between teachers' beliefs and practices in reading comprehension. *American Educational Research Journal, 28*, 559-586.

Rist, R. (1970). Student social class and teacher expectations: The self-fulfilling prophecy in ghetto education. *Harvard Educational Review, 40*, 417-437.

Safford P. L. & Safford, E. J. (1996). *A history of childhood and disability*. New York, NY: Teachers College Press.

Sailor, W. (1997). Invited commentary. *Journal of the Association for Persons with Severe Handicaps, 22*, 102-103.

Schatzman, L. & Strauss A. L. (1973). *Field research: Strategies for a natural sociology*. Upper Saddle River, NJ: Prentice-Hall, Inc.

Scheerenberger, R. C. (1983). *A history of mental retardation*. Baltimore, MD: Paul H. Brookes Publishing Company.

Scheerenberger, R. C. (1987). *A history of mental retardation: A quartercentury of progress*. Baltimore, MD: Paul H. Brookes Publishing Company.

Scruggs, T. E. & Mastropieri, M. A. (1996). Teacher perceptions of mainstreaming/inclusion, 1958-1995: A research synthesis. *Exceptional Children, 63*, 59-74.

Siegel, E. & Allinder, R. M. (2005). Review of assessment procedures for students with moderate and severe disabilities. *Education and Training in Developmental Disabilities*, 40, 343-351.

Skrtic, T. M. (1991). The special education paradox: Equity as the way to excellence. *Harvard Educational Review*, 61, 148-206.

Smith, A. (2006). Access, participation, and progress in the general education curriculum in the least restrictive environment for students with significant cognitive disabilities. *Research and Practice for Persons with Severe Disabilities*, 31, 331-337.

Soodak, L. C., Podell, D. M., & Lehman, L. R. (1998). Teacher, student, and school attributes as predictors of teachers' responses to inclusion. *The Journal of Special Education, 31*, 480-497.

Spooner, F., Dymond, S. K., Smith, A., & Kennedy, C. H. (2006). What we know and need to know about accessing the general education curriculum. *Research and Practice for Persons with Severe Disabilities, 31*, 277-284.

Spradley, J. P. (1979). *The ethnographic interview*. Philadelphia, PA: Harcourt College Publishers.

Spradley, J. P. (1980) *Participant observation*. Philadelphia, PA: Harcourt College Publishers.

Spradley, J. P. & McCurdy, D. W. (1972). The cultural experience: Ethnography in complex society. Chicago, IL: Science Research Associates, Inc.

Swanson-Owens, D. (1986). Identifying natural sources of resistance: A case study of implementing writing across the curriculum. *Research in the Teaching of English, 20,* 69-97.

Taylor, S. J. (1988). Caught in the continuum: A critical analysis of the principle of the least restrictive environment. *Journal of the Association for Persons with Severe Handicaps,* 13, 41-53.

Thompson, S., Thurlow, M., Parson, L., & Barrow, S. (2000). Initial perceptions of educators as they work toward including students with disabilities in Minnesota's High Standards. State Assessment Series, Minnesota Report 25. St. Paul, MN: Minnesota State Department of Children, Families, and Learning. (ERIC Document Reproduction Service No. ED 446408)

Tyler, R. W. (1949). *Basic principles of curriculum construction.* Chicago,IL: The University of Chicago Press.

Weatherly, R. A. & Lipsky, M. (1977). Street level bureaucrats and institutional innovation: Implementing special education reform. In Thomas Hehir and Thomas Latus (Ed.) *Special education at the century's end: Evolution of theory and practice since 1970,* (pp. 89-119). Cambridge, MA: President and Fellows of Harvard College.

Wehmeyer, M. L. (2006). Beyond access: Ensuring progress in the general education curriculum for students with severe disabilities. *Researchand Practice for Persons with Severe Disabilities, 31,* 322-326.

Williamson, P., Mcleskey, J., Hoppey, D. & Rentz, T. (2006). Educating students with mental retardation in general education classrooms. *Exceptional Children,* 72, 347-361.

Winzer, M.A. (1993). *The history of special education From isolation to integration.* Washington, D. C: Gallaudet University Press.

Wolcott, H. F. (1997). Ethnographic research in education. In R. M. Jaeger (Ed.), *Methods for research in education* (pp. 327-353). Washington, DC: American Educational Research Association
.

Index